Modern Europe and America

Modern Europe and America

Edited by

WILLIAM H. McNEILL

and

SCHUYLER OWEN HOUSER

New York
OXFORD UNIVERSITY PRESS
London 1973 Toronto

Library of Congress Catalogue Card Number: 68:8409
Printed in the United States of America

Preface

The closer one comes to the present and to our own civilization the more difficult it is to arrive at a clear vision of the whole. With the invention of printing, materials from which to choose readings such as these multiply far beyond the capacity of any one person to explore or begin to know what is available. On the other hand, a diligent company of historians has explored the ground; and despite their many disagreements, they have achieved a rough consensus as to what were the most important movements and changes in European and American history since 1500. In selecting the documents for this final book of readings in world history, we have conformed to this established consensus, as the headings of the parts will show.

Two closely connected themes run through the book: man's relationship to his fellows through government and man's relationship to the universe through religion (or some secularized ideological equivalent thereof). The complex and ever-changing connection between government and religion, that is, between human institutions and human beliefs, constitutes the common ground for all the selections reprinted here.

It is possible to organize modern European history around three periods of revolutionary change, separate from one another by times when things were a bit more stable. According to this scheme, the first of these major revolutionary upheavals came in the age of renaissance and reformation, when medieval Europe's intellectual and social patterns were shattered beyond repair by skills and secular viewpoints coming out of Italy on the one hand, and, on the other, by the fierce rejection of routinized piety coming both from Luther's Germany and from Loyola's Spain.

Then, by slow degrees, comparative stability set in under the Old Regime. Efforts to accommodate all the new information that flowed in with dizzying speed from exploration of new lands and new realms of knowledge began to attain some success, aided no doubt by the aristocratic and monarchical stabilization of political and social institutions that began to emerge after about 1650.

This pattern of European civilization in turn gave way after about 1780 before the upheavals of the democratic and industrial revolutions. Then, by 1870, once again, a kind of bourgeois and nationalist "Old Regime" became discernible, at least in the countries of western Europe. But this quickly crumpled with the outbreak of World War I in 1914, followed by the severe economic depression of the 1930's, and renewed world war in the 1940's. Since World War II, however, a new period of relative quiet may have set in. There has not been enough time to be sure.

Obviously, our documents cluster around the periods of revolutionary upheaval. This is not surprising since by definition it is during such times that the patterns of conduct and belief that guided subsequent generations' behavior first emerge. Actually, from a time perspective appropriate for genuine world history, it is very likely (if men survive so long) that a thousand years from now when historians look back on what happened in Europe and America between 1500 and 2000 they will view the entire five hundred years as a single revolutionary age of world-shaking innovation, when new ideas, new techniques, new institution, and new values surged irresistibly through men's lives. Even today we may be sure that the leading fact of modern times is this: since 1500 it has been Europe's fate and fortune to drag the rest of mankind toward a new cosmopolitan and genuinely global pattern of culture, whose lineaments and enduring character we of the twentieth century are not yet in a position to discern.

However unclear the shape of things to come may be, the past, insofar as we are able to apprehend it, remains the only guide men have to future probabilities and possibilities. By trying to understand how our immediate predecessors saw the world, how they acted, and what they achieved and failed to achieve, we may hope to become wiser as well as better informed. Young students may find it hard to take seriously the concerns of Luther or Loyola, of Locke or Robespierre, or even of Hitler and Mussolini. It is only by surrendering their own narrow and time-bound personal points of view about what matters long enough to try seriously and sympathetically to enter into the minds of these (and similar) famous figures of the past that they can expect to understand what bothered, what comforted, and what illumined the creators of the modern world.

Only by trying and succeeding in such an attempt can a young person begin to see himself and his world in the perspective of time, and learn to believe as well as to say that he, too, is time's creature and captive, as all men have been, are, and will remain in time to come. By enlarging and enriching a person's sense of the human condition in this way, the study of history serves one of its principal functions in a liberal education. May those who use this book be successful in the quest for better understanding—of themselves, as well as of the men here represented through their printed words, who did so much to shape the world we all inhabit.

W.H.M.

Chicago, Illinois
February 1972

Contents

I RENAISSANCE AND REFORMATION

A Renaissance Man 3
Giorgio Vasari: Life of Leonardo da Vinci 4
Thoughts on Religion and Government 15
Niccolò Machiavelli: Discourses on Livy 15
Christian Faith and Freedom Reaffirmed 26
Martin Luther: Christian Liberty 27
Songs for Salvation 39
John Hunnis: Metrical Psalms 40
How To Make Soldiers for Christ 43
St. Ignatius Loyola: Spiritual Exercises 45
God's Will Be Done 52
Thomas Harrison: Speech upon the Ladder 53

II EXPLORATION AND DISCOVERY

Terrestrial Exploration 60
Bernal Díaz del Castillo: Memoirs 62
Celestial Exploration 87
Galileo Galilei: The Sidereal Messenger 88
Intellectual Exploration 98
René Descartes: Discourse on Method 99

III GOVERNMENT AND RELIGION IN THE OLD REGIME

Political Right According To Revelation 117
Bishop Bossuet: Politics Derived from the Words of Holy Scripture 118
Political Right According to Nature and Reason 127
John Locke: Of Civil Government 127
Reasonable Religion vs. Superstition 138
Voltaire: Philosophical Dictionary 139

IV THE DEMOCRATIC REVOLUTION

Natural Rights and Revolution in America 145
The Declaration of Independence 146
Democratic Demands in France 147
Abbé Sieyès: What Is the Third Estate? 149
Natural Rights and Revolution in France 166
Declaration of the Rights of Man and of the Citizen 166
Virtue Through Terror, if Need Be 169
Maximilien Robespierre: Report upon the Principles of Political Morality 170

V THE INDUSTRIAL REVOLUTION

How To Be Successful in Business While Still in Your Teens 176
Robert Owen: Autobiography 177
How Capitalism Is Its Own Gravedigger 190
Karl Marx and Friedrich Engels: The Communist Manifesto 191
How To Head off Proletarian Revolution 216
Otto von Bismarck: Speech on Social Insurance 217

VI WORLD WARS I AND II

Shock of Trench Warfare 229
Wilfred Owen: Poems 229
Russian Recipe for Peace 233
Bolshevik Proclamation on Peace 235
American Recipe for Peace 239
Woodrow Wilson: Speech 241
Nation as Refuge for the Lost Soul 247
Benito Mussolini: The Doctrine of Fascism 249
Race as Refuge for the Lost Soul 262
Adolf Hitler: Mein Kampf 263
Freedom as Cure for the World's Ills 279
Franklin D. Roosevelt: State of the Union, 1941 280

VII THE HUMAN CONDITION

A Nineteenth-Century View 289
Winwood Reade: The Martyrdom of Man 289
A Twentieth Century View 294
Pierre Teilhard de Chardin: The Singularities of the Human Species 295

I

Renaissance and Reformation

A Renaissance Man
Giorgio Vasari: Life of Leonardo da Vinci

Thoughts on Religion and Government
Niccolò Machiavelli: Discourses on Livy

Christian Faith and Freedom Reaffirmed
Martin Luther: Christian Liberty

Songs for Salvation
John Hunnis: Metrical Psalms

How To Make Soldiers for Christ
St. Ignatius Loyola: Spiritual Exercises

God's Will Be Done
Thomas Harrison: Speech upon the Ladder

A Renaissance Man

As a painter and architect, Georgio Vasari (1511–74) was both prolific and financially successful. But his modern reputation rests on his abilities as a biographer and historian of art. He was born in the Italian city of Suzzo and began his artistic studies as a small child by copying paintings in local churches. His literary education was not neglected; he studied Latin and memorized long passages of Roman poetry. In 1523 he went to Florence, where he studied for three years with Michaelangelo Buonarroti (1475–1564), most famous painter and sculptor of the Renaissance. The Medici family, rulers of Florence, took Vasari under their protection; they continued as his chief patrons during the remainder of his career.

Vasari dedicated his book, *The Lives of Seventy of the Most Eminent Painters, Sculptors, and Architects of Italy*, to a member of the Medici family. He began the work in order to satisfy the request of a Roman cardinal for information on Italian painters. At the outset, Vasari intended merely to collect notes on the lives of his subjects; but with the encouragement of friends, he expanded the project into a general survey of Italian artists from Cimabue (1240–1302) to his own teacher, Michaelangelo. The work was first published in 1550. Vasari, however, continued his researches and published an expanded second edition in 1568.

Of the men whose works he celebrated, Vasari admired Leonardo da Vinci most. Leonardo's reputation as a "universal man," capable of excelling at everything he undertook, was, if not created, certainly confirmed and magnified by Vasari's biography, extracts from which follow.

GIORGIO VASARI: LIFE OF LEONARDO DA VINCI

Born 1452–Died 1519

The richest gifts are occasionally seen to be showered, as by celestial influence, on certain human beings, nay, they sometimes supernaturally and marvellously congregate in one sole person; beauty, grace, and talent being united in such a manner, that to whatever the man thus favoured may turn himself, his every action is so divine as to leave all other men far behind him, and manifestly to prove that he has been specially endowed by the hand of God himself, and has not obtained his pre-eminence by human teaching, or the power of man. This was seen and acknowledged by all men in the case of Leonardo da Vinci, in whom, to say nothing of his beauty of person, which yet was such that it has never been sufficiently extolled, there was a grace beyond expression which was rendered manifest without thought or effort in every act and deed, and who had besides so rare a gift of talent and ability, that to whatever subject he turned his attention, however difficult, he presently made himself absolute master of it. Extraordinary power was in his case conjoined with remarkable facility, a mind of regal boldness and magnanimous daring; his gifts were such that the celebrity of his name extended most widely, and he was held in the highest estimation, not in his own time only, but also, and even to a greater extent, after his death, nay, this he has continued, and will continue to be by all succeeding ages.

Truly admirable, indeed, and divinely endowed was Leonardo da Vinci; this artist was the son of Ser Piero da Vinci; he would without doubt have made great progress in learning and knowledge of the sciences, had he not been so versatile and changeful, but the instability of his character caused him to undertake many things which having commenced he afterwards abandoned. In arithmetic, for example, he made such rapid progress

From Giorgio Vasari, *Lives of the Most Eminent Painters, Sculptors and Architects*, Vol. II, trans. by Mrs. Jonathan Foster (London: George Bell and Sons, 1892), pp. 366-89.

in the short time during which he gave his attention to it, that he often confounded the master who was teaching him, by the perpetual doubts he started, and by the difficulty of the questions he proposed. He also commenced the study of music, and resolved to acquire the art of playing the lute, when, being by nature of an exalted imagination and full of the most graceful vivacity, he sang to that instrument most divinely, improvising at once the verses and the music.

But, though dividing his attention among pursuits so varied, he never abandoned his drawing, and employed himself much in works of relief, that being the occupation which attracted him more than any other. His father, Ser Piero, observing this, and considering the extraordinary character of his son's genius, one day took some of his drawings and showed them to Andrea del Verrocchio,[1] who was a very intimate friend of his, begging him earnestly to tell him whether he thought that Leonardo would be likely to secure success if he devoted himself to the arts of design. Andrea Verrocchio was amazed as he beheld the remarkable commencement made by Leonardo, and advised Ser Piero to see that he attached himself to that calling, whereupon the latter took his measures accordingly, and sent Leonardo to study in the bottega or workshop of Andrea. Thither the boy resorted therefore, with the utmost readiness, and not only gave his attention to one branch of art, but to all the others, of which design made a portion. Endowed with such admirable intelligence, and being also an excellent geometrician, Leonardo not only worked in sculpture (having executed certain heads in terracotta, of women smiling, even in his first youth, which are now reproduced in gypsum, and also others of children which might be supposed to have proceeded from the hand of a master); but in architecture likewise he prepared various designs for ground-plans, and the construction of entire buildings: he too it was who, though still but a youth, first suggested the formation of a canal from Pisa to Florence, by means of certain changes to be effected on the river Arno. Leonardo likewise made designs for mills, fulling machines, and other engines, which were to be acted on by means of water; but as he had resolved to make

1. Florentine sculptor and painter, lived 1435-88.

painting his profession, he gave the larger portion of time to drawing from nature. He sometimes formed models of different figures in clay, on which he would arrange fragments of soft drapery dipped in plaster; from these he would then set himself patiently to draw on very fine cambric or linen that had already been used and rendered smooth, these he executed in black and white with the point of the pencil in a most admirable manner, as may be seen by certain specimens from his own hand which I have in my book of drawings. He drew on paper also with so much care and so perfectly, that no one has ever equalled him in this respect: I have a head by him in chiaro-scuro, which is incomparably beautiful. Leonardo was indeed so imbued with power and grace by the hand of God, and was endowed with so marvellous a facility in reproducing his conceptions; his memory also was always so ready and so efficient in the service of his intellect, that in discourse he won all men by his reasonings, and confounded every antagonist, however powerful, by the force of his arguments.

This master was also frequently occupied with the construction of models and the preparation of designs for the removal or the perforation of mountains,[2] to the end that they might thus be easily passed from one plain to another. By means of levers, cranes, and screws, he likewise showed how great weights might be raised or drawn; in what manner ports and havens might be cleansed and kept in order, and how water might be obtained from the lowest deeps. From speculations of this kind he never gave himself rest, and of the results of these labours and meditations there are numberless examples in drawings, &c., dispersed among those who practise our arts: I have myself seen very many of them. . . .

Having been placed then by Ser Piero in his childhood with Andrea Verrocchio, as we have said, to learn the art of the painter, that master was engaged on a picture the subject of which was San Giovanni baptizing Jesus Christ; in this Leonardo painted an angel holding some vestments; and although he was but a youth, he completed that figure in such a manner, that the angel of Leonardo was much better than the portion

2. I.e., tunnel building.

executed by his master, which caused the latter never to touch colours more, so much was he displeased to find that a mere child could do more than himself.

. . . .

It is related that Ser Piero da Vinci, being at his country house, was there visited by one of the peasants on his estate, who, having cut down a fig-tree on his farm, had made a shield from part of it with his own hands, and then brought it to Ser Piero, begging that he would be pleased to cause the same to be painted for him in Florence This the latter very willingly promised to do, the countryman having great skill in taking birds and in fishing, and being often very serviceable to Ser Piero in such matters. Having taken the shield with him to Florence therefore, without saying any thing to Leonardo as to whom it was for, he desired the latter to paint something upon it. Accordingly, he one day took it in hand, but finding it crooked, coarse, and badly made, he straightened it at the fire, and giving it to a turner, it was brought back to him smooth and delicately rounded, instead of the rude and shapeless form in which he had received it. He then covered it with gypsum, and having prepared it to his liking, he began to consider what he could paint upon it that might best and most effectually terrify whomsoever might approach it, producing the same effect with that formerly attributed to the head of Medusa. For this purpose therefore, Leonardo carried to one of his rooms, into which no one but himself ever entered, a number of lizards, hedgehogs, newts, serpents, dragon-flies, locusts, bats, glow-worms, and every other sort of strange animal of similar kind on which he could lay his hands; from this assemblage, variously adapted and joined together, he formed a hideous and appalling monster, breathing poison and flames, and surrounded by an atmosphere of fire; this he caused to issue from a dark and rifted rock, with poison reeking from the cavernous throat, flames darting from the eyes, and vapours rising from the nostrils in such sort that the result was indeed a most fearful and monstrous creature: at this he laboured until the odours arising from all those dead animals filled the room with a mortal fetor, to which the zeal of Leonardo and the love which he bore to art rendered him insensible or indifferent. When this work, which neither the countryman nor Ser Piero any longer inquired for, was completed, Leonardo went to his father and told him that he might send for the shield at his earliest convenience, since so far as he was concerned, the work was finished; Ser Piero went accordingly one morning to the room for the shield, and having knocked at the door, Leonardo opened it to him, telling him nevertheless to wait a little without, and having returned into the room he placed the shield on the easel, and shading the window so that the light falling on the painting was somewhat dimmed, he made Ser Piero step within to look at it. But the latter, not expecting any such thing, drew back, startled at the first glance, not supposing that to be the shield, or believing the monster he beheld to be a painting, he therefore turned to rush out, but Leonardo withheld him, saying:—The shield will serve the purpose for which it has been executed, take it therefore and carry it away, for this is the effect it was designed to produce. The work seemed something more than wonderful to Ser Piero, and he highly commended the fanciful idea of Leonardo, but he afterwards silently bought from a merchant another shield, whereon there was painted a heart transfixed with an arrow, and this he gave to the countryman, who considered himself obliged to him for it to the end of his life. Some time after Ser Piero secretly sold the shield painted by Leonardo to certain merchants for one hundred ducats, and it subsequently fell into the hands of the Duke of Milan, sold to him by the same merchants for three hundred ducats.

. . . .

Leonardo was so much pleased when he encountered faces of extraordinary character, or heads, beards or hair of unusual appearance, that he would follow any such, more than commonly attractive, through the whole day, until the figure of the person would become so well impressed on his mind that, having returned home, he would draw him as readily as though he stood before him. Of heads thus obtained there exist many, both masculine and feminine; and I have myself several of them drawn with a pen by his own hand, in the book of drawings so frequently cited. . . .

On the death of Giovanni Galeazzo, Duke of Milan, in the year 1493, Ludovico Sforza was chosen in the same year to be his successor, when Leonardo was invited with great honour to Milan by the Duke, who delighted greatly in the music of the lute, to the end that the master might play before him; Leonardo therefore took with him a certain instrusment which he had himself constructed almost wholly of silver, and in the shape of a horse's head, a new and fanciful form calculated to give more force and sweetness to the sound. Here Leonardo surpassed all the musicians who had assembled to perform before the Duke; he was besides one of the best *improvisatori* in verse existing at that time, and the Duke, enchanted with the admirable conversation of Leonardo, was so charmed by his varied gifts that he delighted beyond measure in his society, and prevailed on him to paint an altar-piece, the subject of which was the Nativity of Christ, which was sent by the Duke as a present to the Emperor. For the Dominican monks of Santa Maria delle Grazie at Milan, he also painted a Last Supper, which is a most beautiful and admirable work; to the heads of the Apostles in this picture the master gave so much beauty and majesty that he was constrained to leave that of Christ unfinished, being convinced that he could not impart to it the divinity which should appertain to and distinguish an image of the Redeemer. But this work, remaining thus in its unfinished state, has been ever held in the highest estimation by the Milanese, and not by them only, but by foreigners also: Leonardo succeeded to perfection in expressing the doubts and anxiety experienced by the Apostles, and the desire felt by them to know by whom their Master is to be betrayed; in the faces of all appear love, terror, anger, or grief and bewilderment, unable as they are to fathom the meaning of their Lord. Nor is the spectator less struck with admiration by the force and truth with which, on the other hand, the master has exhibited the impious determination, hatred, and treachery of Judas. The whole work indeed is executed with inexpressible diligence even in its most minute part, among other things may be mentioned the table-cloth, the texture of which is copied with such exactitude, that the linen-cloth itself could scarcely look more real.

It is related that the Prior of the Monastery was excessively importunate in pressing Leonardo to complete the picture; he could in no way comprehend wherefore the artist should sometimes remain half a day together absorbed in thought before his work, without making any progress that he could see; this seemed to him a strange waste of time, and he would fain have had him work away as he could make the men do who were digging in his garden, never laying the pencil out of his hand. Not content with seeking to hasten Leonardo, the Prior even complained to the Duke, and tormented him to such a degree that the latter was at length compelled to send for Leonardo, whom he courteously entreated to let the work be finished, assuring him nevertheless that he did so because impelled by the importunities of the Prior. Leonardo, knowing the Prince to be intelligent and judicious, determined to explain himself fully on the subject with him, although he had never chosen to do so with the Prior. He therefore discoursed with him at some length respecting art, and made it perfectly manifest to his comprehension, that men of genius are sometimes producing most when they seem to be labouring least, their minds being occupied in the elucidation of their ideas, and in the completion of those conceptions to which they afterwards give form and expression with the hand. He further informed the Duke that there were still wanting to him two heads, one of which, that of the Saviour, he could not hope to find on earth, and had not yet attained the power of presenting it to himself in imagination, with all that perfection of beauty and celestial grace which appeared to him to be demanded for the due representation of the Divinity incarnate. The second head still wanting was that of Judas, which also caused him some anxiety, since he did not think it possible to imagine a form of feature that should properly render the countenance of a man who, after so many benefits received from his master, had possessed a heart so depraved as to be capable of betraying his Lord and the Creator of the world. With regard to that second, however, he would make search, and after all—if he could find no better, he need never be at any great loss, for there would always be the head of that troublesome and impertinent Prior. This made the Duke laugh with all his heart, he declared Leonardo to be completely in the right, and the poor Prior, utterly confounded, went away to drive on the digging in his garden, and left Leonardo in peace: the head of Judas was then finished so successfully, that it is indeed the true image of treachery and wickedness; but that of the Redeemer remained, as we have said, incomplete.

. . . .

While still engaged with the paintings of the refectory, Leonardo proposed to the Duke to cast a horse in bronze of colossal size, and to place on it a figure of the Duke, by way of monument to his memory: this he commenced, but finished the model on so large a scale that it never could be completed, and there were many ready to declare (for the judgments of men are various, and are sometimes rendered malignant by envy) that Leonardo had begun it, as he did others of his labours, without intending ever to finish it. The size of the work being such, insuperable difficulties presented themselves, as I have said, when it came to be cast; nay, the casting could not be effected in one piece, and it is very probable that, when this result was known, many were led to form the opinion alluded to above, from the fact that so many of Leonardo's works had failed to receive completion. But of a truth, there is good reason to believe that the very greatness of his most exalted mind, aiming at more than could be effected, was itself an impediment; perpetually seeking to add excellence to excellence, and perfection to perfection; this was, without doubt, the true hindrance, so that, as our Petrarch has it, the work was retarded by desire. All who saw the large model in clay which Leonardo made for this work, declared that they had never seen anything more beautiful or more majestic; this model remained as he had left it until the French, with their King Louis, came to Milan, when they destroyed it totally. A small model of the same work, executed in wax, and which was considered perfect, was also lost, with a book containing studies of the anatomy of the horse, which Leonardo had prepared for his own use. He afterwards gave his attention, and with increased earnestness, to the anatomy of the human frame, a study wherein Messer Marcantonio della Torre, an eminent philosopher, and himself, did mutually assist and encourage each other.

Messer Marcantonio was at that time holding lectures in Pavia, and wrote on the same subject; he was one of the first, as I have heard say, who began to apply the doctrines of Galen to the elucidation of medical science, and to diffuse light over the science of anatomy, which, up to that time, had been involved in the almost total darkness of ignorance. In this attempt Marcantonio was wonderfully aided by the genius and labour of Leonardo, who filled a book with drawings in red crayons, outlined with the pen, all copies made with the utmost care from bodies dissected by his own hand. In this book he set forth the entire structure, arrangement, and disposition of the bones, to which he afterwards added all the nerves, in their due order, and next supplied the muscles, of which the first are affixed to the bones, the second give the power of cohesion or holding firmly, and the third impart that of motion. Of each separate part he wrote an explanation in rude characters, written backwards and with the left-hand, so that whoever is not practised in reading cannot understand them, since they are only to be read with a mirror. . . .

[Leonardo took service in France for a while, then returned to Florence, where he painted the Mona Lisa and started other projects.]

On the exaltation of Pope Leo X to the chair of St. Peter,[3] Leonardo accompanied the Duke Giuliano de' Medici to Rome: the Pontiff was much inclined to philosophical inquiry, and was more especially addicted to the study of alchemy: Leonardo, therefore, having composed a kind of paste from wax, made of this, while it was still in its half-liquid state, certain figures of animals, entirely hollow and exceedingly slight in texture, which he then filled with air. When he blew into these figures he could make them fly through the air, but when the air within had escaped from them they fell to the earth. One day the vine-dresser of the Belvedere found a very curious lizard, and for this creature Leonardo constructed wings, made from the skins of other lizards, flayed for the purpose; into these wings he put quicksilver, so that when the animal walked, the wings moved

3. Pope Leo X, son of Lorenzo the Magnificent of Florence, reigned 1513-21.

also, with a tremulous motion: he then made eyes, horns, and a beard for the creature, which he tamed and kept in a case; he would then show it to the friends who came to visit him, and all who saw it ran away terrified. . . . He made numbers of these follies in various kinds, occupied himself much with mirrors and optical instruments, and made the most singular experiments in seeking oils for painting, and varnishes to preserve the work when executed. About this time he painted a small picture for Messer Baldassare Turini, of Pescia, who was Datary to Pope Leo: the subject of this work was Our Lady, with the Child in her arms, and it was executed by Leonardo with infinite care and art, but whether from the carelessness of those who prepared the ground, or because of his peculiar and fanciful mixtures for colours, varnishes, &c., it is now much deteriorated. In another small picture he painted a little Child, which is graceful and beautiful to a miracle. These paintings are both in Pescia, in the possession of Messer Giulio Turini. It is related that Leonardo, having received a commission for a certain picture from Pope Leo, immediately began to distil oils and herbs for the varnish, whereupon the pontiff remarked, "Alas! the while, this man will assuredly do nothing at all, since he is thinking of the end before he has made a beginning to his work." There was perpetual discord between Michelagnolo Buonarroti and Leonardo, and the competition between them caused Michelagnolo to leave Florence, the Duke Giuliano framing an excuse for him, the pretext for his departure being that he was summoned to Rome by the Pope for the Façade of San Lorenzo. When Leonardo heard of this, he also departed and went to France, where the king, already possessing several of his works, was most kindly disposed towards him, and wished him to paint the cartoon of Sant' Anna, but Leonardo, according to his custom, kept the king a long time waiting with nothing better than words. Finally, having become old, he lay sick for many months, and, finding himself near death, wrought diligently to make himself acquainted with the Catholic ritual, and with the good and holy path of the Christian religion: he then confessed with great penitence and many tears, and although he could not support himself on his feet, yet, being sustained in the arms of his servants and friends, he devoutly received the Holy Sacrament, while thus out of his bed. The king, who was accustomed frequently and affectionately to visit him, came immediately afterwards to his room, and he, causing himself out of reverence to be raised up, sat in his bed describing his malady and the different circumstances connected with it, lamenting, besides, that he had offended God and man, inasmuch as that he had not laboured in art as he ought to have done. He was then seized with a violent paroxysm, the forerunner of death, when the king, rising and supporting his head to give him such assistance and do him such favour as he could, in the hope of alleviating his sufferings, the spirit of Leonardo, which was most divine, conscious that he could attain to no greater honour, departed in the arms of the monarch, being at that time in the seventy-fifth year of his age.

Thoughts on Religion and Government

Niccolò Machiavelli (1469–1527) spent most of his life in the Italian city of Florence. His father was a lawyer; otherwise little is known of Niccolò's childhood or education. In 1498, Machiavelli obtained two posts in the Florentine city government: he was both secretary to the Council of Ten (the war council) and chief of the Second Chancellery, which handled domestic correspondence for the city government. In his daily work, therefore, Machiavelli handled all of the city's official correspondence for domestic and foreign affairs.

During Machiavelli's career, Florence was an independent city-state, whose republican government ruled both the city itself and towns and countryside nearby. Similar states rivaled Florence throughout northern Italy; to the south the Papal States, governed from Rome, behaved just like the other states of the peninsula, despite the fact that the Pope also was religious head of Latin Christendom as a whole. In the conduct of state business, Machiavelli learned much at first hand about diplomacy, war, and the internal strength of states.

Then, in 1512, Machiavelli lost his job. A revolution in Florence brought the once-dominant Medici family back into control; Machiavelli, a leader of the anti-Medici republican forces, withdrew to his estate. He occupied his time by writing—several poems and plays, a history of Florence, stories, and brief biographies. But his most important works from this period concerned politics and statecraft. The most famous is *The Prince*, written in 1513 for Lorenzo de Medici, perhaps in the hope that Lorenzo would employ him once again. It was not published until after Machiavelli's death. In *The Prince* Machiavelli rejected traditional Christian morality as impractical for rulers; instead he coolly analyzed the pros and cons of deceit, treachery, generosity, display, and any other sort of behavior known to princes. The book was shocking to most who read it when it was new; it gave Machiavelli a bad name, though he professed only to be describing what men and rulers did and assessing what worked best.

A longer and quite different work is Machiavelli's *Discourses on Livy*. This takes the form of a commentary on events of Roman history as described by the historian Titus Livius (59 B.C.–17 A.D.) Machiavelli was interested in drawing practical lessons from the past, and frequently, as in the first two chapters reprinted below, moves from remarks about ancient Rome to discussion of the affairs of Italy in his own day. Machiavelli's republican preferences appear more clearly in the *Discourses* than in *The Prince*. Machiavelli never finished the *Discourses*, which, like *The Prince*, was published only after his death.

NICCOLO MACHIAVELLI: DISCOURSES ON LIVY

Chapter XI
Of the Religion of the Romans

Although the founder of Rome was Romulus, to whom like a daughter, she owed her birth and her education, yet the gods did not judge the laws of this prince sufficient for so great an empire, and therefore inspired the Roman Senate to elect Numa Pompilius as his successor, so that he might regulate all those things that had been omitted by Romulus. Numa, finding a very savage people, and wishing to reduce them to civil obedience by

From the *Historical, Political and Diplomatic Writings of Nicollò Machiavilli*, Vol. II, trans. by Christian E. Detmold (Boston: J. R. Osgood Co., 1882).

the arts of peace, had recourse to religion as the most necessary and assured support of any civil society; and he established it upon such foundations that for many centuries there was nowhere more fear of the gods than in that republic, which greatly facilitated all the enterprises which the Senate or its great men attempted. Whoever will examine the actions of the people of Rome as a body, or of many individual Romans, will see that these citizens feared much more to break an oath than the laws; like men who esteem the power of the gods more than that of men. This was particularly manifested in the conduct of Scipio and Manlius Torquatus; for after the defeat which Hannibal had inflicted upon the Romans at Cannæ many citizens had assembled together, and, frightened and trembling, agreed to leave Italy and fly to Sicily. When Scipio heard of this, he went to meet them, and with his drawn sword in hand he forced them to swear not to abandon their country. Lucius Manlius, father of Titus Manlius, who was afterwards called Torquatus, had been accused by Marcus Pomponius, one of the Tribunes of the people. Before the day of judgment Titus went to Marcus and threatened to kill him if he did not promise to withdraw the charges against his father; he compelled him to take an oath, and Marcus, although having sworn under the pressure of fear, withdrew the accusation against Lucius. And thus these citizens, whom neither the love of country nor the laws could have kept in Italy, were retained there by an oath that had been forced upon them by compulsion; and the Tribune Pomponius disregarded the hatred which he bore to the father, as well as the insult offered him by the son for the sake of complying with his oath and preserving his honor; which can be ascribed to nothing else than the religious principles which Numa had instilled into the Romans. And whoever reads Roman history attentively will see in how great a degree religion served in the command of the armies, in uniting the people and keeping them well conducted, and in covering the wicked with shame. So that if the question were discussed whether Rome was more indebted to Romulus or to Numa, I believe that the highest merit would be conceded to Numa; for where religion exists it is easy to introduce armies and discipline, but where there are armies and no religion it is difficult to introduce the latter. And although we have seen that Romulus could organize the Senate and establish other civil and militiary institutions without the aid of divine authority, yet it was very necessary for Numa, who feigned that he held converse with a nymph, who dictated to him all that he wished to persuade the people to; and the reason for all this was that Numa mistrusted his own authority, lest it should prove insufficient to enable him to introduce new and unaccustomed ordinances in Rome. In truth, there never was any remarkable lawgiver amongst any people who did not resort to divine authority, as otherwise his laws would not have been accepted by the people; for there are many good laws, the importance of which is known to the sagacious lawgiver, but the reasons for which are not sufficiently evident to enable him to persuade others to submit to them; and therefore do wise men, for the purpose of removing this difficulty, resort to divine authority. Thus did Lycurgus and Solon[1] and many others who aimed at the same thing.

The Roman people, then, admiring the wisdom and goodness of Numa, yielded in all things to his advice. It is true that those were very religious times, and the people with whom Numa had to deal were very untutored and superstitious, which made it easy for him to carry out his designs, being able to impress upon them any new form. And doubtless, if any one wanted to establish a republic at the present time, he would find it much easier with the simple mountaineers, who are almost without any civilization, than with such as are accustomed to live in cities, where civilization is already corrupt; as a sculptor finds it easier to make a fine statue out of a crude block of marble than out of a statue badly begun by another. Considering then, all these things, I conclude that the religion introduced by Numa into Rome was one of the chief causes of the prosperity of that city; for this religion gave rise to good laws, and good laws bring good fortune, and from good fortune results happy success in all enterprises. And as the observance of divine institutions is the cause of the greatness of republics, so the disregard of them produces their ruin; for where the fear of God is wanting, there

1. Lawgivers for Sparta and Athens, respectively.

the country will come to ruin, unless it be sustained by the fear of the prince, which may temporarily supply the want of religion. But as the lives of princes are short, the kingdom will of necessity perish as the prince fails in virtue. Whence it comes that kingdoms which depend entirely upon the virtue of one man endure but for a brief time, for his virtue passes away with his life, and it rarely happens that it is renewed in his successor. . . .

The welfare, then, of a republic or a kingdom does not consist in having a prince who governs it wisely during his lifetime, but in having one who will give it such laws that it will maintain itself even after his death. And although untutored and ignorant men are more easily persuaded to adopt new laws or new opinions, yet that does not make it impossible to persuade civilized men who claim to be enlightened. The people of Florence are far from considering themselves ignorant and benighted, and yet Brother Girolamo Savonarola[2] succeeded in persuading them that he held converse with God. I will not pretend to judge whether it was true or not, for we must speak with all respect of so great a man; but I may well say that an immense number believed it, without having seen any extraordinary manifestations that should have made them believe it; but it was the purity of his life, the doctrines he preached, and the subjects he selected for his discourse, that sufficed to make the people have faith in him. Let no one, then, fear not to be able to accomplish what others have done, for all men (as we have said in our Preface) are born and live and die in the same way, and therefore resemble each other.

Chapter XII
The Importance of Giving Religion a Prominent Influence in a State, and How Italy Was Ruined Because She Failed in This Respect Through the Conduct of the Church of Rome

Princes and republics who wish to maintain themselves free from corruption must above all things preserve the purity of all

2. Savonarola was a Dominican Friar whose impassioned preaching provoked a revolution in Florence in 1494. He lost power in 1497 and was executed in 1498.

religious observances, and treat them with proper reverence; for there is no greater indication of the ruin of a country than to see religion contemned. And this is easily understood, when we know upon what the religion of a country is founded; for the essence of every religion is based upon some one main principle. The religion of the Gentiles[3] had for its foundation the responses of the oracles, and the tenets of the augurs and aruspices; upon these alone depended all their ceremonies, rites, and sacrifices. For they readily believed that the Deity which could predict their future good or ill was also able to bestow it upon them. Thence arose their temples, their sacrifices, their supplications, and all the other ceremonies; for the oracle of Delphos, the temple of Jupiter Ammon, and other celebrated oracles, kept the world in admiration and devoutness. But when these afterwards began to speak only in accordance with the wishes of the princes, and their falsity was discovered by the people, then men became incredulous, and disposed to disturb all good institutions. It is therefore the duty of princes and heads of republics to uphold the foundations of the religion of their countries, for then it is easy to keep their people religious, and consequently well conducted and united. And therefore everything that tends to favor religion (even though it were believed ot be false) should be received and availed of to strengthen it; and this should be done the more, the wiser the rulers are, and the better they understand the natural course of things. Such was, in fact, the practice observed by sagacious men; which has given rise to the belief in the miracles that are celebrated in religions, however false they may be. For the sagacious rulers have given these miracles increased importance, no matter whence or how they originated; and their authority afterwards gave them credence with the people. Rome had many such miracles; and one of the most remarkable was that which occurred when the Roman soldiers sacked the city of Veii; some of them entered the temple of Juno, and, placing themselves in front of her statue, said to her, "Will you come to Rome?" Some imagined that they observed the statue make a sign of assent, and others pretended to have heard her reply, "Yes." Now these men, being very reli-

3. I.e., Greeks and Romans.

gious, as reported by Titus Livius, and having entered the temple quietly, they were filled with devotion and reverence, and might really have believed that they had heard a reply to their question, such as perhaps they could have presupposed. But this opinion and belief was favored and magnified by Camillus and the other Roman chiefs.

And certainly, if the Christian religion had from the beginning been maintained according to the principles of its founder, the Christian states and republics would have been much more united and happy than what they are. Nor can there be a greater proof of its decadence than to witness the fact that the nearer people are to the Church of Rome, which is the head of our religion, the less religious are they. And whoever examines the principles upon which that religion is founded, and sees how widely different from those principles its present practice and application are, will judge that her ruin or chastisement is near at hand. But as there are some of the opinion that the well-being of Italian affairs depends upon the Church of Rome, I will present such arguments against that opinion as occur to me; two of which are most important, and cannot according to my judgment be controverted. The first is, that the evil example of the court of Rome has destroyed all piety and religion in Italy, which brings in its train infinite improprieties and disorders; for as we may presuppose all good where religion prevails, so where it is wanting we have the right to suppose the very opposite. We Italians then owe to the Church of Rome and to her priests our having become irreligious and bad; but we owe her a still greater debt, and one that will be the cause of our ruin, namely, that the Church has kept and still keeps our country divided. And certainly a country can never be united and happy, except when it obeys wholly one government, whether a republic or a monarchy, as is the case in France and in Spain; and the sole cause why Italy is not in the same condition, and is not governed by either one republic or one sovereign, is the Church; for having acquired and holding a temporal dominion, yet she has never had sufficient power or courage to enable her to seize the rest of the country and make herself sole sovereign of all Italy. And on the other hand she has not been so feeble that the fear of losing her temporal power prevented her from calling in the aid of a foreign power to defend her against such others as had become too powerful in Italy; as was seen in former days by many sad experiences, when through the intervention of Charlemagne she drove out the Lombards, who were masters of nearly all Italy; and when in our times she crushed the power of the Venetians by the aid of France, and afterwards with the assistance of the Swiss drove out in turn the French. The Church, then, not having been powerful enough to be able to master all Italy, nor having permitted any other power to do so, has been the cause why Italy has never been able to unite under one head, but has always remained under a number of princes and lords, which occasioned her so many dissensions and so much weakness that she became a prey not only to the powerful barbarians, but of whoever chose to assail her. This we other Italians owe to the Church of Rome, and to none other. And any one, to be promptly convinced by experiment of the truth of all this, should have the power to transport the court of Rome to reside, with all the power it has in Italy, in the midst of the Swiss, who of all peoples nowadays live most according to their ancient customs so far as religion and their military system are concerned; and he would see in a very little while that the evil habits of that court would create more confusion in that country than anything else that could ever happen there.

Chapter LVIII
The People Are Wiser and More Constant Than Princes

Titus Livius as well as all other historians affirm that nothing is more uncertain and inconstant than the multitude; for it appears from what he relates of the actions of men, that in many instances the multitude, after having condemned a man to death, bitterly lamented it, and most earnestly wished him back. This was the case with the Roman people and Manlius Capitolinus, whom they had condemned to death and afterwards most earnestly desired him back, as our author says in the following words: "No sooner had they found out that they had nothing to fear from him, than they began to regret and to wish him back."

And elsewhere, when he relates the events that occurred in Syracuse after the death of Hieronymus, nephew of Hiero, he says: "It is the nature of the multitude either humbly to serve or insolently to dominate." I know not whether, in undertaking to defend a cause against the accusations of all writers, I do not assume a task so hard and so beset with difficulties as to oblige me to abandon it with shame, or to go on with it at the risk of being weighed down by it. Be that as it may, however, I think, and ever shall think, that it cannot be wrong to defend one's opinions with arguments founded upon reason, without employing force or authority.

I say, then, that individual men, and especially princes, may be charged with the same defects of which writers accuse the people; for whoever is not controlled by laws will commit the same errors as an unbridled multitude. This may easily be verified, for there have been and still are plenty of princes, and a few good and wise ones, such, I mean, as needed not the curb that controlled them. Amongst these, however, are not to be counted either the kings that lived in Egypt at that ancient period when that country was governed by laws, or those that arose in Sparta; neither such as are born in our day in France, for that country is more thoroughly regulated by laws than any other of which we have any knowledge in modern times. And those kings that arise under such constitutions are not to be classed amongst the number of those whose individual nature we have to consider, and see whether it resembles that of the people; but they should be compared with a people equally controlled by law as those kings were, and then we shall find in that multitude the same good qualities as in those kings, and we shall see that such a people neither obey with servility nor command with insolence. Such were the people of Rome, who, so long as that republic remained uncorrupted, neither obeyed basely nor ruled insolently, but rather held its rank honorably, supporting the laws and their magistrates. And when the unrighteous ambition of some noble made it necessary for them to rise up in self-defence, they did so, as in the case of Manlius, the Decemvirs, and others who attempted to oppress them; and so when the public good required them to obey the Dictators and Consuls, they promptly yielded obedience. And if the Roman people regretted Manlius Capitolinus after his death, it is not to be wondered at; for they regretted his virtues, which had been such that the remembrance of them filled every one with pity, and would have had the power to produce the same effect upon any prince; for all writers agree that virtue is to be admired and praised, even in one's enemies. And if intense desire could have restored Manlius to life, the Roman people would nevertheless have pronounced the same judgment against him as they did the first time, when they took him from prison and condemned him to death. And so we have seen princes that were esteemed wise, who have caused persons to be put to death and afterwards regretted it deeply; such as Alexander the Great with regard to Clitus and other friends, and Herod with his wife Mariamne. But what our historian says of the character of the multitude does not apply to a people regulated by laws, as the Romans were, but to an unbridled multitude, such as the Syracusans; who committed all the excesses to which infuriated and unbridled men abandon themselves, as did Alexander the Great and Herod in the above-mentioned cases.

Therefore, the character of the people is not to be blamed any more than that of princes, for both alike are liable to err when they are without any control. Besides the examples already given, I could adduce numerous others from amongst the Roman Emperors and other tyrants and princes, who have displayed as much inconstancy and recklessness as any populace ever did. Contrary to the general opinion, then, which maintains that the people, when they govern, are inconsistent, unstable, and ungrateful, I conclude and affirm that these defects are not more natural to the people than they are to princes. To charge the people and princes equally with them may be the truth, but to except princes from them would be a great mistake. For a people that governs and is well regulated by laws will be stable, prudent, and grateful, as much so, and even more, according to my opinion, than a prince, although he be esteemed wise; and, on the other hand, a prince, freed from the restraints of the law, will be more ungrateful, inconstant, and imprudent than a people similarly situated. The difference in their conduct is not due to any difference in their nature (for that is the same, and if there be any difference for good, it is on the side of the people); but to the greater or less respect they have for the laws under which they respectively live. And whoever studies the Roman people will see that for four hundred years they have been haters of royalty, and lovers of the glory and common good of their country; and he will find any number of examples that will prove both the one and the other. And should any one allege the ingratitude which the Roman people displayed towards Scipio, I shall reply the same as I have said in another place on this subject, where I have demonstrated that the people are less ungrateful than princes. But as regards prudence and stability, I say that the people are more prudent and stable, and have better judgment than a prince; and it is not without good reason that it is said, "The voice of the people is the voice of God"; for we see popular opinion prognosticate events in such a wonderful manner that it would almost seem as if the people had some occult virtue, which enables them to foresee the good and the evil. As to the people's capacity of judging of things, it is exceedingly rare that, when they hear two orators of equal talents advocate different measures, they do not decide in favor of the best of the two; which proves their ability to discern the truth of what they hear. And if occasionally they are misled in matters involving questions of courage or seeming utility (as has been said above), so is a prince also many times misled by his own passions, which are much greater than those of the people. We also see that in the election of their magistrates they make far better choice than princes; and no people will ever be persuaded to elect a man of infamous character and corrupt habits to any post of dignity, to which a prince is easily influenced in a thousand different ways. When we see a people take an aversion to anything, they persist in it for many centuries, which we never find to be the case with princes. Upon both these points the Roman people shall serve me as a proof, who in the many elections of Consuls and Tribunes had to regret only four times the choice they had made. The Roman people held the name of king in such detestation, as we have said, that no extent of services rendered by any of its citizens who attempted to usurp that title could save him from his merited punishment. We furthermore see the cities where the people are masters make the greatest progress in the least possible time, and much greater than such as have always been governed by princes; as was the case with Rome after the expulsion of the kings; and with Athens after they rid themselves of Pisistratus; and this can be attributed to no other cause than that the governments of the people are better than those of princes.

It would be useless to object to my opinion by referring to what our historian has said in the passages quoted above, and elsewhere; for if we compare the faults of a people with those of princes, as well as their respective good qualities, we shall find the people vastly superior in all that is good and glorious. And if princes show themselves superior in the making of laws, and in the forming of civil institutions and new statutes and ordinances, the people are superior in maintaining those institutions, laws, and ordinances, which certainly places them on a par with those who established them.

And finally to sum up this matter, I say that both governments of princes and of the people have lasted a long time, but both required to be regulated by laws. For a prince who knows no other control but his own will is like a madman, and a people that can do as it pleases will hardly be wise. If now we compare a prince who is controlled by laws, and a people that is untrammeled by them, we shall find more virtue in the people than in the prince; and if we compare them when both are freed from such control, we shall see that the people are guilty of fewer excesses than the prince, and that the errors of the people are of less importance, and therefore more easily remedied. For a licentious and mutinous people may easily be brought back to good conduct by the influence and persuasion of a good man, but an evil-minded prince is not amenable to such influences, and therefore there is no other remedy against him but cold steel. We may judge then from this of the relative defects of the one and the other; if words suffice to correct those of the people, whilst those of the prince can only be remedied by violence, no one can fail to see that where the greater remedy is required, there also the defects must be greater. The follies which a people commits at the moment of its greatest license are not what is most to be feared; it is not the immediate evil that may result from them that inspires apprehension, but the fact that such general confusion might afford the opportunity for a tyrant to seize the government. But with evil-disposed princes the contrary is the case; it is the immediate present that causes fear, and there is hope only in the future; for men will persuade themselves that the termination of his wicked life may give them a chance of liberty. Thus we see the difference between the one and the other to be, that the one touches the present and the other the future. The excesses of the people are directed against those whom they suspect of interfering with the public good; whilst those of princes are against apprehended interference with their individual interests. The general prejudice against the people results from the fact that everybody can freely and fearlessly speak ill of them in mass, even whilst they are at the height of their power; but a prince can only be spoken of with the greatest circumspection and apprehension. . . .

Christian Faith and Freedom Reaffirmed

Martin Luther (1483–1546) originally planned to become a lawyer; at his father's urging he took a master's degree from the University of Erfurth, in central Germany, in 1505. But shortly thereafter Martin went through a spiritual crisis: uncertain about his future and worried about the state of his soul, he dropped out of the university and entered an Augustinian monastery. He studied for the priesthood and then went on to take a doctorate in theology. In 1512 he became a professor of Biblical studies at the newly founded University of Wittenberg, in the Electorate of Saxony.

He did not, however, manage to resolve his spiritual crisis. He was constantly plagued by an awareness of his own sinfulness and weakness. For these feelings of inadequacy the Church offered a series of remedies—prayer, penances, and the performance of good works—designed to ensure forgiveness for the sinner. But none of these provided Luther with the assurance of salvation which he demanded.

In studying the Bible, especially the Epistles written by St. Paul, Luther finally found a Scriptural basis for a new view of salvation and man's relationship to God. Good works, indeed any human actions, Luther argued, were insufficient for salvation; man could be saved only by faith in God. No action, nothing which man could do by himself, would be enough to earn God's forgiveness.

Luther's theological position led him to attack several of the Church's practices, chief among them the sale of indulgences. The purchase of an indulgence supposedly freed the soul of the buyer (or of someone else designated by the buyer) from the punishments of purgatory. Before 1519 Luther hoped that by attacking such abuses, he could reform the Church from within. While arguing with the defenders of the Papacy, however, he began to realize the radical implications of his own views. He gave up the attempt to work within the Roman Church; he and his followers began to build a new organization.

Luther's doctrines appealed to many Germans, at least partly for nationalistic reasons. He used all available means to spread his views. By reorganizing the liturgy to emphasize the sermon, doubtful points of doctrine could be made clear. Luther also introduced congregational singing as a regular part of the service. An able musician himself, he understood the emotional and aesthetic energies the could be tapped by singing in a group. But most of all Luther used the newly invented printing press, writing vigorous pamphlets in popular speech to explain his views, which were then disseminated throughout German-speaking lands. One of the most important of these pamphlets is reproduced in part below. Luther wrote it in 1520, when his break with the Papacy had become irreparable. It offers a concise statement of Luther's most important ideas.

MARTIN LUTHER: CHRISTIAN LIBERTY

One thing and one only is necessary for Christian life, righteousness, and liberty. That one thing is the most holy Word of God, the Gospel of Christ, as he says, John 11, "I am the resurrection and the life: he that believeth in me shall not die forever"; and John 8, "If the Son shall make you free, you shall be free in-

From Martin Luther, *Christian Liberty* (Philadelphia: Muhlenberg Press, 1947), pp. 7-21. Reprinted by permission of Fortress Press.

deed"; and Matthew 4, "Not in bread alone doth man live; but in every word that proceedeth from the mouth of God." Let us then consider it certain and conclusively established that the soul can do without all things except the Word of God, and that where this is not there is no help for the soul in anything else whatever. But if it has the Word it is rich and lacks nothing, since this Word is the Word of life, of truth, of light, of peace, of righteousness, of salvation, of joy, of liberty, of wisdom, of power, of grace, of glory, and of every blessing beyond our power to estimate. This is why the prophet in the entire One Hundred and Nineteenth Psalm, and in many other places of Scripture, with so many sighs yearns after the Word of God and applies so many names to it. On the other hand, there is no more terrible plague with which the wrath of God can smite men than a famine of the hearing of His Word, as He says in Amos, just as there is no greater mercy than when He sends forth His Word, as we read in Psalm 107, "He sent His word and healed them, and delivered them from their destructions." Nor was Christ sent into the world for any other ministry but that of the Word, and the whole spiritual estate, apostles, bishops and all the priests, has been called and instituted only for the ministry of the Word.

You ask, "What then is this Word of God, and how shall it be used, since there are so many words of God?" I answer, the Apostle explains that in Romans 1. The Word is the Gospel of God concerning His Son, who was made flesh, suffered, rose from the dead, and was glorified through the Spirit who sanctifies. For to preach Christ means to feed the soul, to make it righteous, to set it free, and to save it, if it believe the preaching. For faith alone is the saving and efficacious use of the Word of God, Romans 10, "If thou confess with thy mouth that Jesus is Lord, and believe with thy heart that God hath raised Him up from the dead, thou shalt be saved"; and again, "The end of the law is Christ, unto righteousness to everyone that believeth"; and, in Romans 1, "The just shall live by his faith." The Word of God cannot be received and cherished by any works[1] what-

1. A technical term in medieval theology, meaning such acts as prayer, charitable deeds, penances.

ever, but only by faith. Hence it is clear that, as the soul needs only the Word for its life and righteousness, so it is justified by faith alone and not by any works; for if it could be justified by anything else, it would not need the Word, and therefore it would not need faith. But this faith cannot at all exist in connection with works, that is to say, if you at the same time claim to be justified[2] by works, whatever their character; for that would be to halt between two sides, to worship Baal[3] and to kiss the hand, which, as Job says, is a very great iniquity. Therefore the moment you begin to believe, you learn that all things in you are altogether blameworthy, sinful, and damnable, as Romans 3 says, "For all have sinned and lack the glory of God"; and again, "There is none just, there is none that doeth good, all have turned out of the way: they are become unprofitable together." When you have learned this, you will know that you need Christ, who suffered and rose again for you, that, believing in Him, you may through this faith become a new man, in that all your sins are forgiven, and you are justified by the merits of another, namely, of Christ alone.

Since, therefore, this faith can rule only in the inward man, as Romans 10 says, "With the heart we believe unto righteousness"; and since faith alone justifies, it is clear that the inward man cannot be justified, made free, and be saved by any outward work or dealing whatsoever and that works, whatever their character, have nothing to do with this inward man. On the other hand, only ungodliness and unbelief of heart, and no outward work, make him guilty and a damnable servant of sin. Wherefore it ought to be the first concern of every Christian to lay aside all trust in works, and more and more to strengthen faith alone, and through faith to grow in the knowledge, not of works, but of Christ Jesus, who suffered and rose for him, as Peter teaches, in the last chapter of his first Epistle; since no other work makes a Christian. Thus when the Jews asked Christ,

2. Another technical term in medieval theology meaning "made just," i.e., to have one's sins somehow canceled so as to deserve salvation. God, being just, could only save those who were justified; the question for Luther had been how any man, being sinful, could ever deserve to be saved.

3. Canaanitish deity, abhorrent to the ancient Hebrews.

John 6, what they should do that they might work the works of God, He brushed aside the multitude of works in which He saw that they abounded, and enjoined upon them a single work, saying, "This is the work of God, that you believe in Him whom He hath sent. For Him hath God the Father sealed."

Hence true faith in Christ is a treasure beyond comparison, which brings with it all salvation and saves from every evil, as Christ says in the last chapter of Mark, "He that believeth and is baptized, shall be saved; but he that believeth not, shall be condemned." . . .

Should you ask how it comes that faith alone justifies and without works offers us such a treasury of great benefits, when so many works, ceremonies, and laws are prescribed in the Scriptures, I answer: First of all, remember what has been said: faith alone, without works, justifies, makes free and saves, as we shall later make still more clear. Here we must point out that all the Scriptures of God are divided into two parts—commands and promises. The commands indeed teach things that are good, but the things taught are not done as soon as taught; for the commands show us what we ought to do, but do not give us the power to do it: they are intended to teach a man to know himself, that through them he may recognize his inability to do good and may despair of his powers. That is why they are called and are the Old Testament. For example: "Thou shalt not covet" is a command which convicts us all of being sinners, since no one is able to avoid coveting, however much he may struggle against it. Therefore, in order not to covet, and to fulfill the command, a man is compelled to despair of himself, and to seek elsewhere and from someone else the help which he does not find in himself, as is said in Hosea, "Destruction is thy own, O Israel: thy help is only in Me." And as we fare with this one command, so we fare with all; for it is equally impossible for us to keep any of them.

But when a man through the commands has learned to know his weakness, and has become troubled as to how he may satisfy the law, since the law must be fulfilled so that not a jot or tittle shall perish, otherwise man will be condemned without hope; then, being truly humbled and reduced to nothing in his own eyes, he finds in himself no means of justification and salvation. Here the second part of the Scriptures stands ready—the promises of God, which declare the glory of God and say, "If you wish to fulfill the law, and not to covet, as the law demands, come, believe in Christ, in whom grace, righteousness, peace, liberty and all things are promised you; if you believe you shall have all, if you believe not you shall lack all." For what is impossible for you in all the works of the law, many as they are, but all useless, you will accomplish in a short and easy way through faith. For God our Father has made all things depend on faith, so that whoever has faith, shall have all, and whoever has it not, shall have nothing. "For He has concluded all under unbelief, that He might have mercy on all," Romans 11. Thus the promises of God give what the commands of God ask, and fulfill what the law prescribes, that all things may be of God alone, both the commands and the fulfilling of the commands. He alone commands, He also alone fulfills. Therefore the promises of God belong to the New Testament, nay, they are the New Testament.

And since these promises of God are holy, true, righteous, free and peaceful words, full of all goodness, it comes to pass that the soul which clings to them with a firm faith is so united with them, nay, altogether taken up into them, that it not only shares in all their power, but is saturated and made drunken with it. For if a touch of Christ healed, how much more will this most tender touch in the spirit, rather this absorbing of the Word, communicate to the soul all things that are the Word's. This, then, is how through faith alone without works the soul is justified by the Word of God, sanctified, made true and peaceful and free, filled with every blessing and made truly a child of God, as John 1 says, "To them gave he power to become the sons of God, even to them that believe on his name."

From what has been said it is easily seen whence faith has such great power, and why no good work nor all good works together can equal it: no work can cling to the Word of God nor be in the soul; in the soul faith alone and the Word have sway. As the Word is, so it makes the soul, as heated iron glows like fire because of the union of fire with it. It is clear then that a Christian man has in his faith all that he needs, and needs no works to justify him. And if he has no need of works, neither does he need the law; and if he has no need of the law, surely he is free from the law, and it is true, "the law is not made for a righteous man." And this is that Christian liberty, even our faith, which does not indeed cause us to live in idleness or in wickedness, but makes the law and works unnecessary for any man's righteousness and salvation.

This is the first power of faith. Let us now examine the second also. For it is a further function of faith, that whom it trusts it also honors with the most reverent and high regard, since it considers him truthful and trustworthy. For there is no other honor equal to the estimate of truthfulness and righteousness with which we honor him whom we trust. Or could we ascribe to a man anything greater than truthfulness, and righteousness, and perfect goodness? On the other hand, there is no way in which we can show greater contempt for a man than to regard him as false and wicked and to suspect him, as we do when we do not trust him. So when the soul firmly trusts God's promises, it regards Him as truthful and righteous, than which nothing more excellent can be ascribed to God. This is the very highest worship of God, that we ascribe to Him truthfulness, righteousness, and whatever else ought to be ascribed to one who is trusted. Then the soul consents to all His will, then it hallows His name and suffers itself to be dealt with according to God's good pleasure, because, clinging to God's promises, it does not doubt that He, who is true, just and wise, will do, dispose, and provide all things well. And is not such a soul, by this faith, in all things most obedient to God? What commandment is there that such obedience has not abundantly fulfilled? What more complete fulfillment is there than obedience in all things? But this obedience is not rendered by works, but by faith alone. . . .

The third incomparable benefit of faith is this, that it unites the soul with Christ as a bride is united with her bridegroom. And by this mystery, as the Apostle teaches, Christ and the soul become one flesh. And if they are one flesh and there is between them a true marriage, nay, by far the most perfect of all marriages, since human marriages are but frail types of this one true marriage, it follows that all they have they have in common, the good as well as the evil, so that the believing soul can boast of and glory in whatever Christ has as if it were its own, and whatever the soul has Christ claims as His own. Let us compare these and we shall see things that cannot be estimated. Christ is full of grace, life, and salvation; the soul is full of sins, death, and condemnation. Now let faith come between them, and it shall come to pass that sins, death, and hell are Christ's, and grace, life, and salvation are the soul's. For it behooves Him, if He is a bridegroom, to take upon Himself the things which are His bride's, and to bestow upon her the things that are His. For if He gives her His body and His very self, how shall He not give her all that is His? And if He takes the body of the bride, how shall He not take all that is hers?

Lo! here we have a pleasant vision not only of communion, but of a blessed strife and victory and salvation and redemption. For Christ is God and man in one person, who has neither sinned nor died, and is not condemned, and who cannot sin, die, or be condemned; His righteousness, life, and salvation are unconquerable, eternal, omnipotent; and He by the wedding ring of faith shares in the sins, death, and pains of hell which are His bride's, nay, makes them His own, and acts as if they were His own, and as if He Himself had sinned; He suffered, died, and descended into hell that He might overcome them all. Now since it was such a one who did all this, and death and hell could not swallow Him up, they were of necessity swallowed up of Him in a mighty duel. For His righteousness is greater than the sins of all men, His life stronger than death, His salvation more invincible than hell. Thus the believing soul by the pledge of its faith is free in Christ, its Bridegroom, from all sins, secure against death and against hell, and is endowed with the eternal righteousness, life and salvation of Christ, its Bridegroom. So He presents to Himself a glorious bride, without spot or wrinkle, cleansing her with the washing in the Word of life, that is, by faith in the Word of life, of righteousness, and of salvation. Thus He marries her to Himself in faith, in loving kindness, and in mercies, in righteousness and in judgment, as Hosea 2 says.

Who, then, can fully appreciate what this royal marriage means? Who can understand the riches of the glory of this grace? Here this rich and godly Bridegroom, Christ, marries this poor, wicked harlot, redeems her from all her evil and adorns her with all His good. It is now impossible that her sins should destroy her, since they are laid upon Christ and swallowed up in Him, and she has that righteousness in Christ her husband of which she may boast as of her own, and which she can confidently set against all her sins in the face of death and hell, and say, "If I have sinned, yet my Christ, in Whom I believe, has not sinned, and all His is mine, and all mine is His"—as the bride in the Song of Solomon says, "My beloved is mine, and I am his." This is what Paul means when he says, in 1 Corinthians 15, "Thanks be to God, which giveth us the victory through our Lord Jesus Christ"—that is, the victory over sin and death, as he there says, "the sting of death is sin, and the strength of sin is the law."

From this you see once more why so much is ascribed to faith, that it alone may fulfill the law and justify without works. You see that the First Commandment, which says, "Thou shalt worship one God," is fulfilled by faith alone. For though you were nothing but good works from the sole of your foot to the crown of your head, yet you would not be righteous, nor worship God, nor fulfill the First Commandment, since God cannot be worshiped unless you ascribe to Him the glory of truthfulness and of all goodness, which is due Him. And this cannot be done by works, but only by the faith of the heart. For not by the doing of works, but by believing, do we glorify God and acknowledge that He is truthful. Therefore, faith alone is the righteousness of a Christian man and the fulfilling of all the commandments. For he who fulfills the First, has no difficulty in fulfilling all the rest. But works, being insensate things, cannot glorify God, although they can, if faith be present, be done to the glory of God. At present, however, we are not inquiring what works and what sort of works are done, but who it is that does them, who glorifies God and brings forth the works. This is faith which dwells in the heart, and is the head and substance of all our righteousness. Hence, it is a blind and dangerous doctrine which teaches that the commandments must be fulfilled by works. The commandments must be fulfilled before any works can be done, and the works proceed from the fulfillment of the commandments, as we shall hear.

But that we may look more deeply into that grace which our inward man has in Christ, we must consider that in the Old Testament God sanctified to Himself every first-born male, and the birthright was highly prized, having a two-fold honor, that of priesthood, and that of kingship. For the first-born brother was priest and lord over all the others, and was a type of Christ, the true and only First-born of God the Father and of the Virgin Mary, and true King and Priest, not after the fashion of the flesh and of the world. For His kingdom is not of this world. He reigns in heavenly and spiritual things and consecrates them—such as righteousness, truth, wisdom, peace, salvation, etc. Not as if all things on earth and in hell were not also subject to Him—else how could He protect and save us from them?—but His kingdom consists neither in them nor of them. Nor does His priesthood consist in the outward splendor of robes and postures, like that human priesthood of Aaron and of our present-day Church; but it consists in spiritual things, through which He by an unseen service intercedes for us in heaven before God, there offers Himself as a sacrifice and does all things a priest should do, as Paul in the epistle to the Hebrews describes him under the type of Melchizedek. Nor does He only pray and intercede for us, but within our soul He teaches us through the living teaching of His Spirit, thus performing the two real functions of a priest, of which the prayers and the preaching of human priests are visible types.

Now, just as Christ by his birthright obtained these two prerogatives, so He imparts them to and shares them with everyone who believes on Him according to the law of the aforesaid marriage, by which the wife owns whatever belongs to the husband. Hence we are all priests and kings in Christ, as many as believe on Christ, as 1 Peter 2 says, "Ye are a chosen generation, a peculiar people, a royal priesthood and priestly kingdom, that ye should show forth the virtues of him who hath called you out of darkness into his marvelous light."

This priesthood and kingship we explain as follows: First, as to the kingship, every Christian is by faith so exalted above all things that by a spiritual power he is lord of all things without exception, so that nothing can do him any harm whatever, nay, all things are made subject to him and compelled to serve him to his salvation. Thus Paul says in Romans 8, "All things work together for good to them who are called." And, in 1 Corinthians 3, "All things are yours, whether life or death, or things present or things to come, and ye are Christ's." Not as if every Christian were set over all things, to possess and control them by physical power—a madness with which some churchmen are afflicted—for such power belongs to kings, princes, and men on earth. Our ordinary experience in life shows us that we are subjected to all, suffer many things and even die; nay, the more Christian a man is, the more evils, sufferings, and deaths is he made subject to, as we see in Christ the first-born Prince Himself, and in all His brethren, the saints. The power of which we speak is spiritual; it rules in the midst of enemies, and is mighty in the midst of oppression, which means nothing else than that strength is made perfect in weakness, and that in all things I can find profit unto salvation, so that the cross and death itself are compelled to serve me and to work together with me for my salvation. This is a splendid prerogative and hard to attain, and a true omnipotent power, a spiritual dominion, in which there is nothing so good and nothing so evil, but that it shall work together for good to me, if only I believe. And yet, since faith alone suffices for salvation, I have need of nothing, except that faith exercise the power and dominion of its own liberty. Lo, this is the inestimable power and liberty of Christians.

Not only are we the freest of kings, we are also priests forever, which is far more excellent than being kings, because as priests we are worthy to appear before God to pray for others and to teach one another the things of God. For these are the functions of priests, and cannot be granted to any unbeliever. Thus Christ has obtained for us, if we believe on Him, that we are not only His brethren, co-heirs and fellow-kings with Him, but also fellow-priests with Him, who may boldly come into the present of God in the spirit of faith and cry, "Abba, Father!" pray for one another and do all things which we see done and prefigured in the outward and visible works of priests. But he who does not believe is not served by anything, nor does anything work for good to him, but he himself is a servant of all, and all things become evils to him, because he wickedly uses them to his own profit and not to the glory of God. And so he is no priest, but a profane man, whose prayer becomes sin and never comes into the presence of God, because God does not hear sinners. Who then can comprehend the lofty dignity of the Christian? Through his kingly power he rules over all things, death, life, and sin, and through his priestly glory is all-powerful with God, because God does the things which he asks and desires, as it is written, "He will fulfill the desire of them that fear Him; He also will hear their cry, and will save them." To this glory a man attains, surely not by any works of his, but by faith alone.

From this anyone can clearly see how a Christian man is free from all things and over all things, so that he needs no works to make him righteous and to save him, since faith alone confers all these things abundantly. But should he grow so foolish as to presume to become righteous, free, saved, and a Christian by means of some good work, he would on the instant lose faith and all its benefits: a foolishness aptly illustrated in the fable of the dog who runs along a stream with a piece of meat in his mouth, and, deceived by the reflection of the meat in the water, opens his mouth to snap at it, and so loses both the meat and the reflection.

You will ask, "If all who are in the Church are priests, how do those whom we now call priests differ from laymen?" I answer: "Injustice is done those words, 'priest,' 'cleric,' 'spiritual,' 'ecclesiastic,' when they are transferred from all other Christians to those few who are now by a mischievous usage called 'ecclesiastics.' For Holy Scripture makes no distinction between them, except that it gives the name 'ministers,' 'servants,' 'stewards,' to those who are now proudly called popes, bishops, and lords, and who should by the ministry of the Word serve others and teach them the faith of Christ and the liberty of believers. For although we are all equally priests, yet we cannot all publicly minister and teach, nor ought we if we could." Thus Paul writes in 1 Corinthians 4, "Let a man so account of us, as of the ministers of Christ, and stewards of the mysteries of God."

But that stewardship has now been developed into so great a pomp of power and so terrible a tyranny, that no heathen empire or earthly power can be compared with it, just as if laymen were not also Christians. Through this perversion the knowledge of Christian grace, faith, liberty, and of Christ Himself has altogether perished, and its place has been taken by an unbearable bondage of human words and laws, until we have become, as the Lamentations of Jeremiah say, servants of the vilest men on earth, who abuse our misfortune to serve only their base and shameless will.

To return to our purpose, I believe it has now become clear that it is not enough, nor is it Christian, to preach the works, life, and words of Christ as historical facts, as if the knowledge of these would suffice for the conduct of life, although this is the fashion of those who must today be regarded as our best preachers; and far less is it enough or Christian to say nothing at all about Christ and to teach instead the laws of men and the decrees of the Fathers. And now there are not a few who preach Christ and read about Him that they may move men's affections to sympathy with Christ, to anger against the Jews and such like childish and womanish nonsense. Rather ought Christ to be preached to the end that faith in Him may be established, that He may not only be Christ, but be Christ for thee and for me, and that what is said of Him and what His Name denotes may be effectual in us. And such faith is produced and preserved in us by preaching why Christ came, what He brought and bestowed, what benefit it is to us to accept Him. This is done when that Christian liberty which He bestows is rightly taught, and we are told in what way we who are Christians are all kings and priests and so are lords of all, and may firmly believe that whatever we have done is pleasing and acceptable in the sight of God, as I have said.

What man is there whose heart, hearing these things, will not rejoice to its very core, and in receiving such comfort grow tender so as to love Christ, as he never could be made to love by any laws or works? Who would have power to harm such a heart or to make it afraid? If the knowledge of sin or the fear of death break in upon it, it is ready to hope in the Lord; it does not grow afraid when it hears tidings of evil, nor is it disturbed until it shall look down upon its enemies. For it believes that the righteousness of Christ is its own, and that its sin is not its own, but Christ's; and that all sin is swallowed up by the righteousness of Christ is, as has been said above, a necessary consequence of faith in Christ. So the heart learns to scoff at death and sin, and to say with the Apostle, "Where, O death, is thy victory? where, O death, is thy sting? The sting of death is sin, and the strength of sin is the law. But thanks be to God, which giveth us the victory through our Lord Jesus Christ." For death is swallowed up not only in the victory of Christ, but also by our victory, because through faith His victory has become ours, and in that faith we also are conquerors.

Let this suffice concerning the inward man, his liberty and its source, the righteousness of faith, which needs neither laws nor good works, nay, is rather injured by them, if a man trusts that he is justified by them.

Songs for Salvation

Luther's successful attack on the Roman Church encouraged reformers in other parts of Europe—especially Switzerland and England—to challenge papal authority as well. Later generations of Protestant leaders developed their own theologies, which differed from Luther's. But Luther's propaganda techniques—the use of hymns and pamphlets, sermons and cartoons—were widely copied.

The hymn texts below were written by John Hunnis (died 1597), an English follower of the French reformer John Calvin (1509–64). A minor composer and musician, Hunnis became a well-paid musician in the chapel of the Protestant King Edward VI (ruled 1547–53). During the reign of Edward's Catholic successor, Mary I, Hunnis was implicated in Protestant plots against the government and was dismissed from his post. After Mary's death, however, the Protestant Queen Elizabeth I restored Hunnis to his old job. In 1560, as an additional mark of royal favor, she made him Keeper of the Gardens and Orchards at Greenwich, a royal palace east of London;

in 1566 she gave him charge over the children's choir in the royal chapel.

Hunnis wrote both texts and music for hymns. They dealt with themes common in Calvinist literature—the weakness and basic sinfulness of man, and his need for God's forgiveness. The first of the texts reprinted here is a paraphrase of Psalm 6; it could have been used in church services or sung at home for private devotions. The second text was set for two voices or for choirs and was probably intended solely for church use; it is a dialogue between Christ and a sinful man.

JOHN HUNNIS: A METRICAL PSALM AND A HYMN

Psalm 6

Oh Lord when I myself behold,
How wicked I have been;
And, view the paths and ways I went,
Wandring from sin to sin;

Again to think upon thy power,
Thy judgement, and thy might,
And how that nothing can be hid,
Or close kept from thy sight.

A Dialogue between Christ and a Sinner

Christ: Arise from sin thou wicked man,
Before the trump doth sound:
Lest thou among the guilty sort,
A damned soul be found.
My sheep why dost thou persecute
My lambs why dost thou kill?
Myself why dost thou crucify,

From *English and Scottish Psalm and Hymn Tunes, c. 1543-1677* by Maurice Frost (London: Oxford University Press, 1953), pp. 460, 463-64.

And guiltless blood thus spill?
Arise, I say, arise, arise.

Sinner: What fearful thundering voice is this,
That soundeth in mine ear:
Which bids me rise, and brings my soul,
And all her power in fear?

Christ: It is the voice of him thy judge,
That shall thy judger be
Which bids thee rise while sun doth shine,
That thou thyself mayst see:
For after sun be set in shade,
And darksome clouds appear:
Too late is then for to arise,
If thou arise not here.
Arise, I say, arise, arise.

Sinner: O Lord by grace I now behold,
Where I did offend.

Christ: What made thee thus against my saints,
Such cruelty extend?

DOMINE NE IN FURORE. Psal. 6.

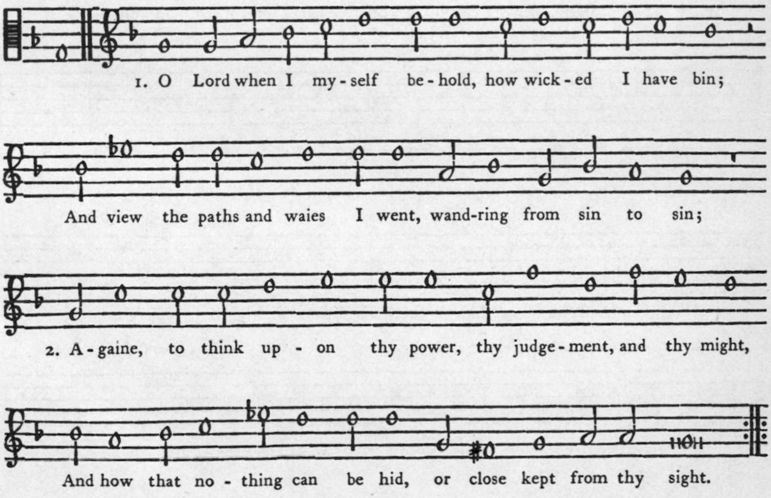
1. O Lord when I my-self be-hold, how wick-ed I have bin;
And view the paths and waies I went, wand-ring from sin to sin;
2. A-gaine, to think up-on thy power, thy judge-ment, and thy might,
And how that no-thing can be hid, or close kept from thy sight.

A Dialog. betweene Christ and a Sinner.

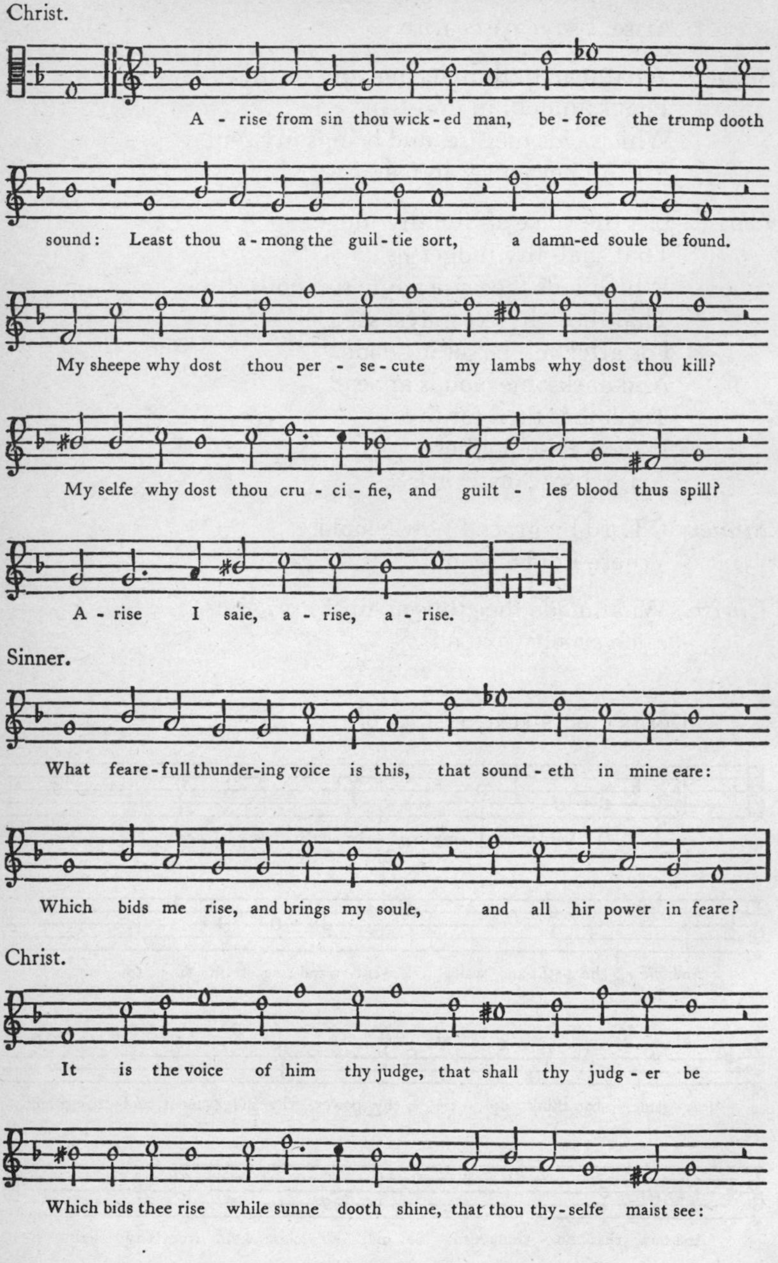
Christ.
A - rise from sin thou wick - ed man, be - fore the trump dooth
sound: Least thou a - mong the guil - tie sort, a damn - ed soule be found.
My sheepe why dost thou per - se - cute my lambs why dost thou kill?
My selfe why dost thou cru - ci - fie, and guilt - les blood thus spill?
A - rise I saie, a - rise, a - rise.
Sinner.
What feare - full thunder - ing voice is this, that sound - eth in mine eare:
Which bids me rise, and brings my soule, and all hir power in feare?
Christ.
It is the voice of him thy judge, that shall thy judg - er be
Which bids thee rise while sunne dooth shine, that thou thy - selfe maist see:

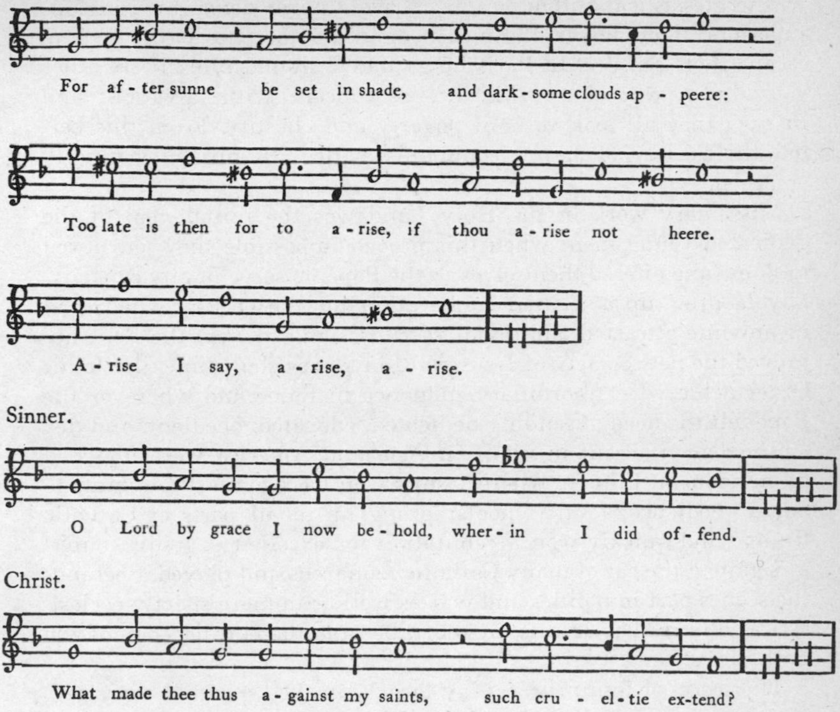
For af - ter sunne be set in shade, and dark - some clouds ap - peere:
Too late is then for to a - rise, if thou a - rise not heere.
A - rise I say, a - rise, a - rise.
Sinner.
O Lord by grace I now be - hold, wher - in I did of - fend.
Christ.
What made thee thus a - gainst my saints, such cru - el - tie ex-tend?

How To Make Soldiers for Christ

Inigo Lopez de Loyola (1491–1556) was born a petty nobleman in Spain and started a military career. In 1521 he was wounded and while recovering in a hospital experienced a religious conversion. Loyola was not the man to do things half-heartedly. He launched upon a rigorously ascetic discipline, scourging himself and praying seven hours a day. Later he relaxed the severity of his self-inflicted punishments, made pilgrimage to Jerusalem. On his return he started to study Latin and theology in Barcelona and Salamanca. He continued his studies in Paris arriving there in 1528.

His personal experience of conversion and self-discipline provided him with the basis for "spiritual exercises" which he began to administer to others while still a student. This created some difficulties with ecclesiastical authorities, but Loyola never defied his religious superiors, though several times he found it best to leave town to escape their censure. In Paris he gathered around himself six other young men who shared his intense concern with salvation; and in 1534 they all took vows of poverty and chastity. From this kernel the Society of Jesus (commonly called "Jesuits") eventually emerged.

Missionary work in the Holy Land was the initial goal of the dedicated young men; when this proved impossible they journeyed to Rome and offered themselves to the Pope, to serve in any capacity. Loyola drew up a written constitution for the Order (which had meanwhile attracted additional recruits), and in 1540 the Pope approved the new Society of Jesus. Within a very short time, the Jesuit Order achieved extraordinary influence in Rome and wherever the Pope felt the need of sending dedicated, educated, obedient, and disciplined men. Jesuit missions in Asia and America were matched by missions in Europe, where Jesuits won back many Protestants to papal obedience. Jesuit schools sprang up in all parts of Catholic Europe and quickly won a reputation for excellence. Jesuit confessors gained the ear of many Catholic monarchs and played a behind-the-scenes part in politics and war as well as in more strictly ecclesiastical affairs. The Jesuits, in short, became the cutting edge of the Catholic reform.

The secret of Jesuit success lay largely in the "spiritual exercises" which, when skilfully administered by an experienced supervisor, had the effect of reshaping men to make them into dedicated "soldiers of Christ." The exercises reached down toward the deepest psychic structures of those who took them, for St. Ignatius wished to duplicate in others the sort of shattering and revivifying experience he had been through himself. Having supervised many conversions personally, in 1549 he put the final touches on the little handbook reproduced in part below, which explained in exact detail how to go about changing men's lives by directing them in "spiritual exercises." Loyola's *Spiritual Exercises* have remained ever since an important and influential element in Catholic piety and practice the world around.

The exercises were designed to last four weeks. Each week a different aspect of Christian doctrine was emphasized: Sin during the first week; the Incarnation during the second week; the Crucifixion during the third week; the Resurrection during the fourth week. Over-all, the pattern is, therefore, one of sadness and despair alternating with joy and hope. Throughout, St. Ignatius emphasized the need for touching the emotions and reducing the exercitant to tears, both of desolation and of joy.

ST. IGNATIUS LOYOLA: SPIRITUAL EXERCISES

First Week.

THE FIRST EXERCISE

The First Exercise is a meditation by means of the three powers of the soul upon the first, the second, and the third sin. It contains in itself, after a preparatory prayer and two preludes, three principal points and a colloquy.

The preparatory prayer is to ask our Lord God for grace that all my intentions, actions, and operations may be ordained purely to the service and praise of His Divine Majesty.

The first prelude is a composition of place, seeing the spot. Here it is to be observed that in contemplation or meditation on visible matters, such as the contemplation of Christ our Lord, Who is visible, the composition will be to see with the eyes of the imagination the corporeal place where the thing I wish to contemplate is found. I say the corporeal place, such as the Temple or the mountain, where Jesus Christ or our Lady is found, according to what I desire to contemplate. In meditation on invisible things, such as the present meditation on sins, the composition will be to see with the eyes of the imagination and to consider that my soul is imprisoned in this corruptible body, and my whole self in this vale of misery, as it were in exile among brute beasts; I say my whole self, that is, soul and body.

The second prelude is to ask of God our Lord that which I wish and desire. The petition ought to be according to the subject-matter, *i.e.*, if the contemplation is on the Resurrection, the

From *The Text of the Spiritual Exercises of Saint Ignatius,* 4th edition (Westminster Maryland: The Newman Press, 1949), pp. 20-31. Reprinted by permission of Paulist/Newman Press.

petition ought to be to ask for joy with Christ rejoicing; if it be on the Passion, to ask for grief, tears, and pain in union with Christ in torment; here it will be to ask for shame and confusion at myself, seeing how many have been lost for one sole mortal sin, and how many times I have merited to be lost eternally for my so many sins.

Before all the contemplations or meditations the preparatory prayer must always be the same, without any alteration. There must also be the two above-named preludes, which are changed from time to time according to the subject-matter.

The first point will be to apply the memory to the first sin, which was that of the angels;[1] and then immediately to employ the understanding on the same by turning it over in the mind: and then the will, desiring to remember and understand the whole, in order to put myself to the blush, and to be confounded, bringing my many sins into comparison with the one sole sin of the angels; and while they have gone to Hell for one sin, how often I have deserved the same for so many. I say, to bring to memory the sin of the angels, how they were created in grace, yet not willing to help themselves by the means of their liberty in the work of paying reverence and obedience to their Creator and Lord, falling into pride, they were changed from grace into malice, and hurled from Heaven to Hell; and then in turn to reason more in particular with the understanding, and thus in turn to move still more the affections by means of the will.

The second point will be to do the same, *i.e.*, to apply the three powers, to the sin of Adam and Eve; bringing before the memory how for that sin they did such long penance, and how much corruption came upon the human race, so many men being put on the way to Hell. I say, to bring to memory the second sin, that of our first parents; how, after Adam had been created in the plain of Damascus, and placed in the terrestrial Paradise, and Eve had been formed out of his rib, when they had been forbidden to eat of the tree of knowledge, yet eating of it, and so sinning, they were afterwards clothed in garments made of skins, and driven out of Paradise, lived without original justice, which they had lost, all their life long in many travails and

1. I.e., the fallen angels, whose chief was Satan.

much penance; and in turn with the understanding to discuss all this, making more especially use of the will, as has been said before.

The third point will be to do in like manner also in regard to the third sin, *i.e.*, the particular sin of some one person who for one mortal sin has gone to Hell; and many others without number have been condemned for fewer sins than I have committed. I say, to do the same in regard to the third particular sin, bringing before the memory the gravity and malice of sin committed by man against his Creator and Lord; then to discuss with the understanding, how in sinning and acting against the Infinite Goodness, such a person has justly been condemned for ever; and to conclude with acts of the will, as has been said.

Colloquy. Imagining Christ our Lord before us and placed on the Cross, to make a colloquy with Him, asking Him how, being our Creator, He had come to this, that He has made Himself Man, and from eternal life has come to temporal death, thus to die for my sins. Again, to look at myself, asking what I have done for Christ, what I am doing for Christ, what I ought to do for Christ; and then seeing Him that which He is, and thus fixed to the Cross, to give expression to what shall present itself to my mind.

The colloquy is made properly by speaking as one friend speaks to another, or as a servant to his master; at one time asking for some favour, at another blaming oneself for some evil committed, now informing him of one's affairs, and seeking counsel in them. And at the end let a *Pater noster* be said.

THE SECOND EXERCISE

The Second Exercise is a meditation upon sins; it contains, after the preparatory prayer and the two preludes, five points and a colloquy.

Let the preparatory prayer be the same.

The first prelude will be the same composition of place.

The second is to ask for what I desire; it will be here to beg great and intense grief, and tears for my sins.

The first point is the series of sins, that is to say, to recall to memory all the sins of my life, looking at them from year to year or from period to period. Three things help in this: the first, to behold the place and the house where I have dwelt; the second, the conversation I have had with others; the third, the calling in which I have lived.

The second point is to weigh the sins, looking at the foulness and the malice that every mortal sin committed contains in itself, even supposing that it were not forbidden.

The third point is to consider who I am, abasing myself by examples; first, how little I am in comparison with all men; secondly, what men are in comparison with all the angels and saints of Paradise; thirdly, to consider what all that is created is in comparison with God; then I alone, what can I be? fourthly, to consider all my corruption and foulness of body; fifthly, to see myself as an ulcer and abscess whence have issued so many sins and so many iniquities, and such vile poison.

The fourth point is to consider who God is, against Whom I have sinned, looking at His attributes, comparing them with their contraries in myself: His wisdom with my ignorance, His omnipotence with my weakness, His justice with my iniquity, His goodness with my malice.

The first point is an exclamation of wonder, with intense affection, running through all creatures in my mind, how they have suffered me to live, and have preserved me in life; how the angels, who are the sword of the Divine Justice, have borne with me, and have guarded and prayed for me; how the saints have been interceding and praying for me; and the heavens, the sun, the moon, the stars, and the elements, the fruits of the earth, the birds, the fishes, and the animals; and the earth, how it is it has not opened to swallow me up, creating new hells that I might suffer in them for ever.

The whole to conclude with a colloquy of mercy, reasoning and giving thanks to God our Lord, for having given me life till now, and proposing through His grace to amend henceforward. *Pater noster*.

THE THIRD EXERCISE

The Third Exercise is a repetition of the first and second Exercise; making three colloquies.

THE FOURTH EXERCISE

The Fourth Exercise is made by resuming the third.

I have said resuming, in order that the understanding without distraction may turn over assiduously the remembrance of the matters contemplated in the preceding Exercises; then making the three same colloquies.

THE FIFTH EXERCISE

The Fifth Exercise is a meditation on Hell. It contains, after a preparatory prayer and two preludes, five points and a colloquy.

Let the preparatory prayer be the usual one.

The first prelude is a composition of place, which is here to see with the eyes of the imagination the length, breadth, and depth of Hell.

The second prelude is to ask for that which I desire. It will be here to ask for an interior sense of the pains which the lost suffer, in order that if I through my faults forget the love of the Eternal Lord, at least the fear of punishment may help me not to fall into sin.

The first point will be to see with the eyes of the imagination those great fires, and the souls as it were in bodies of fire.

The second will be to hear with the ears of the imagination the wailings, the howlings, the cries, the blasphemies against Christ our Lord and against all His saints.

The third will be to smell the smoke, the sulphur, the filth, and the putrid matter.

The fourth will be to taste with the taste of the imagination bitter things, such as tears, sadness, and the worm of conscience.

The fifth will be to feel with the touch of the imagination how those fires touch and burn the souls.

Making a colloquy to Christ our Lord, to bring to memory the souls which are in Hell, some because they did not believe His coming, others because believing they did not act according to His commandments; making of them three classes: the first, those who lived before His coming; the second, those who were alive during His lifetime; and the third, those who lived after His life in this world: and then give thanks that He has not, by putting an end to my life, permitted me to fall into any of these classes. In like manner to consider how up till now He has always had towards me such pity and mercy; and then I will finish by once saying a *Pater noster*.

Additions

FOR THE PURPOSE OF HELPING THE EXERCITANT TO MAKE THE EXERCISES BETTER, AND TO FIND MORE EASILY WHAT HE WANTS

I. After having lain down, when I want to go to sleep, to think for the space of an *Ave Maria* of the hour when I have to rise, and for what purpose, briefly recapitulating the Exercise which I have to make.

II. When I awake, not admitting other thoughts, immediately to turn my mind to that which I am going to contemplate in the first Exercise at midnight, bringing myself to confusion for my many sins, proposing examples to myself, as if a knight were to stand before his king and all his court, covered with shame and confusion, because he had grievously offended him, from whom he had first received many gifts and many favours. And thus too in the second Exercise, considering myself as a great sinner, and in chains, imagining, namely, that bound in fetters I am about to appear before the Supreme, Eternal Judge, taking an example from how prisoners bound in chains, and deserving of death, appear before their temporal judge; and I will dress myself, turning over these or other like thoughts, according to the subject-matter.

III. I will stand for the space of a *Pater noster* one or two paces from the place in which I am about to contemplate or meditate, and with my mind raised on high consider how God our Lord sees me, and I will make an act of reverence and humiliation.

IV. The fourth Addition is to enter on the contemplation, at one time kneeling, at another prostrate on the earth, or stretched on the ground with my face upwards, now seated, now standing, ever intent on seeking that which I desire. Two things are to be noticed: first, if kneeling, or if prostrate, &c., I find that which I want, I will not try any other position; secondly, that in the point on which I shall find what I desire, there I will rest, without being anxious to proceed to another, until I have satisfied myself.

V. After having finished the Exercise, for the space of a quarter of an hour, sitting or walking, I will examine how I have succeeded in the contemplation or meditation; if badly, I will look for the cause whence it proceeds, and when I have seen it I will be sorry for it, so as to amend in future; if well, I will thank God our Lord, and proceed in the same manner another time.

VI. The sixth Addition is not to desire to think on pleasant and joyful subjects, as, for example, on the glory of Paradise, the Resurrection, &c., because any consideration of joy and delight hinders the feeling of pain, grief, and tears for our sins; but rather to keep before my mind my wish to grieve and to feel pain, for that purpose rather calling to mind death and judgment.

VII. The seventh is for this same end, to deprive myself of all light, shutting the shutters and doors during the time that I am in the room, if it be not to say prayers, to read, or to eat.

VIII. The eighth is not to laugh or to say anything that may provoke laughter.

IX. The ninth is to restrain my eyes, except in receiving or dismissing the person with whom I shall speak.

X. The tenth is penance, which is divided into interior and exterior penance: the interior consists in grieving for one's sins, with a firm resolution not to commit them or any others; the exterior, which is the fruit of the interior, consists in chastisement for sins committed, and this is inflicted chiefly in three ways:

The first is in regard to food; that is to say, when we cut off what is superfluous, this is not penance but temperance: it is penance when we retrench from what is suitable, and the more and more we retrench, the greater and better is the penance, provided only the person be not injured, and no notable weakness ensue.

The second is in regard to our method of taking sleep; and here again it is not penance to leave off what is superfluous in delicate and soft things; it is penance rather when in it we leave off conveniences, and the more and more this is done, the better is the penance, provided only the person be not injured, and no notable weakness ensue; and also let nothing be retrenched from the fit time for sleep, unless perchance one have an ill habit of sleeping too much, and this in order to arrive at the mean.

The third manner is to chastise the flesh; that is to say, by causing it sensible pain, which is inflicted by wearing a hair-cloth, cords, or iron chains, next to the skin, by disciplining or bruising the body, and by other kinds of austerities. What seems to be most convenient and safe in the matter of penance is that the pain should be sensible to the flesh, and not penetrate to the bone, so that pain, and not sickness, be the result. For which purpose it seems to be more convenient to discipline oneself with small cords, which cause pain exteriorly, than to do so in any other way, from which may result any notable injury to the health.

God's Will Be Done

The Restoration brought Charles II to the English throne in 1660. His father, Charles I, had been executed by the leaders of parliament in 1649 during the English Civil War. When King Charles II assumed power, he sought out and punished those responsible for the death of his father. One of the men condemned to execution was Thomas Harrison (1606–60), whose speech, given on the gallows, appears below.

Harrison's father was a prosperous butcher. Thomas studied law at the Inns of Court in London. He joined the parliamentary armies in the early 1640's and by 1650 had become a major-general. When Oliver Cromwell, commander of the Parliamentary armies, went to Scotland in 1651, he left Harrison in charge of military forces in England.

In 1647, when Cromwell's armies captured Charles I, Harrison argued that the king should be tried and punished for his misdeeds. Harrison guarded Charles on his land journey to London, sat on the court which tried the king, and signed the royal death sentence.

After 1653, Harrison withdrew his support from Cromwell. As a member of the religious group known as Fifth Monarchists, he believed that in accordance with the prophecies of the Book of Daniel the saints of the Lord were about to descend from heaven to take over the earth and rule in glory. Harrison therefore objected to Cromwell's effort to set up a more permanent form of government; this, he argued, was a betrayal of faith in the Lord and unworthy of a Christian. Cromwell eventually imprisoned Harrison and deprived him of his commission.

In 1660 Harrison realized that Charles II intended to punish his father's executioners, but he refused to flee the country. As his speech makes clear, Harrison continued to believe that God would soon break in upon the world with the Day of Judgment. With that impending, it seemed silly to flee the vengeance of a mere mortal like King Charles.

It was customary in seventeenth-century England to permit condemned criminals to make a final speech to the crowds that came to watch public executions. They were sometimes recorded in shorthand and published. This text, therefore, is probably quite close to Major-General Harrison's actual words.

THOMAS HARRISON: SPEECH UPON THE LADDER

On Saturday the 13th of October, 1660, betwixt Nine and Ten of the Clock in the Morning, Mr. Thomas Harrison, or Major-General Harrison, according to his Sentence, was upon a Hurdle drawn from Newgate to the Place called Charing-Cross, where within certain Rails lately there made, a Gibbet was erected, and he hanged with his Face looking towards the Banqueting-House at Whitehall, (the Place where our late Sovereign of Eternal Memory[1] was sacrificed;) being half dead, he was cut down by the common Executioner, his Privy Members cut off before his Eyes, his Bowels burned, his Head severed from his Body, and his Body divided into Quarters, which were returned back to

From *The Indictment, Arraignment, Tryal and Judgement at Large of Twenty Nine Regicides* (London, 1724), pp. 277, 284-87.

1. I.e., Charles I.

Newgate upon the same Hurdle that carried it. His Head is since set on a Pole on the Top of the South-East End of Westminister-Hall, looking towards London. The Quarters of his Body are in like manner exposed upon some of the City Gates.

. . .

Having mounted the ladder for his execution, he spoke as follows:

Gentlemen,

I Did not expect to have spoken a Word to you at this Time, but seeing there is a Silence commanded, I will speak something of the Work God had in Hand in our Days.

Many of you have been Witnesses of the Finger of God, that hath been seen amongst us of late Years, in the Deliverance of his People from their Oppressors; and in bringing to Judgement those that were Guilty of the precious Blood of the dear Servants of the Lord. And how God did witness thereto, by many wonderful and evident Testimonies, as it were immediately from Heaven; insomuch, that many of our Enemies, who were Persons of no mean Quality, were forc'd to confess, That God was with us: And if God did but stand Neuter, they should not value us. And therefore seeing the Finger of God hath been pleading this Cause, I shall not need to speak much to it: In which Work I with others were engaged; for the which I do from my Soul, bless the Name of God, who, out of the exceeding Riches of his Grace, accounted me worthy to be instrumental in so glorious a Work; and though I am wrongfully charged with Murther and Blood-shed, yet I must tell you, I have kept a good Conscience, both towards God, and towards Man. I never had Malice against any Man; neither did I act maliciously towards any Person, but as I judged them to be Enemies to God and his People: And the Lord is my Witness, that I have done what I did out of the Sincerity of my Heart to the Lord. I bless God I have no Guilt upon my Conscience, but the Spirit of God beareth witness, that my Actions are acceptable to the Lord through Jesus Christ: Though I have been compassed about with manifold Infirmities, Failings and Imperfections in my holiest Duties; but in this I have Comfort and Consolation, that I have Peace with God, and do see all my Sins wash'd away in the Blood of my dear Saviour. And I do declare, as before the Lord, that I would not be guilty wittingly nor willingly of the Blood of the meanest Man, no not for ten thousand Worlds, much less of the Blood of such as I am charged with.

I have again and again besought the Lord with Tears to make known his Will and Mind unto me concerning it; and to this Day he hath rather confirmed me in the Justice of it; and therefore I leave it to him, and to him I commit my Ways; but some that were eminent in the Work, did wickedly turn aside themselves, and set up their Nests on high,[2] which caused great Dishonour to the Name of God, and the Profession they had made. And the Lord knows I could have suffered more than this, rather than have fallen in with them in that Iniquity; though I was offered what I would if I would have joined with them: My Aim in all my Proceedings was the Glory of God, and the Good of his People, and the Welfare of the whole Commonwealth.

[The People observing him to tremble in his Hands and Legs, he taking notice of it, said,]

Gentlemen, By reason of some scoffing that I do hear, I judge, that some do think I am afraid to die, by the shaking I have in my Hands and Knees; I tell you, No, but it is by reason of much Blood I have lost in the Wars, and many Wounds I have received in my Body, which caused this Shaking and Weakness in my Nerves. I have had it this Twelve Years; I speak this to the Praise and Glory of God; he hath carried me above the Fear of Death; and I value not my Life, because I go to my Father, and am assured I shall take it up again.

Gentlemen, Take notice, that for being instrumental in that Cause and Interest of the Son of God, which hath been pleaded amongst us, and which God hath witnessed to by Appeals and wonderful Victories, I am brought to this Place to suffer Death this Day; and if I had Ten thousand Lives, I would freely and chearfully lay them down all to witness to this Matter.

Oh! what am I, poor Worm, that I should be accounted

2. Harrison refers to Oliver Cromwell and others who helped set up the revolutionary governments, 1649-58.

worthy to suffer any Thing for the Sake of my Lord and Saviour Jesus Christ! I have gone joyfully and willingly many a Time to lay down my Life upon the Account of Christ, but never with so much Joy and Freedom as at this Time. I do not lay down my Life by constraint but willingly; for if I had been minded to have run away, I might have had many Opportunities; but being so clear in the Thing, I durst not turn my Back, nor step a Foot out of the Way, by reason I had been engaged in the Service of so glorious and great a God: However Men presume to call it by hard Names, yet, I believe, e'er it be long the Lord will make it known from Heaven, that there was more of God in it, than Men are now aware of. All the Gods of the Nations are but Idols, they have Eyes but see not, and Mouths but speak not, and cannot save those that trust in them. But my God is the King of Kings, and Lord of Lords; before whom all you here, and all Nations, are but as a Drop of a Bucket. And he will never leave those that truly trust in him, unto whose Glory I shall surely go, and shall sit on the Right Hand of Christ in Heaven; it may be, to judge those that have unjustly judged me, Matth. 25. 33, 34. I Cor. 6.2.

[The Sheriff minding him of the Shortness of Time; if he had any Thing to say to the People, he might. He said,]

I do desire, as from my own Soul, that they and every one may fear the Lord, that they may consider their latter End, and so it may be well with them; and even for the worst of those that have been most malitious against me, from my Soul I would forgive them all. So far as any Thing concerns me, and so far as it concerns the Cause and Glory of God, I leave for him to plead: And as for the Cause of God, I am willing to justify it by my Sufferings, according to the good Pleasure of his Will.

I have been this Morning, before I came hither, so hurried up and down Stairs, (the Meaning whereof I knew not,) that my Spirits are almost spent; therefore you may not expect much from me.

Oh, the Greatness of the Love of God to such a poor, vile, and nothing-creature as I am! What am I, that Jesus Christ should shed his Heart's Blood for me, that I might be happy to all Eternity; that I might be made a Son of God, and an Heir of Heaven! Oh, that Christ should undergo so great Sufferings and Reproaches for me, and should not I be willing to lay down my Life, and suffer Reproaches for him that hath so loved me! Blessed be the Name of God that I have a Life to lose upon so glorious, and so honourable an Account.

[Then praying to himself, with Tears; and having ended, the Hangman pull'd down his Cap; but he thrust it up again, saying,]

I have one Word more to the Lord's People, that desire to serve him with an upright Heart: Let them not think hardly of any of the good Ways of God for all this; for I have been near this Seven Years a suffering Person, and have found the Way of God to be a perfect Way, his Word a tried Word, a Buckler to them that trust in him, and will make known his glorious Arm in the Sight of all Nations. And though we may suffer hard Things, yet he hath a gracious End, and will make a good End for his own Glory, and the Good of his People; therefore be chearful in the Lord your God, hold fast that which you have, and be not afraid of suffering; for God will make hard and bitter Things sweet and easy to all those that trust in him. Keep close to the good Confession you have made of Jesus Christ, and look to the Recompence of Reward: Be not discouraged, by reason of the Cloud that now is upon you; for the Sun will shine, and God will give a Testimony unto what he hath been a doing, in a short Time.

And now I desire to commit my Concernments into the Hands of my Lord and Saviour Jesus Christ; he that hath delivered himself for the Chief of Sinners; he that came into the World, was made Flesh, and was crucified, that hath loved me, and washed me from my Sins in his own Blood, and is risen again, sitting at the Right-Hand of God, making Intercession for me.

And as for me, Oh, who am I, poor, Base, vile Worm, that God should deal thus by me? for this will make me come the sooner into his Glory, and to inherit the Kingdom, and the Crown prepared for me! Oh, I have served a good Lord and Master, which hath helped me from my Beginning to this Day, and hath carried me through many Difficulties, Trials, Straits and Temptations, and hath always been a very present Help in Time of Trouble; he hath covered my Head many Times in the Day of Battle: By God, I have leaped over a Wall; by God I have run through a Troop; and by my God I will go through this Death, and he will make it easy for me. Now into thy Hand, O Lord Jesus, I commit my Spirit.

II

Exploration and Discovery

Terrestrial Exploration
    Bernal Díaz del Castillo: Memoirs

Celestial Exploration
    Galileo Galilei; Sidereal Messenger

Intellectual Exploration
    René Descartes: Discourse on Method

Terrestrial Exploration

Bernal Díaz del Castillo (ca. 1492–1581) was a Spanish soldier who accompanied Hernando Cortez on the expedition that climaxed in the conquest of Mexico (1521). Cortez started out with only 600 men and sixteen horses; by the time the Spaniards reached the Aztec capital, modern Mexico City, their numbers had shrunk to about 450. Yet when the Spaniards quarreled with the Aztecs, they were able first to flee the city, and then came back, to beseige and eventually to conquer it again. The aid of Indian allies eager to rebel against the Aztec rule was important; so was the effect of a smallpox epidemic that led to very heavy mortality among the Indians; but the brute courage and fighting skills of Cortez and his men were also decisive in permitting such a small number of men to conquer such a mighty empire.

After the re-entry into Mexico City, Bernal Díaz left Cortez and eventually settled on a plantation in Honduras. He became a writer late in life, deciding to correct rhetorically exaggerated accounts of Cortez' career by writing down what he remembered, simply and without literary embellishment. Modern scholars believe that his information was quite correct, save for a few slips of memory. His work was published only in 1632; it is a lengthy and vivid narrative of which the portion reprinted below is only a small part. It describes the first arrival of the Spaniards in Mexico City in 1519.

BERNAL DIAZ DEL CASTILLO: MEMOIRS

Chapter LXXXVIII

The magnificent and pompous reception which the powerful Motecusuma gave to Cortes and all of us, on our entrance into the great city of Mexico

The following morning we left Iztapalapan accompanied by all the principal caziques[1] above mentioned. The road along which we marched was eight paces in breadth, and if I still remember ran in a perfectly straight line to Mexico. Notwithstanding the breadth, it was much too narrow to hold the vast crowds of people who continually kept arriving from different parts to gaze upon us, and we could scarcely move along. Besides this, the tops of all the temples and towers were crowded, while the lake beneath was completely covered with canoes filled with Indians, for all were curious to catch a glimpse of us. And who can wonder at this, as neither men like unto ourselves, nor horses, had ever been seen here before!

When we gazed upon all this splendour at once, we scarcely knew what to think, and we doubted whether all that we beheld was real. A series of large towns stretched themselves along the banks of the lake, out of which still larger ones rose magnificently above the waters. Innumerable crowds of canoes were plying everywhere around us; at regular distances we continually passed over new bridges, and before us lay the great city of Mexico in all its splendour.

And we who were gazing upon all this, passing through innumerable crowds of human beings, were a mere handful of men, in all 450, our minds still full of the warnings which the inhabitants of Huexotzinco, Tlascalla, and Tlalmanalco, with the caution they had given us not to expose our lives to the

From *The Memoirs of the Conquistador Bernal Díaz del Castillo, Written by Himself Containing a True and Full Account of the Discovery and Conquest of Mexico and New Spain,* trans. by John Ingram Lockhart (London: J. Hatchard and Sons, 1884), pp. 220-43.

1. Indian chieftains.

treachery of the Mexicans. I may safely ask the kind reader to ponder a moment, and say whether he thinks any men in this world ever ventured so bold a stroke as this?

When we had arrived at a spot where another narrow causeway led towards Cojohuacan we were met by a number of caziques and distinguished personages, all attired in their most splendid garments. They had been despatched by Motecusuma[2] to meet us and bid us welcome in his name; and in token of peace they touched the ground with their hands and kissed it. Here we halted for a few minutes, while the princes of Tetzcuco, Iztapalapan, Tlacupa, and Cojohuacan hastened in advance to meet Motecusuma, who was slowly approaching us, surrounded by other grandees of the kingdom, seated in a sedan of uncommon splendour. When we had arrived at a place not far from the town, where several small towers rose together, the monarch raised himself in his sedan, and the chief caziques supported him under the arms, and held over his head a canopy of exceedingly great value, decorated with green feathers, gold, silver, chalchihuis stones, and pearls, which hung down from a species of bordering, altogether curious to look at.

Motecusuma himself, according to his custom, was sumptuously attired, had on a species of half boot, richly set with jewels, and whose soles were made of solid gold. The four grandees who supported him were also richly attired, which they must have put on somewhere on the road, in order to wait upon Motecusuma; they were not so sumptuously dressed when they first came out to meet us. Besides these distinguished caziques, there were many other grandees around the monarch, some of whom held the canopy over his head, while others again occupied the road before him, and spread cotton cloths on the ground that his feet might not touch the bare earth. No one of his suite ever looked at him full in the face; every one in his presence stood with eyes downcast, and it was only his four nephews and cousins who supported him that durst look up.

When it was announced to Cortes that Motecusuma himself was approaching, he alighted from his horse and advanced to meet him. Many compliments were now passed on both sides.

2. Aztec ruler. His name is often spelled Montezuma.

Motecusuma bid Cortes welcome, who, through Marina,[3] said, in return, he hoped his majesty was in good health. If I still remember rightly, Cortes, who had Marina next to him, wished to concede the place of honour to the monarch, who, however, would not accept of it, but conceded it to Cortes, who now brought forth a necklace of precious stones, of the most beautiful colours and shapes, strung upon gold wire, and perfumed with musk, which he hung about the neck of Motecusuma. Our commander was then going to embrace him, but the grandees by whom he was surrounded held back his arms, as they considered it improper. Our general then desired Marina to tell the monarch how exceedingly he congratulated himself upon his good fortune of having seen such a powerful monarch face to face, and of the honour he had done us by coming out to meet us himself. To all this Motecusuma answered in very appropriate terms, and ordered his two nephews, the princes of Tetzuco and Cojohuacan, to conduct us to our quarters. He himself returned to the city, accompanied by his two other relatives, the princes of Cuitlahuac and Tlacupa, with the other grandees of his numerous suite. As they passed by, we perceived how all those who composed his majesty's retinue held their heads bent forward, no one daring to lift up his eyes in his presence; and altogether what deep veneration was paid him.

The road before us now became less crowded, and yet who would have been able to count the vast numbers of men, women, and children who filled the streets, crowded the balconies, and the canoes in the canals, merely to gaze upon us? Indeed, at the moment I am writing this, everything comes as lively to my eyes as if it had happened yesterday; and I daily become more sensible of the great mercy of our Lord Jesus Christ, that he lent us sufficient strength and courage to enter this city: for my own person, I have particular reason to be thankful that he spared my life in so many perils, as the reader will sufficiently see in the course of this history: indeed I cannot sufficiently praise him that I have been allowed to live thus long to narrate these adventures, although they may not turn out so perfect as I myself could wish.

3. An Indian princess who acted as translator for Cortez.

We were quartered in a large building where there was room enough for us all, and which had been occupied by Axayacatl, father of Motecusuma, during his life-time. Here the latter had likewise a secret room full of treasures, and where the gold he had inherited from his father was hid, which he had never touched up to this moment. Near this building there were temples and Mexican idols, and this place had been purposely selected for us because we were termed teules,[4] or were thought to be such, and that we might dwell among the latter as among our equals. The apartments and halls were very spacious, and those set apart for our general were furnished with carpets. There were separate beds for each of us, which could not have been better fitted up for a gentleman of the first rank. Every place was swept clean, and the walls had been newly plastered and decorated.

When we had arrived in the great court-yard adjoining this palace, Motecusuma came up to Cortes, and, taking him by the hand, conducted him himself into the apartments where he was to lodge, which had been beautifully decorated after the fashion of the country. He then hung about his neck a chaste necklace of gold, most curiously worked with figures all representing crabs. The Mexican grandees were greatly astonished at all these uncommon favours which their monarch bestowed upon our general.

Cortes returned the monarch many thanks for so much kindness, and the latter took leave of him with these words: "Malinche,[5] you and your brothers must now do as if you were at home, and take some rest after the fatigues of the journey," then returned to his own palace, which was close at hand.

We allotted the apartments according to the several companies, placed our cannon in an advantageous position, and made such arrangements that our cavalry, as well as the infantry, might be ready at a moment's notice. We then sat down to a plentiful repast, which had been previously spread out for us, and made a sumptuous meal.

This our bold and memorable entry into the large city of

4. I.e., supernatural beings.
5. The title by which the Indians knew Cortez.

Temixtitlan-Mexico took place on the 8th of November, 1519. Praise be to the Lord Jesus Christ for all this. If, however, I have not exactly related every circumstance that transpired at the moment, the reader must pardon me for the present.

Chapter LXXXIX

How Motecusuma, accompanied by several caziques, pays us a visit in our quarters, and of the discourse that passed between him and our general

After Motecusuma had dined, and was informed that we had likewise left table, he set out from his palace in great pomp, accompanied by a number of his grandees and all his relations, to pay us a visit. Cortes, being apprized of his approach, advanced to the middle of the apartment to receive him. Motecusuma took him by the hand, while others brought in a species of chair of great value, decorated, according to Mexican fashion, with gold beautifully worked into various shapes; the monarch then invited our general to seat himself next to him.

Motecusuma then began a very excellent discourse, and, first of all, expressed his delight to entertain in his kingdom and city such courageous cavaliers as Cortes and all of us were. . . . He had long desired to see Cortes, and, since his wishes were now fulfilled, he was ready to render us any services, and provide us with everything we might require. He was now convinced that we were those people of whom his earliest forefathers had spoken,—a people that would come from the rising of the sun and conquer these countries. After the battles we had fought at Potonchan, Tabasco, and those against the Tlascallans, which had been represented to him by pictures, all further doubt had vanished from his mind.

To which Cortes answered, that we should never be able to repay him for all the kindnesses he had shown us. We indeed came from the rising of the sun, and were servants and subjects of a powerful monarch, called Don Carlos,[6] who had numerous distinguished princes among his vassals. Our monarch had received intelligence of him, Motecusuma, and of his great

6. Charles V, King of Spain, 1516-56; Holy Roman Emperor, 1519-56.

power, and had expressly sent us to his country to beg of him and his subjects to become converts to the Christian faith, for the salvation of their souls. . . . When this discourse was ended, Motecusuma presented to our general various kinds of valuable gold trinkets, and a smaller portion of the same kind to each of our officers, with three packages of cotton stuffs, splendidly interwoven with feathers; and to every soldier two similar packages. All this he gave with every appearance of delight, and in all he did he showed his excellent breeding. He likewise inquired, after the presents had been distributed, whether we were all brothers, and subjects of our great emperor? To which Cortes replied in the affirmative, assuring him we were all united in love and friendship towards each other. In this way a pleasant discourse was kept up between Motecusuma and Cortes, though it was of short duration, as this was the monarch's first, and he was unwilling to be too troublesome thus early. He then ordered his house steward to provide us the necessary provisions, consisting in maise, fowls, and fruits, and also grass for our horses; to furnish women to grind our corn with stones, and bake the bread: after which the monarch took leave of us with great courtesy, Cortes and all of us conducting him to the door.

Our general now issued strict commands that no one should stir from head-quarters until we had gained some certain knowledge as to how matters really stood.

Chapter XC

How our general, the day following, paid a visit to Motecusuma, and of the discourse that passed between them

The next day Cortes determined to visit Motecusuma in his own palace. He therefore first sent to inquire after his health, and whether it would be agreeable to the monarch to receive a visit from him. Our general took with him four of our principal officers, namely, Alvarado, Leon, Ordas, and Sandoval, besides five soldiers, of whom I was one.

When our arrival was announced to Motecusuma, he advanced to the middle of the apartment to meet us, being solely attended by his nephew, as the other grandees were only allowed to enter his apartments upon very important occasions. After the first compliments had passed between the monarch and our general, they shook hands, and Motecusuma conducted Cortes to an elevated seat, and placed him at his right hand. The rest of us were also desired to sit down on chairs which were brought in for us. Cortes then, by means of our interpreters, addressed Motecusuma at considerable length: "He said that all his and our wishes were now fulfilled, as he had reached the end of his journey, and obeyed the commands of our great emperor. There only now remained to disclose to him the commandments of our God. We were Christians, believing in one true God only, Jesus Christ, who suffered and died for our salvation. We prayed to the cross as an emblem of that cross on which our Lord and Saviour was crucified. By his death the whole human race was saved. He rose on the third day, and was received into heaven. By him, heaven, earth, and sea, and every living creature was formed: and nothing existed but by his divine will. Those figures, on the contrary, which he considered as gods, were no gods, but devils, which were evil spirits. It was very evident how powerless and what miserable things they were, since in all those places where we had planted the cross, those gods no longer durst make their appearance. Of this his ambassadors were fully convinced, and he himself would, in the course of time, be convinced of this truth. He begged he would also pay particular attention to something else he had to communicate." Here Cortes very intelligently explained to him how the world was created, how all people were brothers, and sons of one father and mother, called Adam and Eve, and how grieved our emperor was to think that so many human souls should be lost, and sent to hell by those false idols, where they would be tormented by everlasting fire; for this reason he had sent us hither to put an end to so much misery, and to exhort the inhabitants of this country no longer to adore such gods, nor sacrifice human beings to them; and also to abstain from robbery and committing unnatural offences. In a very short time our emperor would send to this country men of great piety and virtue, of whom there were numbers in our country, and who would explain these things more fully to them. Of all this we were merely the first messengers, and could only beg of them to support us in our labours, and assist us in their completion.

As Motecusuma was about to answer, Cortes stopped short, and, turning to us, said, "Verily, I am determined they shall comply with this, and let this be the commencement of our work!"

Motecusuma, in reply, expressed himself as follows: "Malinche! What you have just been telling me of your God has, indeed, been mentioned to me before by my servants, to whom you made similar disclosures immediately upon your arrival off the coast. Neither am I ignorant of what you have stated concerning the cross and everything else in the towns you passed through. We, however, maintained silence, as the gods we adore were adored in bygone ages by our ancestors. We have, once for all, acknowledged them as good deities, in the same way as you have yours, and therefore let us talk no further on this subject. Respecting the creation of the world, we likewise believe it was created many ages ago. We likewise believe that you are those people whom our ancestors prophecied would come from the rising of the sun, and I feel myself indebted to your great emperor, to whom I will send a present of the most valuable things I possess. It is now two years ago that I received the first intelligence of him by some vessels which appeared off my coast belonging to your country, the people on board of which likewise called themselves subjects of your great emperor. Tell me, now, do you really all belong to the same people?"

Cortes assured him we were all servants of the same emperor; that those vessels were merely sent out in advance to explore the seas and the harbours, to make the necessary preparations for our present expedition.

Motecusuma likewise remarked that then even he had contemplated allowing some of those men to penetrate into the interior of his country, from his great desire to see them, and had intended to pay them great honours. Since the gods had now fulfilled his greatest desires, and we now inhabited his dwellings, which we might look upon as our own, we could rest from our fatigues and enjoy ourselves, and we should not want for anything. Although he had sometimes sent us word not to repair to his metropolis, he had done so with great reluctance. He had been forced to act so on account of his subjects, who stood in great awe of us, and believed that we whirled fire and lightning around us, and killed numbers of men with our horses; that we were wild and unruly teules, and such like nonsense: as he had now gained personal knowledge of us, and convinced himself that we were likewise formed of flesh and bone, and men of great understanding, with great courage, he entertained even a more elevated opinion of us than he had previously, and was ready to share all he possessed with us.

Upon this, Cortes assured him that we felt ourselves vastly indebted to him for the very kind feeling he evinced on our behalf.

Motecusuma, who was always of a merry disposition, though never, for an instant, forgetful of his high station, now continued in a more humorous style, as follows: "I am perfectly well aware, Malinche, what the people of Tlascalla, with whom you are so closely allied, have been telling you respecting myself. They have made you believe that I am a species of god, or teule, and that my palaces are filled with gold, silver, and jewels. I do not think, for an instant, that reasonable men as you are can put any faith in all their talk, but that you look upon all this as nonsense: besides which, you can now convince yourself, Malinche, that I am made of flesh and bone as you are, and that my palaces are built of stone, lime, and wood. I am, to be sure, a powerful monarch; it is likewise true that I have inherited vast treasures from my ancestors; but with regard to anything else they may have told you respecting me, it is all nonsense. You must just think of that as I think of the lightning and burning flames which you are said to whirl about in all directions."

To this Cortes answered, likewise laughingly, "We knew, from old experience, that enemies neither tell the truth nor speak well of each other. We had, however, long ago convinced ourselves that there was not another such a noble-minded and illustrious monarch as himself in this quarter of the world, and that the great idea our emperor had formed of him was well founded."

During this discourse, Motecusuma secretly desired his

nephew to order his house-steward to bring in some gold trinkets and ten packages of fine stuffs, which he divided among Cortes and the four officers who were present. We five soldiers obtained each two gold chains for the neck, in value about ten pesos each, besides two packages of cotton stuffs.

The gold which Motecusuma gave away upon this occasion was estimated at above 1000 pesos. But what was more, everything he gave away was given with the best of good will, and with an air of dignity which you might expect in so great a monarch.

As it was already past noon, Cortes began to fear that any longer stay might be troublesome to the monarch, and said to him, in rising from his seat, "We are daily becoming more and more indebted to your majesty for so many kindnesses; at present it is time to think of dinner."

The monarch, in return, thanked us for our visit, and we took leave of each other in the most courteous manner imaginable. We now returned to our quarters, and acquainted our fellow-soldiers with the kind reception the monarch had given us.

Chapter XCI
Of Motecusuma's person, disposition, habits, and of his great power

The mighty Motecusuma may have been about this time in the fortieth year of his age. He was tall of stature, of slender make, and rather thin, but the symmetry of his body was beautiful. His complexion was not very brown, merely approaching to that of the inhabitants in general. The hair of his head was not very long, excepting where it hung thickly down over his ears, which were quite hidden by it. His black beard, though thin, looked handsome. His countenance was rather of an elongated form, but cheerful; and his fine eyes had the expression of love or severity, at the proper moments. He was particularly clean in his person, and took a bath every evening. Besides a number of concubines, who were all daughters of persons of rank and quality, he had two lawful wives of royal extraction, whom, however, he visited secretly without any one daring to observe it, save his most confidential servants. He was perfectly innocent of any unnatural crimes. The dress he had on one day was not worn again until four days had elapsed. In the halls adjoining his own private apartments there was always a guard of 2000 men of quality, in waiting: with whom, however, he never held any conversation unless to give them orders or to receive some intelligence from them. Whenever for this purpose they entered his apartment, they had first to take off their rich costumes and put on meaner garments, though these were always neat and clean; and were only allowed to enter into his presence barefooted, with eyes cast down. No person durst look at him full in the face, and during the three prostrations which they were obliged to make before they could approach him, they pronounced these words: "Lord! my Lord! sublime Lord!" Everything that was communicated to him was to be said in few words, the eyes of the speaker being constantly cast down, and on leaving the monarch's presence he walked backwards out of the room. I also remarked that even princes and other great personages who come to Mexico respecting law-suits, or on other business from the interior of the country, always took off their shoes and changed their whole dress for one of a meaner appearance when they entered his palace. Neither were they allowed to enter the palace straightway, but had to show themselves for a considerable time outside the doors; as it would have been considered want of respect to the monarch if this had been omitted.

Above 300 kinds of dishes were served up for Motecusuma's dinner from his kitchen, underneath which were placed pans of porcelain filled with fire, to keep them warm. Three hundred dishes of various kinds were served up for him alone, and above 1000 for the persons in waiting. He sometimes, but very seldom, accompanied by the chief officers of his household, ordered the dinner himself, and desired that the best dishes and various kinds of birds should be called over to him. We were told that the flesh of young children, as a very dainty bit, was also set before him sometimes by way of a relish. Whether there was any truth in this we could not possibly discover; on account of the great variety of dishes, consisting in fowls, turkeys, pheasants, partridges, quails, tame and wild geese, venison, musk swine, pigeons, hares, rabbits, and of numerous other birds and beasts; besides which there were various other kinds of provisions, indeed it would have been no easy task to call them all over by name. This I know, however, for certain, that after Cortes had reproached him for the human sacrifices and the eating of human flesh, he issued orders that no dishes of that nature should again be brought to his table. I will, however, drop this subject, and rather relate how the monarch was waited on while he sat at dinner. If the weather was cold a large fire was made with a kind of charcoal made of the bark of trees, which emitted no smoke, but threw out a delicious perfume; and that his majesty might not feel any inconvenience from too great a heat, a screen was placed between his person and the fire, made of gold, and adorned with all manner of figures of their gods. The chair on which he sat was rather low, but supplied with soft cushions, and was beautifully carved; the table was very little higher than this, but perfectly corresponded with his seat. It was covered with white cloths, and one of a larger size. Four very neat and pretty young women held before the monarch a species of round pitcher, called by them Xicales, filled with water to wash his hands in. The water was caught in other vessels, and then the young women presented him with towels to dry his hands. Two other women brought him maise-bread baked with eggs. Before, however, Motecusuma began his dinner, a kind of wooden screen, strongly gilt, was placed before him, that no one might see him while eating, and the young women stood at a distance. Next four elderly men, of high rank, were admitted to his table; whom he addressed from time to time, or put some questions to them. Sometimes he would offer them a plate of some kind of his viands, which was considered a mark of great favour. These grey-headed old men, who were so highly honoured, were, as we subsequently learnt, his nearest relations, most trustworthy counsellors and chief justices. Whenever he ordered any victuals to be presented them, they ate it standing, in the deepest veneration, though without daring to look at him full in the face. The dishes in which the dinner was served up were of variegated and black porcelain, made at Cholulla. While the monarch was at table, his courtiers, and those who were in waiting in the halls adjoining, had to maintain strict silence.

After the hot dishes had been removed, every kind of fruit which the country produced were set on the table; of which, however, Motecusuma ate very little. Every now and then was handed to him a golden pitcher filled with a kind of liquor made from the cacao, which is of a very exciting nature. Though we did not pay any particular attention to the circumstance at the time, yet I saw about fifty large pitchers filled with the same liquor brought in all frothy. This beverage was also presented to the monarch by women, but all with the profoundest veneration.

Sometimes during dinner time, he would have ugly Indian hump-backed dwarfs, who acted as buffoons and performed antics for his amusement. At another time he would have jesters to enliven him with their witticisms. Others again danced and sung before him. Motecusuma took great delight in these entertainments, and ordered the broken victuals and pitchers of cacao liquor to be distributed among these performers. As soon as he had finished his dinner the four women cleared the cloths and brought him water to wash his hands. During this interval he discoursed a little with the four old men, and then left table to enjoy his afternoon's nap.

After the monarch had dined, dinner was served up for the men on duty and the other officers of his household, and I have often counted more than 1000 dishes on the table, of the kinds above mentioned. These were then followed, according to the Mexican custom, by the frothing jugs of cacao liquor; certainly 2000 of them, after which came different kinds of fruit in great abundance.

Next the women dined, who superintended the baking department; and those who made the cacao liquor, with the young women who waited upon the monarch. Indeed, the daily expense of these dinners alone must have been very great!

Besides these servants there were numerous butlers, house-stewards, treasurers, cooks, and superintendents of maise-magazines. Indeed there is so much to be said about these that I scarcely knew where to commence, and we could not help wondering that everything was done with such perfect order. I had almost forgotten to mention, that during dinner-time, two other young women of great beauty brought the monarch small cakes, as white as snow, made of eggs and other very nourishing ingredients, on plates covered with clean napkins; also a kind of long-shaped bread, likewise made of very substantial things, and some pachol, which is a kind of wafer-cake. They then presented him with three beautifully painted and gilt tubes, which were filled with liquid amber, and a herb called by the Indians tabaco. After the dinner had been cleared away and the singing and dancing done, one of these tubes was lighted, and the monarch took the smoke into his mouth, and after he had done this a short time, he fell asleep.

About this time a celebrated cazique, whom we called Tapia, was Motecusuma's chief steward: he kept an account of the whole of Motecusuma's revenue, in large books of paper which the Mexicans call *Amatl*. A whole house was filled with such large books of accounts.

Motecusuma had also two arsenals filled with arms of every description, of which many were ornamented with gold and precious stones. These arms consisted in shields of different sizes, sabres, and a species of broadsword, which is wielded with both hands, the edge furnished with flint stones, so extremely sharp that they cut much better than our Spanish swords: further, lances of greater length than ours, with spikes at their end, full one fathom in length, likewise furnished with several sharp flint stones. The pikes are so very sharp and hard that they will pierce the strongest shield, and cut like a razor; so that the Mexicans even shave themselves with these stones. Then there were excellent bows and arrows, pikes with single and double points, and the proper thongs to throw them with; slings with round stones purposely made for them; also a species of large shield, so ingeniously constructed that it could be rolled up when not wanted: they are only unrolled on the field of battle, and completely cover the whole body from the head to the feet. Further, we saw here a great variety of cuirasses made of quilted cotton, which were outwardly adorned with soft feathers of different colours, and looked like uniforms; morions and helmets constructed of wood and bones, likewise adorned with feathers.

There were always artificers at work, who continually augmented this store of arms; and the arsenals were under the care of particular personages, who also superintended the works.

Motecusuma had likewise a variety of aviaries, and it is indeed with difficulty that I constrain myself from going into too minute a detail respecting these. I will confine myself by stating that we saw here every kind of eagle, from the king's eagle to the smallest kind included, and every species of bird, from the largest known to the little colibris, in their full splendour of plumage. Here were also to be seen those birds from which the Mexicans take the green-coloured feathers of which they manufacture their beautiful feathered stuffs. These last-mentioned birds very much resemble our Spanish jays, and are called by the Indians quezales. The species of sparrows were particularly curious, having five distinct colours in their plumage—green, red, white, yellow, and blue; I have, however, forgotten their Mexican name. There were vast numbers of parrots, and such a variety of species, that I cannot remember all their names; and geese of the richest plumage, and other large birds. These were, at stated periods, stripped of their feathers, in order that new ones might grow in their place. All these birds had appropriate places to breed in, and were under the care of several Indians of both sexes, who had to keep the nests clean, give to each kind its proper food, and set the birds for breeding. In the court-yard belonging to this building, there was a large basin of sweet water, in which, besides other water fowls, there was a particularly beautiful bird, with long legs, its body, wings, and tail variously coloured, and is called at Cuba, where it is also found, the ipiris.

In another large building, numbers of idols were erected, and these, it is said, were the most terrible of all their gods. Near these were kept all manner of beautiful animals, tigers, lions of two different kinds, of which one had the shape of a wolf, and was called a jackal; there were also foxes, and other small beasts of prey. Most of these animals had been bred here, and were fed with wild deers' flesh, turkeys, dogs, and sometimes, as I have been assured, with the offal of human beings.

Respecting the abominable human sacrifices of these people,

the following was communicated to us: The breast of the unhappy victim destined to be sacrificed was ripped open with a knife made of sharp flint; the throbbing heart was then torn out, and immediately offered to the idol-god in whose honour the sacrifice had been instituted. After this, the head, arms, and legs were cut off and eaten at their banquets, with the exception of the head, which was saved, and hung to a beam appropriated for that purpose. No other part of the body was eaten, but the remainder was thrown to the beasts which were kept in those abominable dens, in which there were also vipers and other poisonous serpents, and, among the latter in particular, a species at the end of whose tail there was a kind of rattle. This last-mentioned serpent, which is the most dangerous, was kept in a cabin of a diversified form, in which a quantity of feathers had been strewed: here it laid its eggs, and it was fed with the flesh of dogs and of human beings who had been sacrificed. . . .

I will now, however, turn to another subject, and rather acquaint my readers with the skilful arts practised among the Mexicans: among which I will first mention the sculptors, and the gold and silversmiths, who were clever in working and smelting gold, and would have astonished the most celebrated of our Spanish goldsmiths: the number of these was very great, and the most skilful lived at a place called Ezcapuzalco, about four miles from Mexico. After these came the very skilful masters in cutting and polishing precious stones, and the calchihuis, which resemble the emerald. Then follow the great masters in painting, and decorators in feathers, and the wonderful sculptors. Even at this day there are living in Mexico three Indian artists, named Marcos de Aguino, Juan de la Cruz, and El Crespello, who have severally reached to such great proficiency in the art of painting and sculpture, that they may be compared to an Apelles, or our contemporaries Michael Angelo and Berruguete.[7]

The women were particularly skilful in weaving and embroidery, and they manufactured quantities of the finest stuffs,

7. Spanish artist, ca. 1486–1561, pupil of Michaelangelo and court sculptor to Charles V. Apelles was the most famous painter of classical Greece, court painter to Philip of Macedon.

interwoven with feathers. The commoner stuffs, for daily use, came from some townships in the province of Costatlan, which lay on the north coast, not far from Vera Cruz, where we first landed with Cortes.

The concubines in the palace of Motecusuma, who were all daughters of distinguished men, were employed in manufacturing the most beautiful stuffs, interwoven with feathers. Similar manufactures were made by certain kind of women who dwelt secluded in cloisters, as our nuns do. Of these nuns there were great numbers, and they lived in the neighbourhood of the great temple of Huitzilopochtli. Fathers sometimes brought their daughters from a pious feeling, or in honour of some female idol, the protectress of marriage, into these habitations, where they remained until they were married.

The powerful Motecusuma had also a number of dancers and clowns: some danced in stilts, tumbled, and performed a variety of other antics for the monarch's entertainment: a whole quarter of the city was inhabited by these performers, and their only occupation consisted in such like performances. Lastly, Motecusuma had in his service great numbers of stone-cutters, masons, and carpenters, who were solely employed in the royal palaces. Above all, I must not forget to mention here his gardens for the culture of flowers, trees, and vegetables, of which there were various kinds. In these gardens were also numerous baths, wells, basins, and ponds full of limpid water, which regularly ebbed and flowed. All this was enlivened by endless varieties of small birds, which sang among the trees. Also the plantations of medical plants and vegetables are well worthy of our notice: these were kept in proper order by a large body of gardeners. All the baths, wells, ponds, and buildings were substantially constructed of stonework, as also the theatres where the singers and dancers performed. There were upon the whole so many remarkable things for my observation in these gardens and throughout the whole town, that I can scarcely find words to express the astonishment I felt at the pomp and splendour of the Mexican monarch.

In the meantime, I am become as tired in noting down these things as the kind reader will be in perusing them: I will, therefore, close this chapter, and acquaint the reader how our general, accompanied by many of his officers, went to view the Tlatelulco, or great square of Mexico; on which occasion we also ascended the great temple, where stood the idols Tetzcatlipuca and Huitzilopochtli. This was the first time Cortes left his headquarters to perambulate the city.

Chapter XCII

Our general takes a walk through Mexico, and views the Tlatelulco, (the great square,) and the chief temple of Huitzilopochtli

We had already been four days in the city of Mexico, and neither our commander nor any of us had, during that time, left our quarters, excepting to visit the gardens and buildings adjoining the palace. Cortes now, therefore, determined to view the city, and visit the great market, and the chief temple of Huitzilopochtli: he accordingly sent Geronimo Aguilar, Doña Marina, and one of his pages named Orteguilla, who, by this time, understood a little of the Mexican language, to Motecusuma, to request his permission to view the different buildings of the city. Motecusuma, in his answer to this, certainly granted us permission to go where we pleased, yet he was apprehensive we might commit some outrage to one or other of his idols: he, therefore, resolved to accompany us himself, with some of his principal officers, and, for this purpose, left his palace with a pompous retinue. Having arrived at a spot about half way between his palace and a temple, he stepped out of his sedan, as he would have deemed it a want of respect towards his gods to approach them any otherwise than on foot. He leant upon the arms of the principal officers of his court; others walked before him, holding up on high two rods, having the appearance of sceptres, which was a sign that the monarch was approaching. He himself, whenever he was carried in his sedan, held a short staff in his hand, one half of gold, the other of wood, very much like that used by our judges. In this way he came up to the temple, which he ascended, in company with many papas.[8] On reaching the

8. Priests of the Aztec gods.

summit he immediately began to perfume Huitzilopochtli, and to perform other ceremonies.

Our commander, attended by the greater part of our cavalry and foot, all well armed, as, indeed, we were at all times, had proceeded to the Tlatelulco: by command of Motecusuma, a number of caziques had come to meet us on our road there. The moment we arrived in this immense market, we were perfectly astonished at the vast numbers of people, the profusion of merchandise which was there exposed for sale, and at the good police and order that reigned throughout. The grandees who accompanied us drew our attention to the smallest circumstance, and gave us full explanation of all we saw. Every species of merchandise had a separate spot for its sale. We first of all visited those divisions of the market appropriated for the sale of gold and silver wares, of jewels, of cloths interwoven with feathers, and of other manufactured goods; besides slaves of both sexes. This slave market was upon as great a scale as the Portuguese market for negro slaves at Guinea. To prevent these from running away, they were fastened with halters about their neck, though some were allowed to walk at large. Next to these came the dealers in coarser wares—cotton, twisted thread, and cacao. In short, every species of goods which New Spain produces were here to be found; and everything put me in mind of my native town Medino del Campo during fair time, where every merchandise has a separate street assigned for its sale. . . . In another division of the market were exposed the skins of tigers, lions, jackals, otters, red deer, wild cats, and of other beasts of prey, some of which were tanned. In another place were sold beans and sage, with other herbs and vegetables. A particular market was assigned for the merchants in fowls, turkeys, ducks, rabbits, hares, deer, and dogs; also for fruit-sellers, pastry-cooks, and tripe-sellers. Not far from these were exposed all manner of earthenware, from the large earthen cauldron to the smallest pitchers. Then came the dealers in honey and honey-cakes, and other sweetmeats. Next to these, the timber-merchants, furniture-dealers, with their stores of tables, benches, cradles, and all sorts of wooden implements, all separately arranged. What can I further add? . . . If I had to enumerate everything singly, I should not so easily get to the end. And yet I have not mentioned the paper, which in this country is called amatl; the tubes filled with liquid amber and tobacco; the various sweet-scented salves, and similar things; nor the various seeds which were exposed for sale in the porticoes of this market, nor the medicinal herbs.

In this market-place there were also courts of justice, to which three judges and several constables were appointed, who inspected the goods exposed for sale. I had almost forgotten to mention the salt, and those who made the flint knives; also the fish, and a species of bread made of a kind of mud or slime collected from the surface of this lake, and eaten in that form, and has a similar taste to our cheese. Further, instruments of brass, copper, and tin; cups, and painted pitchers of wood: indeed, I wish I had completed the enumeration of all this profusion of merchandize. The variety was so great that it would occupy more space than I can well spare to note them down in; besides which, the market was so crowded with people, and the thronging so excessive in the porticoes, that it was quite impossible to see all in one day.

On our proceeding to the great temple, and passing the courtyards adjoining the market, we observed numbers of other merchants, who dealt in gold dust as it is dug of the mines, which was exposed to sale in tubes made of the bones of large geese, which had been worked to such a thin substance, and were so white that the gold shone through them.

. . . .

Before we mounted the steps of the great temple, Motecusuma, who was sacrificing on the top to his idols, sent six papas and two of his principal officers to conduct Cortes up the steps. There were 114 steps to the summit, and, as they feared that Cortes would experience the same fatigue in mounting as Motecusuma had, they were going to assist him by taking hold of his arms. Cortes, however, would not accept of their proffered aid. When we had reached the summit of the temple, we walked across a platform where many large stones were lying, on which those who were doomed for scarifice were stretched out. Near these stood a large idol, in the shape of a dragon, surrounded by various other abominable figures, with a quantity of fresh blood lying in front of it. Motecusuma himself stepped out of a chapel, in which his cursed gods were standing, accompanied by two papas, and received Cortes and the whole of us very courteously. "Ascending this temple, Malinche," said he to our commander, "must certainly have fatigued you!" Cortes, however, assured him, through our interpreters, that it was not possible for anything to tire us. Upon this the monarch took hold of his hand and invited him to look down and view his vast metropolis, with the towns which were built in the lake, and the other towns which surrounded the city. Motecusuma also observed, that from this place we should have a better view of the great market.

Indeed, this infernal temple, from its great height, commanded a view of the whole surrounding neighbourhood. From this place we could likewise see the three causeways which led into Mexico,—that from Iztapalapan, by which we had entered the city four days ago; that from Tlacupa, along which we took our flight eight months after, when we were beaten out of the city by the new monarch Cuitlahuatzin; the third was that of Tepeaquilla. We also observed the aqueduct which ran from Chapultepec, and provided the whole town with sweet water. We could also distinctly see the bridges across the openings, by which these causeways were intersected, and through which the waters of the lake ebbed and flowed. The lake itself was crowded with canoes, which were bringing provisions, manufactures, and other merchandize to the city. From here we also discovered that the only communication of the houses in this city, and of all the other towns built in the lake, was by means of drawbridges or canoes. In all these towns the beautiful white plastered temples rose above the smaller ones, like so many towers and castles in our Spanish towns, and this, it may be imagined, was a splendid sight.

After we had sufficiently gazed upon this magnificent picture, we again turned our eyes toward the great market, and beheld the vast numbers of buyers and sellers who thronged there. The bustle and noise occasioned by this multitude of human beings was so great that it could be heard at a distance of more than four miles. Some of our men, who had been at Constantinople and Rome, and travelled through the whole of Italy, said that they never had seen a market-place of such large dimensions, or which was so well regulated, or so crowded with people as this one at Mexico.

On this occasion Cortes said to father Olmedo, who had accompanied us: "I have just been thinking that we should take this opportunity, and apply to Motecusuma for permission to build a church here."

To which father Olmedo replied, that it would, no doubt, be an excellent thing if the monarch would grant this; but that it would be acting overhasty to make a proposition of that nature to him now, whose consent would not easily be gained at any time.

Cortes then turned to Motecusuma, and said to him, by means of our interpretress, Doña Marina: "Your majesty is, indeed, a great monarch, and you merit to be still greater! It has been a real delight to us to view all your cities. I have now one favour to beg of you, that you would allow us to see your gods and teules."

To which Motecusuma answered, that he must first consult his chief papas, to whom he then addressed a few words. Upon this, we were led into a kind of small tower, with one room, in which we saw two basements resembling altars, decked with coverings of extreme beauty. On each of these basements stood a gigantic, fat-looking figure, of which the one on the right hand represented the god of war Huitzilopochtli. This idol had a very broad face, with distorted and furious-looking eyes, and was covered all over with jewels, gold, and pearls, which were stuck to it by means of a species of paste, which, in this country, is prepared from a certain root. Large serpents, likewise, covered with gold and precious stones, wound round the body of this monster, which held in one hand a bow, and in the other a bunch of arrows. Another small idol which stood by its side, representing its page, carried this monster's short spear, and its golden shield studded with precious stones. Around Huitzilopochtli's neck were figures representing human faces and hearts made of gold and silver, and decorated with blue stones. In front of him stood several perfuming pans with copal, the incense of the country; also the hearts of three Indians, who had that day been slaughtered, were now consuming before him as a burnt-offering. Every wall of this chapel and the whole floor had become almost black with human blood, and the stench was abominable.

On the left hand stood another figure of the same size as Huitzilopochtli. Its face was very much like that of a bear, its shining eyes were made of tetzcat, the looking-glass of the country. This idol, like its brother Huitzilopochtli, was completely covered with precious stones, and was called *Tetzcatlipuca*. This was the god of hell, and the souls of the dead Mexicans stood under him. A circle of figures wound round its body, resembling diminutive devils with serpents' tails. The walls and floor around this idol were also besmeared with blood, and the stench was worse than in a Spanish slaughter-house. Five human hearts had that day been sacrificed to him. On the very top of this temple stood another chapel, the woodwork of which was uncommonly well finished, and richly carved. In this chapel there was also another idol, half man and half lizard, completely covered with precious stones; half of this figure was hidden from view. We were told that the hidden half was covered with the seeds of every plant of this earth, for this was the god of the seeds and fruits: I have, however, forgotten its name, but not that here also everything was besmeared with blood, and the stench so offensive that we could not have staid there much longer. In this place was kept a drum of enormous dimensions, the tone of which, when struck, was so deep and melancholy that it has very justly been denominated the drum of hell. The drumskin was made out of that of an enormous serpent; its sound could be heard at a distance of more than eight miles. This platform was altogether covered with a variety of hellish objects,—large and small trumpets, huge slaughtering knives, and burnt hearts of Indians who had been sacrificed: everything clotted with coagulated blood, cursed to the sight, and creating horror in the mind. Besides all this, the stench was everywhere so abominable that we scarcely knew how soon to get away from this spot of horrors. Our commander here said, smilingly, to Motecusuma: "I cannot imagine that such a powerful and wise monarch as you are, should not have yourself discovered by this time that these idols are not divinities, but evil spirits, called devils. In order that you may be convinced of this, and that your papas may satisfy themselves of this truth, allow me to erect a cross on the summit of this temple; and, in the chapel, where stand your Huitzilopochtli and Tetzcatlipuca, give us a small space that I may place there the image of the holy Virgin; then you will see what terror will seize these idols by which you have been so long deluded."

Motecusuma knew what the image of the Virgin Mary was, yet he was very much displeased with Cortes' offer, and replied, in presence of two papas, whose anger was not less conspicuous, "Malinche, could I have conjectured that you would have used such reviling language as you have just done, I would certainly not have shown you my gods. In our eyes these are good divinities: they preserve our lives, give us nourishment, water, and good harvests, healthy and growing weather, and victory whenever we pray to them for it. Therefore we offer up our prayers to them, and make them sacrifices. I earnestly beg of you not to say another word to insult the profound veneration in which we hold these gods."

As soon as Cortes heard these words and perceived the great excitement under which they were pronounced, he said nothing in return, but merely remarked to the monarch with a cheerful smile: "It is time for us both to depart hence." To which Motecusuma answered, that he would not detain him any longer, but he himself was now obliged to stay some time to atone to his gods by prayer and sacrifice for having committed *gratlatlacol*, by allowing us to ascend the great temple, and thereby occasioning the affronts which we had offered them.

"If that is the case," returned Cortes, "I beg your pardon, great monarch." Upon this we descended the 114 steps, which very much distressed many of our soldiers, who were suffering from swellings in their groins.

. . . .

With respect to the extensive and splendid courtyards belonging to this temple I have said sufficient above. I cannot, however, pass by in silence a kind of small tower standing in its immediate vicinity, likewise containing idols. I should term it a temple of hell; for at one of its doors stood an open-mouthed dragon armed with huge teeth, resembling a dragon of the infernal regions, the devourer of souls. There also stood near this same door other figures resembling devils and serpents, and not far from this an altar encrusted with blood grown black, and some that had recently been spilt. In a building adjoining this we perceived a quantity of dishes and basins, of various shapes. These were filled with water and served to cook the flesh in of the unfortunate beings who had been sacrificed; which flesh was eaten by the papas. Near to the altar were lying several daggers, and wooden blocks similar to those used by our butchers for hacking meat on. At a pretty good distance from this house of horrors were piles of wood, and a large reservoir of water, which was filled and emptied at stated times, and received its supply through pipes underground from the aqueduct of Chapultepec. I could find no better name for this dwelling than the house of satan!

I will now introduce my reader into another temple, in which the grandees of Mexico were buried. The doors of which were of a different form, and the idols were of a totally different nature; but the blood and stench were the same.

Next to this temple was another in which human skulls and bones were piled up, though both apart; their numbers were endless. This place had also its appropriate idols; and in all these temples, we found priests clad in long black mantles, with hoods shaped like those worn by the Dominican friars and choristers; their ears were pierced and the hair of their head was long and stuck together with coagulated blood. . . .

Although this temple on the Tlatelulco, of which I have given such a lengthened description, was the largest in Mexico, yet it was by no means the only one; for there were numbers of other splendid temples in this city, all of which I am unable to describe. . . .

Cortes, and the whole of us at last grew tired at the sight of so many idols and implements used for these sacrifices, and we returned to our quarters accompanied by a great number of chief personages and caziques, whom Motecusuma had sent for that purpose.

Celestial Exploration

In 1543, Nicolaus Copernicus opened the modern discussion of the structure of the universe by the posthumous publication of his book, *On the Revolution of Planets.* Copernicus challenged the notion, defended by the Roman Church, that the Earth stood still at the center of the universe, and that all other heavenly bodies revolved around it. Copernicus argued that the Earth was a planet (literally "a wanderer") like Mars and Venus and moved, as they did, around the Sun.

Copernicus supported his theory with two kinds of evidence—with purely mathematical arguments on the essential simplicity of the universe and with data gathered by observing the heavens with the unaided eye. But such evidence was inconclusive: it neither completely confirmed Copernicus' theories nor completely refuted the orthodox views. After 1543, therefore, Copernicus' followers throughout Europe continued to search for new and more convincing information to support their heliocentric ("Sun-centered") concept of the universe.

Two astronomers of the next generation, Johannes Kepler (1571–1630) and Galileo Galilei (1564–1642), discovered fresh and impressive evidence to support the Copernican theories. Kepler, basing his calculations on a modified version of the heliocentric model, constructed elaborate tables which predicted the location of planets in the heavens. Kepler's charts, later published, were more accurate than any compiled by previous astronomers; both navigators and scientists used them, and they won converts to Kepler's heliocentric astronomy.

In 1609, the Italian Galileo discovered visual evidence to support the Copernican theory. Galileo taught physics at the Italian University of Padua. He studied the motion of physical objects—pendulums, falling objects, balls rolling down inclined planes; he was also an astronomer and optician. In 1609, after he read a description of the new Dutch invention, the telescope, he speedily built himself an improved version and turned it on the heavens. He reported the results of his first observations in a short book, *The Sidereal Messenger*, one-half of the text and one-fourth of the charts of which appear below. He published the work in 1610 and dedicated it to

Cosimo de Medici, Grand Duke of Florence. This bit of flattery won for Galileo an appointment, in the summer of 1610, as Chief Mathematician and Philosopher to the Grand Duke.

Even the patronage of the Medici could not protect Galileo in his old age. In 1630 he completed a major work, the *Dialogue Concerning the Two Chief World Systems,* which defended the heliocentric theory. But Church authorities refused to grant him permission to publish it; instead, at the age of seventy, he was brought to Rome to be tried as a heretic. Under pressure he recanted his statements about the movement of the Earth; nonetheless, he was sentenced to imprisonment for life and his books were banned. The first part of the sentence was not strictly enforced. Galileo returned to his villa outside Florence, where he died in 1642.

GALILEO GALILEI: THE SIDEREAL MESSENGER

In the present small treatise I set forth some matters of great interest for all observers of natural phenomena to look at and consider. They are of great interest, I think, first, from their intrinsic excellence; secondly, from their absolute novelty; and lastly, also on account of the instrument by the aid of which they have been presented to my apprehension.

The number of the Fixed Stars which observers have been able to see without artificial powers of sight up to this day can be counted. It is therefore decidedly a great feat to add to their number, and to set distinctly before the eyes other stars in myriads, which have never been seen before, and which surpass the old, previously known, stars in number more than ten times.

Again, it is a most beautiful and delightful sight to behold the body of the Moon, which is distant from us nearly sixty semi-diameters of the Earth, as near as if it was at a distance of only two of the same measures; so that the diameter of this same Moon appears about thirty times larger, its surface about

From *The Siderial Messenger of Galileo Galilei,* trans. and notes by Edward Stafford Rivington (London: Rivington's, 1880), pp. 7-12, 14-18, 44-49, 68-70, 72-73.

nine hundred times, and its solid mass nearly 27,000 times larger than when it is viewed only with the naked eye; and consequently any one may know with the certainty that is due to the use of our senses, that the Moon certainly does not possess a smooth and polished surface, but one rough and uneven, and, just like the face of the Earth itself, is everywhere full of vast protuberances, deep chasms, and sinuosities.

Then to have got rid of disputes about the Galaxy or Milky Way, and to have made its nature clear to the very senses, not to say to the understanding, seems by no means a matter which ought to be considered of slight importance. In addition to this, to point out, as with one's finger, the nature of those stars which every one of the astronomers up to this time has called nebulous, and to demonstrate that it is very different from what has hitherto been believed, will be pleasant, and very fine. But that which will excite the greatest astonishment by far, and which indeed especially moved me to call the attention of all astronomers and philosophers, is this, namely, that I have discovered four planets, neither known nor observed by any one of the astronomers before my time, which have their orbits round a certain bright star, one of those previously known, like Venus and Mercury round the Sun, and are sometimes in front of it, sometimes behind it, though they never depart from it beyond certain limits. All which facts were discovered and observed a few days ago by the help of a telescope-devised by me, through God's grace first enlightening my mind.

Perchance other discoveries still more excellent will be made from time to time by me or by other observers, with the assistance of a similar instrument, so I will first briefly record its shape and preparation, as well as the occasion of its being devised, and then I will give an account of the observations made by me.

About ten months ago a report reached my ears that a Dutchman had constructed a telescope, by the aid of which visible objects, although at a great distance from the eye of the observer, were seen distinctly as if near; and some proofs of its most wonderful performances were reported, which some gave credence to, but others contradicted. A few days after, I received confirmation of the report in a letter written from Paris by a noble Frenchman, Jaques Badovere, which finally determined me to give myself up first to inquire into the principle of the telescope, and then to consider the means by which I might compass the invention of a similar instrument, which a little while after I succeeded in doing, through deep study of the theory of Refraction; and I prepared a tube, at first of lead, in the ends of which I fitted two glass lenses, both plane on one side, but on the other side one spherically convex, and the other concave. Then bringing my eye to the concave lens I saw objects satisfactorily large and near, for they appeared one-third of the distance off and nine times larger than when they are seen with the natural eye alone. I shortly afterwards constructed another telescope with more nicety, which magnified objects more than sixty times. At length, by sparing neither labour nor expense, I succeeded in constructing for myself an instrument so superior that objects seen through it appear magnified nearly a thousand times, and more than thirty times nearer than if viewed by the natural powers of sight alone.

It would be altogether a waste of time to enumerate the number and importance of the benefits which this instrument may be expected to confer, when used by land or sea. But without paying attention to its use for terrestrial objects, I betook myself to observations of the heavenly bodies; and first of all, I viewed the Moon as near as if it was scarcely two semi-diameters of the Earth distant. After the Moon, I frequently observed other heavenly bodies, both fixed stars and planets, with incredible delight; and, when I saw their very great number, I began to consider about a method by which I might be able to measure their distances apart, and at length I found one. And here it is fitting that all who intend to turn their attention to observations of this kind should receive certain cautions. For, in the first place, it is absolutely necessary for them to prepare a most perfect telescope, one which will show very bright objects distinct and free from any mistiness, and will magnify them at least 400 times, for then it will show them as if only one-twentieth of their distance off. For unless the instrument be of such power, it will be in vain to attempt to view all the things which have been seen by me in the heavens, or which will be enumerated hereafter.

. . . .

Now let me review the observations made by me during the two months just past, again inviting the attention of all who are eager for true philosophy to the beginnings which led to the sight of most important phenomena.

Let me speak first of the surface of the Moon, which is turned towards us. For the sake of being understood more easily, I distinguish two parts in it, which I call respectively the brighter and the darker. The brighter part seems to surround and pervade the whole hemisphere; but the darker part, like a sort of cloud, discolours the Moon's surface and makes it appear covered with spots. Now these spots, as they are somewhat dark and of considerable size, are plain to every one, and every age has seen them, wherefore I shall call them great or ancient spots, to distinguish them from other spots, smaller in size, but so thickly scattered that they sprinkle the whole surface of the Moon, but especially the brighter portion of it. These spots have never been observed by any one before me; and from my observations of them, often repeated, I have been led to that opinion which I have expressed, namely, that I feel sure that the surface of the Moon is not perfectly smooth, free from inequalities and exactly spherical, as a large school of philosophers considers with regard to the Moon and the other heavenly bodies, but that, on the contrary, it is full of inequalities, uneven, full of hollows and protuberances, just like the surface of the Earth itself, which is varied everywhere by lofty mountains and deep valleys.

The appearances from which we may gather these conclusions are of the following nature:—On the fourth or fifth day after new-moon, when the Moon presents itself to us with bright horns, the boundary which divides the part in shadow from the enlightened part does not extend continuously in an ellipse, as would happen in the case of a perfectly spherical body, but it is marked out by an irregular, uneven, and very wavy line . . . for several bright excrescences, as they may be called, extend beyond the boundary of light and shadow into the dark part, and on the other hand pieces of shadow encroach upon the light:—nay, even a great quantity of small blackish spots, altogether separated from the dark part, sprinkle everywhere almost the whole space which is at the time flooded with the Sun's light, with the exception of that part alone which is occupied by the great and ancient spots. I have noticed that the small spots just mentioned have this common characteristic always and in every case, that they have the dark part towards the Sun's position, and on the side away from the Sun they have brighter boundaries, as if they were crowned with shining summits. Now we have an appearance quite similar on the Earth about sunrise, when we behold the valleys, not yet flooded with light, but the mountains surrounding them on the side opposite to the Sun already ablaze with the splendour of his beams; and just as the shadows in the hollows of the Earth diminish in size as the Sun rises higher, so also these spots on the Moon lose their blackness as the illuminated part grows larger and larger. Again, not only are the boundaries of light and shadow in the Moon seen to be uneven and sinuous, but—and this produces still greater astonishment—there appear very many bright points within the darkened portion of the Moon, altogether divided and broken off from the illuminated tract, and separated from it by no inconsiderable interval, which, after a little while, gradually increase in size and brightness, and after an hour or two become joined on to the rest of the bright portion, now become somewhat larger; but in the meantime others, one here and another there, shooting up as if growing, are lighted up within the shaded portion, increase in size, and at last are linked on to the same luminous surface, now still more extended. . . . Now, is it not the case on the Earth before sunrise, that while the level plain is still in shadow, the peaks of the most lofty mountains are illuminated by the Sun's rays? After a little while does not the light spread further, while the middle and larger part of those mountains are becoming illuminated; and at length, when the Sun has risen, do not the illuminated parts of the plains and hills join together? The grandeur, however, of such prominences and depressions in the Moon seems to surpass both in magnitude and extent the ruggedness of the Earth's surface, as I shall hereafter show. And here I cannot refrain from mentioning what a remarkable spectacle I observed while the Moon was rapidly approaching her first quarter. . . . A protuberance of the shadow, of great size, indented the illuminated part in the neighbourhood of the lower cusp; and when I had observed this indentation longer, and had seen that it was dark throughout, at length, after about two hours, a bright peak began to arise a little below the middle of the depression; this by degrees increased, and presented a triangular shape, but was as yet quite detached and separated from the illuminated surface. Soon around it three other small points began to shine, until, when the Moon was just about to set, that triangular figure, having now extended and widened, began to be connected with the rest of the illuminated part, and, still girt with the three bright peaks already mentioned, suddenly burst into the indentation of shadow like a vast promontory of light.

. . . .

I have now finished my brief account of the observations which I have thus far made with regard to the Moon, the Fixed Stars, and the Galaxy. There remains the matter, which seems to me to deserve to be considered the most important in this work, namely, that I should disclose and publish to the world the occasion of discovering and observing four PLANETS, never seen from the very beginning of the world up to our own times, their positions, and the observations made during the last two months about their movements and their changes of magnitude; and I summon all astronomers to apply themselves to examine and determine their periodic times, which it has not been permittted me to achieve up to this day, owing to the restriction of my time. I give them warning however again, so that they may not approach such an inquiry to no purpose, that they will want a very accurate telescope, and such as I have described in the beginning of this account.

On the 7th day of January in the present year, 1610, in the first[1] hour of the following night, when I was viewing the constellations of the heavens through a telescope, the planet Jupiter

1. The times of Galileo's observations are to be understood as reckoned from sunset.

Original Configurations of Jupiter's Satellites observed by Galileo in the months of January, February, and March 1610, and published with the 1st edition of his book *Sidereus Nuncius*, Venice, 1610.

Figure	Date	East	West
1	Jan. 7	• • ○	•
2	8	○	• • •
3	10	• • ○	
4	11	• • ○	
5	12	• •○	•
6	13	• ○	• • •
7	15	○	• • • •
8	15	○	• • • •
9	16	•○	• •
10	17	• ○	•
11	17	•• ○	•
12	18	• ○	•
13	19	• ○	• •
14	19	• • ○	• •
15	20	• ○	• •
16	20	• ○	••
17	20	• ○	• ••
18	21	•••○	•
19	22	• ○	•• • •
20	22	• ○	• ••
21	23	• • ○	•
22	23	• ○	
23	24	• •• ○	
24	25	• • ○	
25	26	• • ○	•
26	26	• • •○	•
27	27	• ○	
28	30	• ○	•• •
29	31	• •○	•

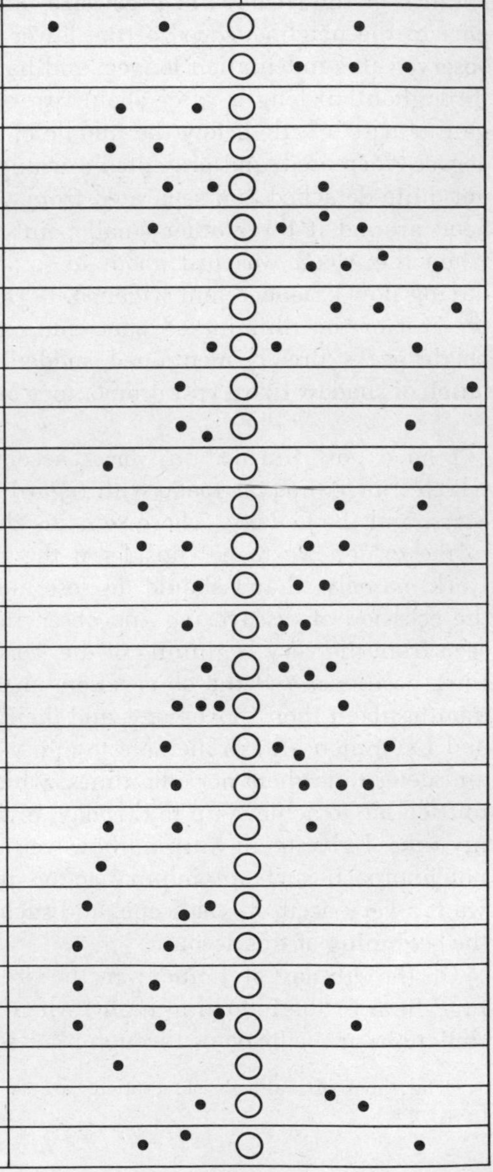

presented itself to my view, and as I had prepared for myself a very excellent instrument, I noticed a circumstance which I had never been able to notice before, owing to want of power in my other telescope, namely, that three little stars, small but very bright, were near the planet; and although I believed them to belong to the number of the fixed stars, yet they made me somewhat wonder, because they seemed to be arranged exactly in a straight line . . . and to be brighter than the rest of the stars, equal to them in magnitude. The position of them with reference to one another and to Jupiter was as follows (Fig. 1).

On the east side there were two stars, and a single one towards the west. The star which was furthest towards the east, and the western star, appeared rather larger than the third.

I scarcely troubled at all about the distance between them and Jupiter, for, as I have already said, at first I believed them to be fixed stars; but when on January 8th, led by some fatality, I turned again to look at the same part of the heavens, I found a very different state of things, for there were three little stars all west of Jupiter, and nearer together than on the previous night, and they were separated from one another by equal intervals, as the accompanying illustration (Fig. 2) shows.

At this point, although I had not turned my thoughts at all upon the approximation of the stars to one another, yet my surprise began to be excited, how Jupiter could one day be found to the east of all the aforesaid fixed stars when the day before it had been west of two of them; and forthwith I became afraid lest the planet might have moved differently from the calculation of astronomers, and so had passed those stars by its own proper motion. I therefore waited for the next night with the most intense longing, but I was disappointed of my hope, for the sky was covered with clouds in every direction.

But on January 10th the stars appeared in the following position with regard to Jupiter; there were two only, and both on the east side of Jupiter, the third, as I thought, being hidden by the planet (Fig. 3). They were situated just as before, exactly in the same straight line with Jupiter, and along the Zodiac.

When I had seen these phenomena, as I knew that corresponding changes of position could not by any means belong to Jupiter, and as, moreover, I perceived that the stars which I saw had been always the same, for there were no others either in front or behind, within a great distance, along the Zodiac,—at length, changing from doubt into surprise, I discovered that the interchange of position which I saw belonged not to Jupiter, but to the stars to which my attention had been drawn, and I thought therefore that they ought to be observed henceforward with more attention and precision.

Accordingly, on January 11th I saw an arrangement of the following kind (Fig. 4), namely, only two stars to the east of Jupiter, the nearer of which was distant from Jupiter three times as far as from the star further to the east; and the star furthest to the east was nearly twice as large as the other one; whereas on the previous night they had appeared nearly of equal magnitude. I therefore concluded, and decided unhesitatingly, that there are three stars in the heavens moving about Jupiter, as Venus and Mercury round the Sun; which at length was established as clear as daylight by numerous other subsequent observations. These observations also established that there are not only three, but four, erratic sidereal bodies performing their revolutions round Jupiter, observations of whose changes of position made with more exactness on succeeding nights the following account will supply. . . . Besides this, I have given the times of observation, especially when several were made in the same night, for the revolutions of these planets are so swift that an observer may generally get differences of position every hour.

Jan. 12.—At the first hour of the next night I saw these heavenly bodies arranged in this manner (Fig. 5). The satellite furthest to the east was greater than the satellite furthest to the west; but both were very conspicuous and bright; the distance of each one from Jupiter was two minutes. A third satellite, certainly not in view before, began to appear at the third hour; it nearly touched Jupiter on the east side, and was exceedingly small. They were all arranged in the same straight line, along the ecliptic.

Jan. 13.—For the first time four satellites were in view in the following position with regard to Jupiter (Fig. 6).

There were three to the west, and one to the east; they made a straight line nearly, but the middle satellite of those to the west deviated a little from the straight line towards the north. The satellite furthest to the east was at a distance of 2′ from Jupiter; there were intervals of 1′ only between Jupiter and the nearest satellite, and between the satellites themselves, west of Jupiter. All the satellites appeared of the same size, and though small they were very brilliant, and far outshone the fixed stars of the same magnitude.

Jan. 14.—The weather was cloudy.

Jan. 15.—At the third hour of the night the four satellites were in the state depicted in the next diagram (Fig. 7) with reference to Jupiter.

All were to the west, and arranged nearly in the same straight line; but the satellite which counted third from Jupiter was raised a little to the north. The nearest to Jupiter was the smallest of all; the rest appeared larger and in order of magnitude; the intervals between Jupiter and the three nearest satellites were all equal, and were of the magnitude of 2′ each; but the satellite furthest to the west was distant 4′ from the satellite nearest to it. They were very brilliant, and not at all twinkling, as they have always appeared both before and since. . . .

These are my observations upon the four Medicean[2] planets, recently discovered for the first time by me; and although it is not yet permitted me to deduce by calculation from these observations the orbits of these bodies, yet I may be allowed to make some statements, based upon them, well worthy of attention.

And, in the first place, since they are sometimes behind, sometimes before Jupiter, at like distances, and withdraw from this planet towards the east and towards the west only within very narrow limits of divergence, and since they accompany this planet alike when its motion is retrograde and direct, it can be a matter of doubt to no one that they perform their revolutions about this planet, while at the same time they all accomplish together orbits of twelve years' length about the centre of

2. Named thus by Galileo as an honor to the Medici family of Florence. The name did not stick; Jupiter's moons now being commonly referred to by Roman numerals.

the world.[3] Moreover, they revolve in unequal circles, which is evidently the conclusion to be drawn from the fact that I have never been permitted to see two satellites in conjunction when their distance from Jupiter was great, whereas near Jupiter two, three, and sometimes all (four), have been found closely packed together. Moreover, it may be detected that the revolutions of the satellites which describe the smallest circles round Jupiter are the most rapid, for the satellites nearest to Jupiter are often to be seen in the east, when the day before they have appeared in the west, and contrariwise. Also the satellite moving in the greatest orbit seems to me, after carefully weighing the occasions of its returning to positions previously noticed, to have a periodic time of half a month. Besides, we have a notable and splendid argument to remove the scruples of those who can tolerate the revolution of the planets round the Sun in the Copernican system, yet are so disturbed by the motion of one Moon about the Earth, while both accomplish an orbit of a year's length about the Sun, that they consider that this theory of the constitution of the universe must be upset as impossible; for now we have not one planet only revolving about another, while both traverse a vast orbit about the Sun, but our sense of sight presents to us four satellites circling about Jupiter, like the Moon about the Earth, while the whole system travels over a mighty orbit about the Sun in the space of twelve years.

3. I.e., the Sun.

Intellectual Exploration

René Descartes (1596–1650) was born and educated in France but in 1628 decided to live in Holland, where he remained until 1649, when he went to Sweden to instruct the young Queen Christiana in philosophy, only to fall sick and die soon after his arrival.

Descartes was a great mathematician, philosopher, and scientist. In his youth he found mathematics to be the only really satisfactory school subject because, once anyone clearly understood the terms being used, results followed logically and everyone had to agree on what the right answer was. How different were such fields as theology and metaphysica, where in Descartes' lifetime men were ready to kill one another over differences of creed!

In 1619, when still a young and unknown man, Descartes conceived the ambition of using the methods of mathematics to discover true knowledge in other fields. By starting with clear and distinct ideas, like the axioms of geometry, he hoped that logical deduction, helped at critical points by experiment, might arrive at propositions as certain and universal as those of mathematical demonstrations. Applied to physics, for instance, this meant analyzing bodies into their simplest elements—pure extension in space. Applied to animals and the human body, it meant analyzing their motions as the motions of a machine. The physical world itself was a vast machine, for that matter. The same method discovered the conscious mind whose existence could not be doubted because the act of doubt itself implied a mind to do the doubting! It was, in fact, from this clear and distinct idea that Descartes was able to deduce all the rest of his philosophy.

Descartes had several treatises ready for the printer when he heard of Galileo's difficulties with the Inquisition in 1630. This caused him to hold back, and it was only in 1637 that he allowed the first of his works to appear. Among them was the *Discourse on Method*, in which he set out to explain the way in which he hoped to straighten out the errors and confusion that had crept into men's ideas. The selection that follows comprises about the first third of the entire work.

RENÉ DESCARTES: DISCOURSE ON METHOD

Part I

Good sense is, of all things among men, the most equally distributed; for every one thinks himself so abundantly provided with it, that those even who are the most difficult to satisfy in

From René Descartes, *Discourse on Method*, trans. by John Veitsch, 2nd edition (Edinburgh: W. Blackwood & Sons, 1863).

everything else, do not usually desire a larger measure of this quality than they already possess. And in this it is not likely that all are mistaken: the conviction is rather to be held as testifying that the power of judging aright and of distinguishing truth from error, which is properly what is called good sense or reason, is by nature equal in all men; and that the diversity of our opinions, consequently, does not arise from some being endowed with a larger share of reason than others, but solely from this, that we conduct our thoughts along different ways, and do not fix our attention on the same objects. For to be possessed of a vigorous mind is not enough; the prime requisite is rightly to apply it. The greatest minds, as they are capable of the highest excellences, are open likewise to the greatest aberrations; and those who travel very slowly may yet make far greater progress, provided they keep always to the straight road, than those who, while they run, forsake it.

For myself, I have never fancied my mind to be in any respect more perfect than those of the generality; on the contrary, I have often wished that I were equal to some others in promptitude of thought, or in clearness and distinctness of imagination, or in fulness and readiness of memory. And besides these, I know of no other qualities that contribute to the perfection of the mind; for as to the reason or sense, inasmuch as it is that alone which constitutes us men, and distinguishes us from the brutes, I am disposed to believe that it is to be found complete in each individual; and on this point to adopt the common opinion of philosophers, who say that the difference of greater and less holds only among the *accidents*, and not among the *forms* or *natures* of *individuals* of the same *species*.

I will not hesitate, however, to avow my belief that it has been my singular good fortune to have very early in life fallen in with certain tracks which have conducted me to considerations and maxims, of which I have formed a method that gives me the means, as I think, of gradually augmenting my knowledge, and of raising it by little and little to the highest point which the mediocrity of my talents and the brief duration of my life will permit me to reach. For I have already reaped from it such fruits that, although I have been accustomed to think lowly enough of myself, and although when I look with the eye of a philosopher at the varied courses and pursuits of mankind at large, I find scarcely one which does not appear vain and useless, I nevertheless derive the highest satisfaction from the progress I conceive myself to have already made in the search after truth, and cannot help entertaining such expectations of the future as to believe that if, among the occupations of men as men, there is any one really excellent and important, it is that which I have chosen.

After all, it is possible I may be mistaken; and it is but a little copper and glass, perhaps, that I take for gold and diamonds. I know how very liable we are to delusion in what relates to ourselves, and also how much the judgments of our friends are to be suspected when given in our favour. But I shall endeavour in this discourse to describe the paths I have followed, and to delineate my life as in a picture, in order that each one may be able to judge of them for himself, and that in the general opinion entertained of them, as gathered from current report, I myself may have a new help towards instruction to be added to those I have been in the habit of employing.

My present design, then, is not to teach the method which each ought to follow for the right conduct of his reason, but solely to describe the way in which I have endeavoured to conduct my own. They who set themselves to give precepts must of course regard themselves as possessed of greater skill than those to whom they prescribe; and if they err in the slightest particular, they subject themselves to censure. But as this tract is put forth merely as a history, or, if you will, as a tale, in which, amid some examples worthy of imitation, there will be found, perhaps, as many more which it were advisable not to follow, I hope it will prove useful to some without being hurtful to any, and that my openness will find some favour with all.

From my childhood, I have been familiar with letters; and as I was given to believe that by their help a clear and certain knowledge of all that is useful in life might be acquired, I was ardently desirous of instruction. But as soon as I had finished the entire course of study, at the close of which it is customary to be admitted into the order of the learned, I completely changed my opinion. For I found myself involved in so many doubts and errors, that I was convinced I had advanced no farther in all my attempts at learning, than the discovery at every turn of my own ignorance. And yet I was studying in one of the most celebrated schools in Europe, in which I thought there must be learned men, if such were anywhere to be found. I had been taught all that others learned there; and not contented with the sciences actually taught us, I had, in addition, read all the books that had fallen into my hands, treating of such branches as are esteemed the most curious and rare. I knew the judgment which others had formed of me; and I did not find that I was considered inferior to my fellows, although there were among them some who were already marked out to fill the places of our instructors. And, in fine, our age appeared to me as flourishing, and as fertile in powerful minds as any preceding one. I was thus led to take the liberty of judging of all other men by myself, and of concluding that there was no science in existence that was of such a nature as I had previously been given to believe.

I still continued, however, to hold in esteem the studies of the schools. I was aware that the languages taught in them are necessary to the understanding of the writings of the ancients; that the grace of fable stirs the mind; that the memorable deeds of history elevate it; and, if read with discretion, aid in forming the judgment; that the perusal of all excellent books is, as it were, to interview with the noblest men of past ages, who have written them, and even a studied interview, in which are discovered to us only their choicest thoughts; that eloquence has incomparable force and beauty; that poesy has its ravishing graces and delights; that in the mathematics there are many refined discoveries eminently suited to gratify the inquisitive, as well as further all the arts and lessen the labour of man; that numerous highly useful precepts and exhortations to virtue are contained in treatises on morals; that theology points out the path to heaven; that philosophy affords the means of discoursing with an appearance of truth on all matters, and commands the admiration of the more simple; that jurisprudence, medicine, and the other sciences, secure for their cultivators honours and riches; and, in fine, that it is useful to bestow some attention upon all, even upon those abounding the most in superstition and error, that we may be in a position to determine their real value, and guard against being deceived.

But I believed that I had already given sufficient time to languages, and likewise to the reading of the writings of the ancients, to their histories and fables. For to hold converse with those of other ages and to travel, are almost the same thing. It is useful to know something of the manners of different nations, that we may be enabled to form a more correct judgment regarding our own, and be prevented from thinking that every thing contrary to our customs is ridiculous and irrational,—a conclusion usually come to by those whose experience has been limited to their own country. On the other hand, when too much time is occupied in travelling, we become strangers to our native country; and the over curious in the customs of the past are generally ignorant of those of the present. Besides, fictitious narratives lead us to imagine the possibility of many events that are impossible; and even the most faithful histories, if they do not wholly misrepresent matters, or exaggerate their importance to render the account of them more worthy of perusal, omit, at least, almost always the meanest and least striking of the attendant circumstances; hence it happens that the remainder does not represent the truth, and that such as regulate their conduct by examples drawn from this source, are apt to fall into the extravagances of the knight-errants of romance, and to entertain projects that exceed their powers.

I esteemed eloquence highly, and was in raptures with poesy; but I thought that both were gifts of nature rather than fruits of study. Those in whom the faculty of reason is predominant, and who most skilfully dispose their thoughts with a view to render them clear and intelligible, are always the best able to persuade others of the truth of what they lay down, though they should speak only in the language of Lower Brittany,[1] and be wholly ignorant of the rules of rhetoric; and those whose minds are stored with the most agreeable fancies, and who can give expression to them with the greatest embellishment and

1. A Celtic dialect.

harmony, are still the best poets, though unacquainted with the art of poetry.

I was especially delighted with the mathematics, on account of the certitude and evidence of their reasonings; but I had not as yet a precise knowledge of their true use; and thinking that they but contributed to the advancement of the mechanical arts, I was astonished that foundations, so strong and solid, should have had no loftier superstructure reared on them. On the other hand, I compared the disquisitions of the ancient moralists to very towering and magnificent palaces with no better foundation than sand and mud: they laud the virtues very highly, and exhibit them as estimable far above anything on earth; but they give us no adequate criterion of virtue, and frequently that which they designate with so fine a name is but apathy, or pride, or despair, or parricide.

I revered our theology, and aspired as much as any one to reach heaven: but being given assuredly to understand that the way is not less open to the most ignorant than to the most learned, and that the revealed truths which lead to heaven are above our comprehension, I did not presume to subject them to the impotency of my reason; and I thought that in order competently to undertake their examination, there was need of some special help from heaven, and of being more than man.

Of philosophy I will say nothing, except that when I saw that it had been cultivated for many ages by the most distinguished men, and that yet there is not a single matter within its sphere which is not still in dispute, and nothing, therefore, which is above doubt, I did not presume to anticipate that my success would be greater in it than that of others; and further, when I considered the number of conflicting opinions touching a single matter that may be upheld by learned men, while there can be but one true, I reckoned as well-nigh false all that was only probable.

As to the other sciences, inasmuch as these borrow their principles from philosophy, I judged that no solid superstructures could be reared on foundations so infirm; and neither the honour nor the gain held out by them was sufficient to determine me to their cultivation: for I was not, thank Heaven, in a condition which compelled me to make merchandise of science for the bettering of my fortune;[2] and though I might not profess to scorn glory as a cynic, I yet made very slight account of that honour which I hoped to acquire only through fictitious titles. And, in fine, of false sciences I thought I knew the worth sufficiently to escape being deceived by the professions of an alchemist, the predictions of an astrologer, the impostures of a magician, or by the artifices and boasting of any of those who profess to know things of which they are ignorant.

For these reasons, as soon as my age permitted me to pass from under the control of my instructors, I entirely abandoned the study of letters, and resolved no longer to seek any other science than the knowledge of myself, or of the great book of the world. I spent the remainder of my youth in travelling, in visiting courts and armies, in holding intercourse with men of different dispositions and ranks, in collecting varied experience, in proving myself in the different situations into which fortune threw me, and, above all, in making such reflection on the matter of my experience as to secure my improvement. For it occurred to me that I should find much more truth in the reasonings of each individual with reference to the affairs in which he is personally interested, and the issue of which must presently punish him if he has judged amiss, than in those conducted by a man of letters in his study, regarding speculative matters that are of no practical moment, and followed by no consequences to himself, farther, perhaps, than that they foster his vanity the better the more remote they are from common sense; requiring, as they must in this case, the exercise of greater ingenuity and art to render them probable. In addition, I had always a most earnest desire to know how to distinguish the true from the false, in order that I might be able clearly to discriminate the right path in life, and proceed in it with confidence.

It is true that, while busied only in considering the manners of other men, I found here, too, scarce any ground for settled conviction, and remarked hardly less contradiction among them than in the opinions of the philosophers. So that the greatest ad-

2. Descartes inherited a small estate, which he sold on taking up residence in Holland.

vantage I derived from the study consisted in this, that, observing many things which, however extravagant and ridiculous to our apprehension, are yet by common consent received and approved by other great nations, I learned to entertain too decided a belief in regard to nothing of the truth of which I had been persuaded merely by example and custom; and thus I gradually extricated myself from many errors powerful enough to darken our natural intelligence, and incapacitate us in great measure from listening to reason. But after I had been occupied several years in thus studying the book of the world, and in essaying to gather some experience, I at length resolved to make myself an object of study, and to employ all the powers of my mind in choosing the paths I ought to follow, an undertaking which was accompanied with greater success than it would have been had I never quitted my country or my books.

Part II

I was then in Germany, attracted thither by the wars in that country, which have not yet been brought to a termination; and as I was returning to the army from the coronation of the emperor, the setting in of winter arrested me in a locality where, as I found no society to interest me, and was besides fortunately undisturbed by any cares or passions, I remained the whole day in seclusion, with full opportunity to occupy my attention with my own thoughts. Of these one of the very first that occurred to me was, that there is seldom so much perfection in works composed of many separate parts, upon which different hands had been employed, as in those completed by a single master. Thus it is observable that the buildings which a single architect has planned and executed, are generally more elegant and commodious than those which several have attempted to improve, by making old walls serve for purposes for which they were not originally built. Thus also, those ancient cities which, from being at first only villages, have become, in course of time, large towns, are usually but ill laid out compared with the regularly constructed towns which a professional architect has freely planned on an open plain; so that although the several buildings of the former may often equal or surpass in beauty those of the latter, yet when one observes their indiscriminate juxtaposition, there a large one and here a small, and the consequent crookedness and irregularity of the streets, one is disposed to allege that chance rather than any human will guided by reason must have led to such an arrangement. And if we consider that nevertheless there have been at all times certain officers whose duty it was to see that private buildings contributed to public ornament, the difficulty of reaching high perfection with but the materials of others to operate on, will be readily acknowledged. . . . And because we have all to pass through a state of infancy to manhood, and have been of necessity, for a length of time, governed by our desires and preceptors (whose dictates were frequently conflicting, while neither perhaps always counselled us for the best), I farther concluded that it is almost impossible that our judgments can be so correct or solid as they would have been, had our reason been mature from the moment of our birth, and had we always been guided by it alone.

It is true, however, that it is not customary to pull down all the houses of a town with the single design of rebuilding them differently, and thereby rendering the streets more handsome; but it often happens that a private individual takes down his own with the view of erecting it anew, and that people are even sometimes constrained to this when their houses are in danger of falling from age, or when the foundations are insecure. With this before me by way of example, I was persuaded that it would indeed be preposterous for a private individual to think of reforming a state by fundamentally changing it throughout, and overturning it in order to set it up amended; and the same I thought was true of any similar project for reforming the body of the sciences, or the order of teaching them established in the schools: but as for the opinions which up to that time I had embraced, I thought that I could not do better than resolve at once to sweep them wholly away, that I might afterwards be in a position to admit either others more correct, or even perhaps the same when they had undergone the scrutiny of reason. I firmly believed that in this way I should much better succeed in the conduct of my life, than if I built only upon old foundations, and leant upon principles which, in my youth, I had taken upon trust. For although I recognised various difficulties in this undertaking, these were not, however, without remedy, nor once to be compared with such as attend the slightest reformation in public affairs. Large bodies, if once overthrown, are with great difficulty set up again, or even kept erect when once seriously shaken, and the fall of such is always disastrous. Then if there are any imperfections in the constitutions of states (and that many such exist the diversity of constitutions is alone sufficient to assure us), custom has without doubt materially smoothed their inconveniences, and has even managed to steer altogether clear of, or insensibly corrected a number which sagacity could not have provided against with equal effect; and, in fine, the defects are almost always more tolerable than the change necessary for their removal; in the same manner that highways which wind among mountains, by being much frequented, become gradually so smooth and commodious, that it is much better to follow them than to seek a straighter path by climbing over the tops of rocks and descending to the bottoms of precipices.

Hence it is that I cannot in any degree approve of those restless and busy meddlers who, called neither by birth nor fortune to take part in the management of public affairs, are yet always projecting reforms; and if I thought that this tract contained aught which might justify the suspicion that I was a victim of such folly, I would by no means permit its publication. I have never contemplated anything higher than the reformation of my own opinions, and basing them on a foundation wholly my own. And although my own satisfaction with my work has led me to present here a draft of it, I do not by any means therefore recommend to every one else to make a similar attempt. Those whom God has endowed with a larger measure of genius will entertain, perhaps, designs still more exalted; but for the many I am much afraid lest even the present undertaking be more than they can safely venture to imitate. The single design to strip one's self of all past beliefs is one that ought not to be taken by every one. The majority of men is composed of two classes, for neither of which would this be at all a befitting resolution: in the *first* place, of those who with more than a due confidence in their own powers, are precipitate in their judgments and want the patience requisite for orderly and circumspect thinking; whence it happens, that if men of this class once take the liberty to doubt of their accustomed opinions, and quit the beaten highway, they will never be able to thread the byway that would lead them by a shorter course, and will lose themselves and continue to wander for life; in the *second* place, of those who, possessed of sufficient sense or modesty to determine that there are others who excel them in the power of discriminating between truth and error, and by whom they may be instructed, ought rather to content themselves with the opinions of such than trust for more correct to their own reason.

For my own part, I should doubtless have belonged to the latter class, had I received instruction from but one master, or had I never known the diversities of opinion that from time immemorial have prevailed among men of the greatest learning. But I had become aware, even so early as during my college life, that no opinion, however absurd and incredible, can be imagined, which has not been maintained by some one of the philosophers; and afterwards in the course of my travels I remarked that all those whose opinions are decidedly repugnant to ours are not on that account barbarians and savages, but on the contrary that many of these nations make an equally good, if not a better, use of their reason than we do. I took into account also the very different character which a person brought up from infancy in France or Germany exhibits, from that which, with the same mind originally, this individual would have possessed had he lived always among the Chinese or with savages, and the circumstance that in dress itself the fashion which pleased us ten years ago, and which may again, perhaps, be received into favour before ten years have gone, appears to us at this moment extravagant and ridiculous. I was thus led to infer that the ground of our opinions is far more custom and example than any certain knowledge. And, finally, although such be the ground of our opinions, I remarked that a plurality of suffrages is no guarantee of truth where it is at all of difficult discovery, as in such cases it is much more likely that it will be found by one than by many. I could, however, select from the crowd no one whose opinions seemed worthy of preference, and thus I found myself constrained, as it were, to use my own reason in the conduct of my life.

But like one walking alone and in the dark, I resolved to proceed so slowly and with such circumspection, that if I did not advance far, I would at least guard against falling. I did not even choose to dismiss summarily any of the opinions that had crept into my belief without having been introduced by reason, but first of all took sufficient time carefully to satisfy myself of the general nature of the task I was setting myself, and ascertain the true method by which to arrive at the knowledge of whatever lay within the compass of my powers.

Among the branches of philosophy, I had, at an earlier period, given some attention to logic, and among those of the mathematics to geometrical analysis and algebra,—three arts or sciences which ought, as I conceived, to contribute something to my design. But, on examination, I found that, as for logic, its syllogisms and the majority of its other precepts are of avail rather in the communication of what we already know, or even as the art of Lully,[3] in speaking without judgment of things of which we are ignorant, than in the investigation of the unkown; and although this science contains indeed a number of correct and very excellent precepts, there are, nevertheless, so many others, and these either injurious or superfluous, mingled with the former, that it is almost quite as difficult to effect a severance of the true from the false as it is to extract a Diana or a Minerva from a rough block of marble. Then as to the analysis[4] of the ancients and the algebra of the moderns, besides that they embrace only matters highly abstract, and, to appearance, of no use, the former is so exclusively restricted to the consideration of figures, that it can exercise the understanding only on condition of greatly fatiguing the imagination; and, in the latter,

3. Raymond Lully (ca. 1235-1315), a scholastic philosopher, poet, mystic, and missionary.

4. Geometry.

there is so complete a subjection to certain rules and formulas, that there results an art full of confusion and obscurity calculated to embarrass, instead of a science fitted to cultivate the mind. By these considerations I was induced to seek some other method which would comprise the advantages of the three and be exempt from their defects. And as a multitude of laws often only hampers justice, so that a state is best governed when, with few laws, these are rigidly administered; in like manner, instead of the great number of precepts of which logic is composed, I believed that the four following would prove perfectly sufficient for me, provided I took the firm and unwavering resolution never in a single instance to fail in observing them.

The *first* was never to accept anything for true which I did not clearly know to be such; that is to say, carefully to avoid precipitancy and prejudice, and to comprise nothing more in my judgment than what was presented to my mind so clearly and distinctly as to exclude all ground of doubt.

The *second*, to divide each of the difficulties under examination into as many parts as possible, and as might be necessary for its adequate solution.

The *third*, to conduct my thoughts in such order that, by commencing with objects the simplest and easiest to know, I might ascend by little and little, and, as it were, step by step, to the knowledge of the more complex; assigning in thought a certain order even to those objects which in their own nature do not stand in a relation of antecedence and sequence.

And the *last*, in every case to make enumerations so complete, and reviews so general, that I might be assured that nothing was omitted.

The long chains of simple and easy reasonings by means of which geometers are accustomed to reach the conclusions of their most difficult demonstrations, had led me to imagine that all things, to the knowledge of which man is competent, are mutually connected in the same way, and that there is nothing so far removed from us as to be beyond our reach, or so hidden that we cannot discover it, provided only we abstain from accepting the false for the true, and always preserve in our thoughts the order necessary for the deduction of one truth from another. And I had little difficulty in determining the objects with which it was necessary to commence, for I was already persuaded that it must be with the simplest and easiest to know, and, considering that of all those who have hitherto sought truth in the sciences, the mathematicians alone have been able to find any demonstrations, that is, any certain and evident reasons, I did not doubt but that such must have been the rule of their investigations. I resolved to commence, therefore, with the examination of the simplest objects, not anticipating, however, from this any other advantage than that to be found in accustoming my mind to the love and nourishment of truth, and to a distaste for all such reasonings as were unsound. But I had no intention on that account of attempting to master all the particular sciences commonly denominated mathematics: but observing that, however different their objects, they all agree in considering only the various relations or proportions subsisting among those objects, I thought it best for my purpose to consider these proportions in the most general form possible, without referring them to any objects in particular, except such as would most facilitate the knowledge of them, and without by any means restricting them to these, that afterwards I might thus be the better able to apply them to every other class of objects to which they are legitimately applicable. Perceiving further, that in order to understand these relations I should sometimes have to consider them one by one, and sometimes only to bear them in mind, or embrace them in the aggregate, I thought that, in order the better to consider them individually, I should view them as subsisting between straight lines, than which I could find no objects more simple, or capable of being more distinctly represented to my imagination and senses;[5] and on the other hand, that in order to retain them in the memory, or embrace an aggregate of many, I should express them by certain characters the briefest possible. In this way I believed that I could borrow all that was best both in geometrical analysis and

5. Descartes invented "analytic geometry," by graphing algebraic functions "between straight lines," i.e., on XY coordinates. He here describes his method of doing so.

in algebra, and correct all the defects of the one by help of the other.

And, in point of fact, the accurate observance of these few precepts gave me, I take the liberty of saying, such ease in unravelling all the questions embraced in these two sciences, that in the two or three months I devoted to their examination, not only did I reach solutions of questions I had formerly deemed exceedingly difficult, but even as regards questions of the solution of which I continued ignorant, I was enabled, as it appeared to me, to determine the means whereby, and the extent to which, a solution was possible; results attributable to the circumstance that I commenced with the simplest and most general truths, and that thus each truth discovered was a rule available in the discovery of subsequent ones. Nor in this perhaps shall I appear too vain, if it be considered that, as the truth on any particular point is one, whoever apprehends the truth, knows all that on that point can be known. The child, for example, who has been instructed in the elements of arithmetic, and has made a particular addition, according to rule, may be assured that he has found, with respect to the sum of the numbers before him, all that in this instance is within the reach of human genius. Now, in conclusion, the method which teaches adherence to the true order, and an exact enumeration of all the conditions of the thing sought includes all that gives certitude to the rules of arithmetic.

But the chief ground of my satisfaction with this method, was the assurance I had of thereby exercising my reason in all matters, if not with absolute perfection, at least with the greatest attainable by me: besides, I was conscious that by its use my mind was becoming gradually habituated to clearer and more distinct conceptions of its objects; and I hoped also, from not having restricted this method to any particular matter, to apply it to the difficulties of the other sciences, with not less success than to those of algebra. I should not, however, on this account have ventured at once on the examination of all the difficulties of the sciences which presented themselves to me, for this would have been contrary to the order prescribed in the method, but observing that the knowledge of such is dependent on principles borrowed from philosophy, in which I found nothing certain, I thought it necessary first of all to endeavour to establish its principles. And because I observed, besides, that an inquiry of this kind was of all others of the greatest moment, and one in which precipitancy and anticipation in judgment were most to be dreaded, I thought that I ought not to approach it till I had reached a more mature age (being at that time but twenty-three), and had first of all employed much of my time in preparation for the work, as well by eradicating from my mind all the erroneous opinions I had up to that moment accepted, as by amassing variety of experience to afford materials for my reasonings, and by continually exercising myself in my chosen method with a view to increased skill in its application.

III

Government and Religion in the Old Regime

Political Right According to Revelation
Bishop Bossuet: Politics Derived from the Words of Holy Scripture

Political Right According to Nature and Reason
John Locke: Of Civil Government

Reasonable Religion vs. Superstition
Voltaire: Philosophical Dictionary

Political Right According To Revelation

Jacques Bénigne Bossuet (1627–1704) was a learned French clergyman, who rose to become Bishop of Meaux (1681–1704). He was a famous orator and controversialist against French Protestants who were still numerous and influential when Bossuet began his career. When King Louis XIV appointed Bossuet as tutor to his son, Bossuet prepared himself for the responsibility of educating the heir to the throne by writing three books. An extract from one of them is reproduced below.

Bossuet recognized that part of his task as tutor was to instruct the future king of France in the rights and duties of his office. (In fact the prince never reigned, dying before his father.) Bossuet set out to discover from texts of Holy Scripture just what royal rights and duties were and set forth his conclusions in what follows. This procedure cut the ground from under Protestants who also claimed to derive truth from God's revelation as recorded in the Bible. For if obedience to the king was a duty prescribed by God, then the defiance of the royal will in matters of religion, which had been a prominent fact of French politics in the century before Bossuet's birth, ceased to be permissible. Conversely, Bossuet argued that royal absolutism *was* justified on what every pious Frenchman, Catholic or Protestant, accepted as the highest possible authority—the word of God itself.

Arguments such as these met a deep-felt need in France and other countries of Europe for some kind of definite political legitimacy. By equating resistance to the king with defiance of God, the consolidation of comparatively large kingdoms like that of France became easier than would otherwise have been the case. Conversely, religious defiance of the monarch became more difficult; in fact, Bossuet was instrumental in converting quite a few influential Protestants to the official Catholic faith of France.

BISHOP JACQUES BÉNIGNE BOSSUET: POLITICS DERIVED FROM THE WORDS OF HOLY SCRIPTURE

Book III

Wherein begins the explanation of the nature and properties of royal authority.

Article I. On distinguishing its essential characteristics.

Proposition I. Royal authority has four essential characteristics or qualities. First, royal authority is sacred; second, it is paternal; third, it is absolute; fourth, it is subordinated to reason. These will be explained in proper order in the following articles.

Article II. Royal authority is sacred.

Proposition I. God establishes kings as His Ministers, and reigns through them over the people. We have already seen that all power comes from God. As St. Paul says, "The King is the minister of God to thee for good. But if thou do that which is evil, be afraid; for he beareth not the sword in vain; for he is the minister of God, a revenger to execute wrath upon him that doeth evil." (Romans, 13:4).

Princes serve therefore as ministers of God and as His lieutenants on earth. It is through them that He rules His empire. "And now ye think to withstand the kingdom of the Lord in the hand of the sons of David"; (II Chronicles, 13:8). That is why we have shown that the royal throne is not that of a man but the throne of God himself. ". . . he hath chosen Solomon my son to sit upon the throne of the kingdom of the Lord over Israel." (I Chronicles, 28:5). And again, "Solomon sat on the throne of the Lord. . . ." (I Chronicles, 24:23). And lest this should be considered somehow peculiar to the Israelites, here is

Translated by Elizabeth D. McNeill from Bishop Bossuet, *Politique Tirée des Propres Paroles de l'Écriture Sainte,* Vol. II, republished in *Oeuvres Choisies de Bossuet* (Paris: Hachette, 1900). Reprinted by permission of University of Chicago Press.

what Ecclesiasticus says: "For every nation He appointed a ruler, but Israel is the Lord's own portion." (The Wisdom of Sirach, 17:14, 15). He therefore rules over all nations and to them all He gives their kings; although He rules over Israel in a more clearly stated and distinctive fashion.

Proposition II. The person of kings is sacred. It is clear from the foregoing that kings' persons are sacred, and that any attack upon them is sacrilege. God causes kings to be anointed by His prophets with a holy anointing, as He does the priests and the altars. But even without the outward application of this anointment, kings are sacred because of their obligations; they are the representatives of Divine majesty, delegated by His providence to execute His commands. Thus God even calls Cyrus His anointed. "Thus saith the Lord to his anointed, to Cyrus, whose right hand I have holden, to subdue nations before him." (Isaiah, 45:1).

The title of Christ is given to the kings, and throughout the Scripture one sees them called Christ, or the Lord's anointed. With this venerable title, even the Prophets revere them, and regard them as associated with the sovereign empire of God, whose authority they wield over the nations. "Witness against me before the Lord, and before his anointed: whose ox have I taken? or whose ass have I taken? or whom have I defrauded? whom have I oppressed? And they said, thou hast not defrauded us, nor oppressed us, neither hast taken aught of any man's hand. And Samuel said unto them, the Lord is witness against you, and his anointed is witness this day, that ye have not found aught in my hand." (I Samuel, 12:3-5). Samuel, after having judged the people with absolute power for twenty-one years on behalf of the Lord, thus accounts for his conduct before God and before Saul, whom he calls upon as witnesses, and by whose testimony he establishes his innocence.

One must guard kings as one would sacred things, and he who neglects thus to guard them is worthy of death. "As the Lord liveth, ye are worthy to die," said David to Saul's captains, "because ye have not kept your master, the Lord's anointed." (I Samuel, 26:16). He who guards the life of a prince, commits his own into God's keeping. David said to King

Saul, "And, behold, as thy life was highly valued this day in mine eyes, so let my life be highly valued in the eyes of the Lord, and let him deliver me out of all tribulation." (I Samuel, 26:24).

Twice God placed Saul in the hands of David; Saul did all he could to cause David's undoing; his men pressed David to rid himself of this unjust and impious prince; but the idea filled him with horror. "And David said unto his men, the Lord forbid that I should do this thing unto my master, the Lord's anointed, to stretch forth mine hand against him, seeing he is the anointed of the Lord." (I Samuel, 24:6). Far from making any attack upon Saul, David was filled with fear at having cut off a piece of Saul's mantle, although he had only done it to show Saul how conscientiously he had spared his life. "And it came to pass afterward, that David's heart smote him, because he had cut off Saul's skirt." (I Samuel, 24:5). So sacred did the king's person seem to David, and so afraid was he of violating, by the slightest irreverence, the respect that was Saul's due.

Proposition III. One must obey the prince according to the principles of religion and of conscience. St. Paul, having said that the prince is the minister of God, concludes thus, "Wherefore ye must needs be subject, not only for wrath, but also for conscience' sake." (Romans, 13:5). . . .

"Servants, obey in all things your masters according to the flesh; not with eyeservice as men-pleasers; but in singleness of heart; fearing God: And whatsoever ye do, do it heartily, as to the Lord and not to men; knowing that of the Lord ye shall receive the reward of the inheritance: for ye serve the Lord Christ." (Colossians, 3:22-24). If the Apostle speaks thus of servitude, a state contrary to nature, what ought we to think about legitimate submission to princes who are magistrates, the protectors of public liberty? That is why St. Peter said, "Submit yourselves to every ordinance of man for the Lord's sake: Whether it be to the king, as supreme; or unto governors, as unto them that are sent by Him for the punishment of evildoers, and for the praise of them that do well." (I Peter, 2:13, 14).

In whatever way kings and magistrates may fulfil their duty, one must respect in them their position and their ministry. "Servants, be subject to your masters with all fear; not only to the good and gentle, but also to the froward. (I Peter 2:18). There is therefore something religious about the respect rendered to a prince. Serving God and respecting kings are interconnected, and St. Peter puts these two duties together: "Fear God. Honor the king." (I Peter 2:17).

Also, God endowed the princes with a divine quality. "I have said, Ye are gods; and all of you are children of the most High." (Psalms 82:6). God Himself is made to speak thus by David.

From this it follows that the servants of God take their oaths upon the well being and life of the king as though upon a divine and sacred thing. Uriah says to David, "As thou livest and as thy soul liveth, I will not do this thing." (II Samuel 11:11). Taken in the light of the Lord's commands this holds true even if the king is an infidel: "By the life of Pharaoh ye shall not go forth hence." (Genesis, 42:15).

We ought to give heed to the early Christians, and especially to Tertullian who here speaks in the name of them all: "We swear, not by the genii of the Caesars, but by their life and their well being, which is more august than all the genii. Do you not know that genii are demons? But we, who see the emperors as the choice and the judgment of God, who gave them command over all nations, respect in them what God put there, and we hold it a solemn oath." And he says further, "What more can I say about our religion and our piety toward the emperor, whom we must respect as him whom our God hath chosen? I can say that the Caesar is more ours than yours, since it was our God who established him." (Tertullian, *Apology*).

It is therefore in the spirit of Christianity to respect kings with the sort of religion which Tertullian most aptly terms "the religion of the second majesty." This second majesty is but an outgrowth of the first, that is, of the divine majesty, which, for the good of human affairs, wished to cast some of its reflected brilliance upon kings.

Proposition IV. Kings must respect their proper power, and only use it for the public good. Their power comes from on High, and as has been said, they must not think that they are the masters of this power, to use it as they please; but they must use it with fear and restraint as they should a thing coming to them from God, and for which God will demand an accounting. . . .

Kings must consequently tremble while using the power which the Lord gives them, and reflect upon how horrible a sacrilege it is to use a power which comes from God for evil ends. We have seen how kings are seated on the throne of God, grasping the sword which He Himself put in their hand. How profane and how audacious of unjust kings, to sit upon the throne of God, ordering arrests contrary to the laws, and using the sword God gave them for doing violence and butchering His children!

Let kings therefore respect their might; for it is not theirs, but the might of the Lord, which must be used in a holy and religious manner. . . .

Article III. Royal authority is paternal, and its true characteristic is goodness. . . .

Proposition I. Goodness is a royal quality, and the true measure of greatness. "For the Lord your God is the God of Gods, and the Lord of Lords, a great God, a mighty, and a terrible, which regardeth not persons, nor taketh reward: He doth execute the judgment of the fatherless and widow, and loveth the stranger, in giving him food and raiment." (Deuteronomy, 10:17, 18). Because God is great and complete in himself, he puts Himself all the way out, as it were, to do good to men, in conformity with these words. "For as His majesty is, So is His mercy also." (The Wisdom of Sirach, 2:18). He imbues kings with an image of His majesty in order to compel them to imitate His goodness. He raises them to a level where they no longer desire anything for themselves. We have heard David saying, "And what can David say more unto Thee? for Thou, Lord God, hast invested Thy servant with all this greatness." (II Samuel, 7:20). And at the same time God told the kings that he gave them this greatness out of love for the people, king over them." (II Chronicles, 2:11). And again, "Blessed be "Because the Lord hath loved his people, he hath made thee the Lord thy God, which delighted in thee, to set thee on the throne of Israel: because the Lord loved Israel for ever, therefore he made thee king, to do judgment and justice." (I Kings 10:9). That is why, in the passages where we read that the kingdom of David was imposed upon the people, the Hebrew and Greek read, for the people. This shows that the purpose of greatness is the good of the subjects. In fact, God, who created all men out of the same earth for a body, and equally placed His image and His likeness in all their souls, did not set up distinctions among men, in order to have on one hand the haughty and on the other slaves and wretches. He raised up the great only for them to protect the common people; He only gave His power to kings in order to procure the public welfare, and for them to be the support of the common people.

Proposition II. The prince is born not for himself but for the public. This is a sequel to the preceding proposition. God confirms this truth with the example of Moses. . . .

If only princes could understand that their true glory lies in not existing for themselves, and that the public welfare which they bring about is a sufficiently worthy recompense on earth, while awaiting the eternal blessings that God reserves for them!

Proposition III. The prince must look after the needs of the people. The Lord said to David, "Thou shalt feed my people Israel, and thou shalt be a captain over Israel." (II Samuel 5:2). . . .

It is a royal prerogative to minister to the needs of the people. Whoever else undertakes this function, to the prejudice of the prince, infringes upon royalty; that is why royalty is established; and the obligation to care for the people is the foundation upon which rest all the rights which sovereigns have over their subjects. That is why, in cases of great need, a people has the right of appeal to its prince. "And when all the land of Egypt was famished, the people cried to Pharaoh for bread." (Genesis, 41:55). . . .

Proposition IV. Among the people, those for whom the prince must provide the most carefully are the poor. For they have the greatest need of him who is, through his position, the father and the protector of all. That is why the care of widows and orphans was entrusted by God principally to judges and magistrates. . . .

Book IV

Continuation of the characteristics of royalty

Article I. Royal authority is absolute.

In order to make this term odious and insupportable, there are many who affect to confuse absolute government with arbitrary government. But in reality no two things are more distinct, as we will demonstrate when we speak of justice.

Proposition I. The prince does not have to justify himself to anyone for what he commands. "I counsel thee to keep the king's commandment, and that in regard to the oath of God. Be not hasty to go out of his sight: stand not in an evil thing; for he doeth whatsoever pleaseth him. Where the word of a king is, there is power: and who may say unto him, what doest thou? Whoso keepeth the commandment shall feel no evil thing." (Ecclesiastes 8:2-5). Without this absolute authority, the prince can neither do good nor repress evil; his power must be such that no one can hope to escape him; and as a matter of fact, the individual's sole defence against the public power must be his innocence. This doctrine conforms to what St. Paul said: "Wilt thou then not be afraid of the power? Do that which is good." (Romans 13:3).

Proposition II. When the prince has judged, there is no other judgment. Sovereigns' judgments are attributed to God himself. . . .

Princes are Gods and participate in some fashion in Divine power. "I have said, Ye are Gods; and all of you are children of the Most High." (Psalms 82:6). Only God can review their judgments and their persons—"God standeth in the congregation of the mighty; he judgeth among the gods." (Psalms 82:1).

That is why St. Gregory, bishop of Tours, said to King Chilperic at a church council, "We speak to you; but you listen to us only if you wish to. If you do not wish to, who will condemn you, if not He who has said that He was justice itself?" It therefore follows that whoever does not wish to obey the king cannot appeal to another tribunal, but is irrevocably condemned to death as the enemy of the public peace and of human society. "And the man that will do presumptuously, and will not hearken unto the priest or unto the judge, even that man shall die: and thou shalt put away the evil from Israel." (Deuteronomy, 17:12). And again, "Whosoever he be that doth rebel against thy commandment, he shall be put to death." (Joshua, 1:18). Thus spake the people to Joshua. The prince can correct himself when he finds he has done wrong, but against his authority there can be no remedy except by his authority. That is why a prince must be very careful what he orders. . . .

Proposition III. There is no coactive force against the prince. A coactive force is a power to compel obedience and to carry out legitimate orders. Legitimate command belongs only to the prince; to him alone also belongs coactive force. This is also why St. Paul gave the sword only to the prince. "But if thou do that which is evil, be afraid; for he beareth not the sword in vain." (Romans, 13:4). In a state only the prince is armed; otherwise everything is in confusion and the state collapses into anarchy.

Whoever makes himself a sovereign prince takes everything into his own hands, the supreme judicial authority as well as all the forces of the state. . . .

This is what may be called the royal law of the Jews, where all the powers of kings are excellently set forth. To the prince alone belongs the general care of the people: that is the first article and basis of all the others; to him belong public works; to him belong defence and offence; to him belong decrees and ordinances; to him belong honorific titles; there is no power which is not dependent on his, no assembly but by his authority. Thus for the good of the state, all power is united into a single whole. For power to exist outside of this is to divide the state, to ruin the public peace, to create two masters, which is in contradiction to the word of the Gospel, "No man can serve two masters." (Matthew, 6:24).

The prince is by virtue of his obligations the father of his people; by his majesty he is above petty interests; more than this, all his majesty and his natural interest is directed toward the preservation of the people, since, in short, if the people are in want, he is no longer king. There is therefore nothing better than to leave all the power of the state to him who has the greatest interest in the preservation and grandeur of the state.

Proposition IV. The kings are not, however, therefore freed from all laws. . . . [Here follows a long quotation from Deuteronomy.]

One must observe that this law included not only the religion but also the law of the kingdom, to which the king was subject as much as others, or more than others, through the righteousness of his will. This is what princes find so hard to understand. As St. Ambrose said: "Where will you find a prince who believes that what is not good is not permitted; who holds himself bound by his own laws; who believes that a ruler ought not to permit himself to do what is contrary to justice? But authority does not destroy the obligations of justice; on the contrary, it is by observing the prescriptions of justice that authority avoids criminal behaviour. And the king is not exempt from the law; for if he sins, he destroys the law by his example." St. Ambrose adds, "Can he who judges others escape his own judgment? And ought he to do that which he himself condemns?" Hence a Roman emperor's dictum, "It is worthy of the majesty of a ruler to recognize his submission to the laws."

The kings are therefore subject, like others, to the equity of the laws, both because they ought to be just, and because they owe it to the people to give an example by maintaining justice; but they are not subject to the penalties of the law. . . .

Proposition V. The people must remain peaceable under the authority of the king. . . .

Proposition VI. The people must fear the prince; but the prince need only fear to do evil. . . .

Fear is a necessary brake for the people, because of their presumptuousness and their natural intractability. Therefore it is necessary for the people to fear the prince; but should the prince fear the people, then all is lost. . . .

Political Right According to Nature and Reason

John Locke (1632–1704) was an English gentleman, medical doctor, and philosopher. He associated with opponents of the Stuart Kings and in 1683 took refuge in Holland, where he came to know William of Orange and a group of English exiles who gathered at the Dutch court. In 1688, when William of Orange invaded England and drove King James II from the throne, Locke returned to his native land and quickly became the most persuasive apologist for the "Glorious Revolution." Two treatises on government came out in 1689. The selection below is from the second of these treatises.

Locke's purpose was to justify the overthrow of James II, hereditary King of England, Scotland, and Ireland. To do he had to rebut arguments for the legitimacy of royal power based on the Bible (as advanced by Bishop Bossuet) and on reason (as argued by the English philosopher Thomas Hobbes). His empirical method, seeking instances of how governments were in fact established, supplemented by abstract argument from reason and nature, is well illustrated by the chapter reproduced below. John Locke became extremely influential in the American colonies in the eighteenth century when frictions with Great Britain began to develop, leading toward the American Revolution. And through the American Revolution Locke's theories came to play an important role in justifying popular sovereignty elsewhere in the world—both in Europe and beyond.

Locke also exerted great influence through his writings on religious toleration; and among European philosophers his *Essay Concerning Human Understanding* (1690) inaugurated a new, more rigorous examination of how men can know anything about the world.

JOHN LOCKE: OF CIVIL GOVERNMENT

Chapter VIII

Of the beginning of political societies

Men being, as has been said, by nature, all free, equal, and independent, no one can be put out of this estate, and subjected to

From *The Works of John Locke*, 12th edition, Vol. IV (London, 1824), pp. 394-405.

the political power of another, without his own consent. The only way, whereby any one divests himself of his natural liberty, and puts on the bonds of civil society, is by agreeing with other men to join and unite into a community, for their comfortable, safe, and peaceable living one amongst another, in a secure enjoyment of their properties, and a greater security against any, that are not of it. This any number of men may do, because it injures not the freedom of the rest; they are left as they were in the liberty of the state of nature. When any number of men have so consented to make one community or government, they are thereby presently incorporated, and make one body politic, wherein the majority have a right to act and conclude the rest.

For when any number of men have, by the consent of every individual, made a community, they have thereby made that community one body, with a power to act as one body, which is only by the will and determination of the majority: for that which acts any community, being only the consent of the individuals of it, and it being necessary to that which is one body to move one way; it is necessary the body should move that way whither the greater force carries it, which is the consent of the majority: or else it is impossible it should act or continue one body, one community, which the consent of every individual that united into it, agreed that it should; and so every one is bound by that consent to be concluded by the majority. And therefore we see, that in assemblies, impowered to act by positive laws, where no number is set by that positive law which impowers them, the act of the majority passes for the act of the whole, and of course determines; as having, by the law of nature and reason, the power of the whole.

And thus every man, by consenting with others to make one body politic under one government, puts himself under an obligation, to every one of that society, to submit to the determination of the majority, and to be concluded by it; or else this original compact, whereby he with others incorporate into one society, would signify nothing, and be no compact, if he be left free, and under no other ties than he was in before in the state of nature. For what appearance would there be of any compact?

what new engagement if he were no farther tied by any decrees of the society, than he himself thought fit, and did actually consent to? This would be still as great a liberty, as he himself had before his compact, or any one else in the state of nature hath, who may submit himself, and consent to any acts of it if he thinks fit.

For if the consent of the majority shall not, in reason, be received as the act of the whole, and conclude every individual; nothing but the consent of every individual can make any thing to be the act of the whole: but such a consent is next to impossible ever to be had, if we consider the infirmities of health, and avocations of business, which in a number, though much less than that of a commonwealth, will necessarily keep many away from the public assembly. To which if we add the variety of opinions, and contrariety of interest, which unavoidably happen in all collections of men, the coming into society upon such terms would be only like Cato's[1] coming into the theatre, only to go out again. Such a constitution as this would make the mighty leviathan[2] of a shorter duration, than the feeblest creatures, and not let it outlast the day it was born in: which cannot be supposed, till we can think, that rational creatures should desire and constitute societies only to be dissolved; for where the majority cannot conclude the rest, there they cannot act as one body, and consequently will be immediately dissolved again.

Whosoever therefore out of a state of nature unite into a community, must be understood to give up all the power, necessary to the ends for which they unite into society, to the majority of the community, unless they expressly agreed in any number greater than the majority. And this is done by barely agreeing to unite into one political society, which is all the compact that is, or needs be, between the individuals, that enter into, or make

1. Roman patrician, 234-139 B.C., famous for disapproving newfangled customs and corrupt manners among the ancient Romans.

2. I.e., government. The reference is to a work by Thomas Hobbes (1588-1697), *Leviathan*, in which he argued that only absolute monarchy could control men's evil tendencies; his use of the word in turn derived from a verse from *Job*, 41:1.

up a commonwealth. And thus that, which begins and actually constitutes any political society, is nothing, but the consent of any number of freemen capable of a majority, to unite and incorporate into such a society. And this is that, and that only, which did, or could give beginning to any lawful government in the world.

To this I find two objections made.

First, "That there are no instances to be found in story, of a company of men independent and equal one amongst another, that met together, and in this way began and set up a government."

Secondly, "It is impossible of right, that men should do so, because all men being born under government, they are to submit to that, and are not at liberty to begin a new one."

To the first there is this to answer, That it is not at all to be wondered, that history gives us but a very little account of men, that lived together in the state of nature. The inconveniencies of that condition, and the love and want of society, no sooner brought any number of them together, but they presently united and incorporated, if they designed to continue together. And if we may not suppose men ever to have been in the state of nature, because we hear not much of them in such a state; we may as well suppose the armies of Salmanasser or Xerxes[3] were never children, because we hear little of them, till they were men, and embodied in armies. Government is every where antecedent to records, and letters seldom come in amongst a people till a long continuation of civil society has, by other more necessary arts, provided for their safety, ease, and plenty: and then they begin to look after the history of their founders, and search into their original, when they have outlived the memory of it: for it is with commonwealths, as with particular persons, they are commonly ignorant of their own births and infancies: and if they know any thing of their original, they are beholden for it to the accidental records that others have kept of it. And those that we have of the beginning of any politics in the world, excepting that of the Jews, where God himself immediately interposed, and which favours not at all paternal

3. Ancient kings of Assyria and Persia, respectively.

dominion, are all either plain instances of such a beginning as I have mentioned, or at least have manifest footsteps of it.

He must show a strange inclination to deny evident matter of fact, when it agrees not with his hypothesis, who will not allow, that the beginnings of Rome and Venice were by the uniting together of several men free and independent one of another, amongst whom there was no natural superiority or subjection. And if Josephus Acosta's[4] word may be taken, he tells us, that in many parts of America there was no government at all. "These are great and apparent conjectures, says he, that these men, speaking of those of Peru, for a long time had neither kings nor commonwealths, but lived in troops, as they do this day in Florida, the Cheriquanas, those of Brasil, and many other nations, which have no certain kings, but as occasion is offered, in peace or war, they choose their captains as they please." If it be said, that every man there was born subject to his father, or the head of his family; that the subjection due from a child to a father took not away his freedom of uniting into what political society he thought fit, has been already proved. But be that as it will, these men, it is evident, were actually free; and whatever superiority some politicians now would place in any of them, they themselves claimed it not, but by consent were all equal, till by the same consent they set rulers over themselves. So that their politic societies all began from a voluntary union, and the mutual agreement of men freely acting in the choice of their governors, and forms of government.

. . . .

But to conclude, reason being plain on our side, that men are naturally free, and the examples of history showing, that the governments of the world, that were begun in peace, had their beginning laid on that foundation, and were made by the consent of the people; there can be little room for doubt, either where the right is, or what has been the opinion, or practice of mankind, about the first erecting of governments.

I will not deny, that if we look back as far as history will

4. José de Acosta (ca. 1539-1600), author of a widely read book about the Indians of America, *Historia Natural y Moral de las Indians* (1590).

direct us, towards the original of commonwealths, we shall generally find them under the government and administration of one man. And I am also apt to believe, that where a family was numerous enough to subsist by itself, and continued entire together, without mixing with others, as it often happens, where there is much land, and few people, the government commonly began in the father; for the father having, by the law of nature, the same power with every man else to punish, as he thought fit, any offences against that law, might thereby punish his transgressing children, even when they were men, and out of their pupilage; and they were very likely to submit to his punishment, and all join with him against the offender, in their turns, giving him thereby power to execute his sentence against any transgression, and so in effect make him the law maker, and governour over all that remained in conjunction with his family. He was fittest to be trusted; paternal affection secured their property and interest under his care; and the custom of obeying him, in their childhood, made it easier to submit to him, rather than to any other. If, therefore, they must have one to rule them, as government is hardly to be avoided amongst men that live together; who so likely to be the man as he that was their common father; unless negligence, cruelty, or any other defect of mind or body made him unfit for it? But when either the father died, and left his next heir, for want of age, wisdom, courage, or any other qualities, less fit for rule; or where several families met, and consented to continue together; there, it is not to be doubted, but they used their natural freedom to set up him whom they judged the ablest, and most likely to rule well over them. Conformable hereunto we find the people of America, who (living out of the reach of the conquering swords, and spreading domination of the two great empires of Peru and Mexico) enjoyed their own natural freedom, though, cæteris paribus,[5] they commonly prefer the heir of their deceased king; yet, if they find him any way weak, or incapable, they pass him by, and set up the stoutest and bravest man for their ruler.

Thus, though looking back as far as records give us any ac-

5. Latin: "Other things being equal."

count of peopling the world, and the history of nations, we commonly find the government to be in one hand; yet it destroys not that which I affirm, viz. that the beginning of politic society depends upon the consent of the individuals, to join into, and make one society; who, when they are thus incorporated, might set up what form of government they thought fit. But this having given occasion to men to mistake, and think, that by nature government was monarchical, and belonged to the father; it may not be amiss here to consider, why people in the beginning generally pitched upon this form; which though perhaps the father's preeminency might, in the first institution of some commonwealth give rise to, and place in the beginning the power in one hand; yet it is plain that the reason, that continued the form of government in a single person, was not any regard or respect to paternal authority; since all petty monarchies, that is, almost all monarchies, near their original, have been commonly, at least upon occasion, elective.

First then, in the beginning of things, the father's government of the childhood of those sprung from him, having accustomed them to the rule of one man, and taught them that where it was exercised with care and skill, with affection and love to those under it, it was sufficient to procure and preserve to men all the political happiness they sought for in society. It was no wonder that they should pitch upon, and naturally run into that form of government, which from their infancy they had been all accustomed to; and which, by experience, they had found both easy and safe. To which, if we add, that monarchy being simple, and most obvious to men, whom neither experience had instructed in forms of government, nor the ambition or insolence of empire had taught to beware of the encroachments of prerogative, or the inconveniencies of absolute power, which monarchy in succession was apt to lay claim to, and bring upon them; it was not at all strange, that they should not much trouble themselves to think of methods of restraining any exorbitancies of those to whom they had given the authority over them, and of balancing the power of government, by placing several parts of it in different hands. They had neither felt the oppression of tyrannical dominion, nor did the fashion of the age, nor their possessions, or way of living (which afforded little matter for covetousness or ambition) give them any reason to apprehend or provide against it; and therefore it is no wonder they put themselves into such a frame of government, as was not only, as I said, most obvious and simple, but also best suited to their present state and condition; which stood more in need of defence against foreign invasions and injuries, than of multiplicity of laws. The equality of a simple poor way of living, confining their desires within the narrow bounds of each man's small property, made few controversies, and so no need of many laws to decide them, or variety of officers to superintend the process, or look after the execution of justice, where there were but few trespasses, and few offenders. Since then those, who liked one another so well as to join into society, cannot but be supposed to have some acquaintance and friendship together, and some trust one in another; they could not but have greater apprehensions of others, than of one another: and therefore their first care and thought cannot but be supposed to be, how to secure themselves against foreign force. It was natural for them to put themselves under a frame of government which might best serve to that end, and choose the wisest and bravest man to conduct them in their wars, and lead them out against their enemies, and in this chiefly be their ruler.

Thus we see, that the kings of the Indians in America, which is still a pattern of the first ages in Asia and Europe, whilst the inhabitants were too few for the country, and want of people and money gave men no temptation to enlarge their possessions of land, or contest for wider extent of ground, are little more than generals of their armies; and though they command absolutely in war, yet at home and in time of peace they exercise very little dominion, and have but a very moderate sovereignty; the resolutions of peace and war being ordinarily either in the people, or in a council. Though the war itself, which admits not of plurality of governors, naturally devolves the command into the king's sole authority.

And thus, in Israel itself, the chief business of their judges, and first kings, seems to have been to be captains in war, and leaders of their armies; which (besides what is signified by "going out and in before the people," which was to march forth to war, and home again at the heads of their forces) appears plainly in the story of Jephthah. The Ammonites making war upon Israel, the Gileadites in fear sent to Jephthah, a bastard of their family whom they had cast off, and article with him, if he will assist them against the Ammonites, to make him their ruler; which they do in these words, "And the people made him head and captain over them," Judg. xi. 11, which was, as it seems, all one as to be judge. "And he judged Israel," Judg. xii. 7, that is, was their captain-general, "six years." So when Jotham upbraids the Shechemites with the obligation they had to Gideon, who had been their judge and ruler, he tells them, "He fought for you, and adventured his life far, and delivered you out of the hands of Midian," Judg. ix. 17. Nothing is mentioned of him, but what he did as a general: and indeed that is all is found in his history, or in any of the rest of the judges. And Abimelech particularly is called king, though at most he was but their general. And when, being weary of the ill conduct of Samuel's sons, the children of Israel desired a king, "like all the nations, to judge them, and to go out before them, and to fight their battles," 1 Sam. viii. 20. God granting their desire, says to Samuel, "I will send thee a man, and thou shalt anoint him to be captain over my people Israel, that he may save my people out of the hands of the Philistines," ix. 16. As if the only business of a king had been to lead out their armies, and fight in their defence; and accordingly Samuel, at his inauguration, pouring a vial of oil upon him, declares to Saul, that "the Lord had anointed him to be captain over his inheritance," x. 1. And therefore those who, after Saul's being solemnly chosen and saluted king by the tribes of Mispeh, were unwilling to have him their king, made no other objection but this, "How shall this man save us?" v. 27; as if they should have said, this man is unfit to be our king, not having skill and conduct enough in war to be able to defend us. And when God resolved to transfer the government to David, it is in these words, "But now thy kingdom shall not continue: the Lord hath sought him a man after his own heart, and the Lord hath commanded him to be captain over his people," xiii. 14. As if the whole kingly authority were nothing else but to be their general: and therefore the tribes who had stuck to Saul's family, and opposed David's reign, when they came to Hebron with terms of submission to them, they tell him, amongst other arguments, they had to submit to him as their king, that he was in effect their king in Saul's time, and therefore they had no reason but to receive him as their king now. "Also (say they,) in time past, when Saul was king over us, thou wast he that leddest out, and broughtest in Israel, and the Lord said unto thee, Thou shalt feed my people Israel, and thou shalt be a captain over Israel."

Thus, whether a family by degrees grew up into a commonwealth, and the fatherly authority being continued on to the elder son, every one in his turn growing up under it, tacitly submitted to it; and the easiness and equality of it not offending any one, every one acquiesced, till time seemed to have confirmed it, and settled a right of succession by prescription: or whether several families, or the descendants of several families, whom chance, neighbourhood, or business brought together, uniting into society: the need of a general, whose conduct might defend them against their enemies in war, and the great confidence the innocence and sincerity of that poor but virtuous age (such as are almost all those which begin governments, that ever come to last in the world), gave men of one another, made the first beginners of commonwealths generally put the rule into one man's hand, without any other express limitation or restraint, but what the nature of the thing and the end of government required: Whichever of those it was that at first put the rule into the hands of a single person, certain it is that nobody was entrusted with it but for the public good and safety, and to those ends, in the infancies of commonwealths, those who had it, commonly used it. And unless they had done so, young societies could not have subsisted; without such nursing fathers tender and careful of the public weal, all governments would have sunk under the weakness and infirmities of their infancy, and the prince and the people had soon perished together.

But though the golden age (before vain ambition, and "amor sceleratus habendi,"[6] evil concupiscence, had corrupted men's minds into a mistake of true power and honour) had more virtue, and consequently better governors, as well as less vicious subjects; and there was then no stretching prerogative on the one side, to oppress the people; nor consequently on the other, any dispute about privilege, to lessen or restrain the power of the magistrate; and so no contest betwixt rulers and people about governors or government: yet when ambition and luxury in future ages would retain and increase the power, without doing the business for which it was given; and, aided by flattery, taught princes to have distinct and separate interests from their people; men found it necessary to examine more carefully the original and rights of government, and to find out ways to restrain the exorbitancies, and prevent the abuses of that power, which they having entrusted in another's hands only for their own good, they found was made use of to hurt them.

Thus we may see how probable it is, that people that were naturally free, and by their own consent either submitted to the government of their father, or united together out of different families to make a government, should generally put the rule into one man's hands, and choose to be under the conduct of a single person, without so much as by express conditions limiting or regulating his power, which they thought safe enough in his honesty and prudence: though they never dreamed of monarchy being jure divino,[7] which we never heard of among mankind, till it was revealed to us by the divinity[8] of this last age; nor ever allowed paternal power to have a right to dominion, or to be the foundation of all government. And thus much may suffice to show, that, as far as we have any light from history, we have reason to conclude, that all peaceful beginnings of government have been laid in the consent of the people.

6. Latin: "Wicked love of having things."
7. Latin: "By divine right."
8. I.e., theological speculation.

Reasonable Religion vs. Superstition

Voltaire was the name assumed by François Marie Arouet (1694–1778), French playwright, historian, poet, and satirist. His father was a prosperous Parisian bureaucrat. He planned a legal career for his son and sent him to study at a fashionable school run by the Jesuits. But the young man disliked both his teachers and his subject; he abandoned law and attempted to earn a reputation as a poet. His initial efforts were perhaps too successful; in 1717–18 he spent eleven months in jail on account of several satiric verses which had struck too close to their targets.

He went to jail again in 1726, this time after a quarrel with an important young nobleman. Voltaire was released on condition that he leave the country, so he spent the next three years in England. He found the English most congenial; he admired their political institutions, their freedom of speech, their business sense, and their religious tolerance. After his return to Paris in 1729, Voltaire spent much of his literary talent in attempting to transplant these English virtues into French society.

His work as a social critic, however, was not restricted to France. He spent three years (1749–52) as philosopher-in-residence at the court of the Prussian King Frederick the Great (ruled 1740–86). Voltaire originally hoped to remake Frederick into the model of an enlightened ruler—just, tolerant, efficient—and bring corresponding benefits to Prussian society. But king and philosopher tired of each other and quarreled. In 1758 Voltaire moved to Ferney, an estate he purchased where France meets with the Swiss city of Geneva. There he spent a comfortable old age. Even at Ferney, Voltaire kept in touch with affairs in Paris and elsewhere.

In the course of his life, he wrote many plays and aspired above all else to be a great poet. In addition, he produced an enormous number of varied prose works, including satirical novels, polemical attacks against acts of religious bigotry, a notable series of histories, and popularizations of new philosophical and scientific ideas.

The *Philosophical Dictionary* appeared in 1764. At the time the great *Encyclopedie*, to which Voltaire and other philosophes contributed articles, was in trouble with the censors. Voltaire intended these essays, published under rather whimsically chosen headings (the article before "Religion" deals with "relics"; that following is on "Rhyme"), to ridicule the folly of those who were trying to prevent reasonable views from reaching the French public. A somewhat malicious mockery, which enraged pious Christians, runs through many of the articles and is very evident in the selection from Voltaire's remarks on religion reprinted below.

VOLTAIRE: PHILOSOPHICAL DICTIONARY

Religion

SECTION I

The Epicureans, who had no religion, recommended retirement from public affairs, study, and concord. This sect was a society of friends, for friendship was their principal dogma. Atticus, Lucretius, Memmius,[1] and a few other such men, might live very reputably together; this we see in all countries; philosophize as much as you please among yourselves. A set of amateurs may give a concert of refined and scientific music; but let them beware of performing such a concert before the ignorant and brutal vulgar, lest their instruments be broken over their heads. If you have but a village to govern, it *must* have a religion.

. . . .

Had it been possible for the human mind to have admitted a religion—I will not say at all approaching ours—but not so bad as all the other religions in the world—what would that religion have been?

Would it not have been that which should propose to us the adoration of the supreme, only, infinite, eternal Being, the former of the world, who gives it motion and life, "*cui nec simile, nec secundum*"?[2] That which should re-unite us to this Being of beings, as the reward of our virtues, and separate us from Him, as the chastisement of our crimes?

From *Voltaire's Philosophical Dictionary*, Vol. IX (Paris, London, New York, Chicago: E. R. DuMont, 1901), pp. 61-63, 86-88.

1. Roman Epicureans of the first century B.C.
2. Latin: "To whom there is nothing similar nor of the same kind."

That which should admit very few of the dogmas invented by unreasoning pride; those eternal subjects of disputation; and should teach a pure morality, about which there should never be any dispute?

That which should not make the essence of worship consist in vain ceremonies, as that of spitting into your mouth, or that of taking from you one end of your prepuce, or of depriving you of one of your testicles—seeing that a man may fulfil all the social duties with two testicles and an entire foreskin, and without another's spitting into his mouth?

That of serving one's neighbor for the love of God, instead of persecuting and butchering him in God's name? That which should tolerate all others, and which, meriting thus the goodwill of all, should alone be capable of making mankind a nation of brethren?

That which should have august ceremonies, to strike the vulgar, without having mysteries to disgust the wise and irritate the incredulous?

That which should offer men more encouragements to the social virtues than expiations for social crimes?

That which should insure to its ministers a revenue large enough for their decent maintenance, but should never allow them to usurp dignities and power that might make them tyrants?

That which should establish commodious retreats for sickness and old age, but never for idleness?

A great part of this religion is already in the hearts of several princes; and it will prevail when the articles of perpetual peace, proposed by the abbé de St. Pierre,[3] shall be signed by all potentates.

SEVENTH QUESTION

If a man would persuade foreigners, or his own countrymen, of the truth of his religion, should he not go about it with the most insinuating mildness and the most engaging moderation? If he begins with telling them that what he announces is dem-

3. Charles Irenée Castel, Abbé de St. Pierre (1658-1743), author of *Project for Perpetual Peace* (1713).

onstrated, he will find a multitude of persons incredulous; if he ventures to tell them that they reject his doctrine only inasmuch as it condemns their passions; that their hearts have corrupted their minds; that their reasoning is only false and proud, he disgusts them; he incenses them against himself; he himself ruins what he would fain establish.

If the religion he announces be true, will violence and insolence render it more so? Do you put yourself in a rage, when you say that it is necessary to be mild, patient, beneficent, just, and to fulfil all the duties of society? No; because everyone is of your own opinion. Why, then, do you abuse your brother when preaching to him a mysterious system of metaphysics? Because his opinion irritates your self-love. You are so proud as to require your brother to submit his intelligence to yours; humbled pride produces the wrath; it has no other source. A man who has received twenty wounds in a battle does not fly into a passion; but a divine, wounded by the refusal of your assent, at once becomes furious and implacable.

EIGHTH QUESTION

Must we not carefully distinguish the religion of the state from theological religion? The religion of the state requires that the imans[4] keep registers of the circumcised, the vicars or pastors registers of the baptized; that there be mosques, churches, temples, days consecrated to rest and worship, rites established by law; that the ministers of those rites enjoy consideration without power; that they teach good morals to the people, and that the ministers of the law watch over the morals of the ministers of the temples. This religion of the state cannot at any time cause any disturbance.

It is otherwise with theological religion: this is the source of all imaginable follies and disturbances; it is the parent of fanaticism and civil discord; it is the enemy of mankind. A bonze[5] asserts that *Fo*[6] is a God, that he was foretold by fakirs,[7]

4. Moslem religious leaders.
5. Buddhist monk.
6. Nonsense syllable. Voltaire is here, of course, lampooning Christian doctrine.
7. Hindu holy men.

that he was born of a white elephant, and that every bonze can by certain grimaces make a *Fo*. A *talapoin*[8] says, that *Fo* was a holy man, whose doctrine the bonzes have corrupted, and that *Sammonocodom*[8] is the true God. After a thousand arguments and contradictions, the two factions agree to refer the question to the *dalai-lama*,[9] who resides three hundred leagues off, and who is not only immortal, but also infallible. The two factions send to him a solemn deputation; and the *dalai-lama* begins, according to his divine custom, by distributing among them the contents of his close-stool.

The two rival sects at first receive them with equal reverence; have them dried in the sun, and encase them in little chaplets which they kiss devoutly; but no sooner have the *dalai-lama* and his council pronounced in the name of *Fo*, than the condemned party throw their chaplets in the vice-god's face, and would fain give him a sound thrashing. The other party defend their *lama*, from whom they have received good lands; both fight a long time; and when at last they are tired of mutual extermination, assassination, and poisoning, they grossly abuse each other, while the *dalai-lama* laughs, and still distributes his excrement to whosoever is desirous of receiving the good father lama's precious favors.

8. Nonsense syllables.
9. Buddhist leader and civil ruler of Tibet.

IV

The Democratic Revolution

Natural Rights and Revolution in America
    The Declaration of Independence

Democratic Demands in France
    Abbé Sieyès: What Is the Third Estate?

Natural Rights and Revolution in France
    Declaration of the Rights of Man and of the Citizen

Virtue Through Terror, if Need Be
    Maximilien Robespierre: Report upon the Principles of Political Morality

Natural Rights and Revolution in America

The American Declaration of Independence was promulgated at Philadelphia on July 4, 1776, by a Congress of representatives from thirteen of the fifteen English colonies of North America. The date has since become the recognized birthdate of the United States of America.

The phrases of the Declaration of Independence have become so familiar that it is difficult to understand their original meanings. It is even harder to realize how fascinating such (to us, shopworn) phrases were to "enlightened" Europeans of the 1770's, who had hitherto treated the principles of reason and natural right more as matters for theoretical discussion than as a basis for political action and rebellion.

The language of the Declaration of Independence was revised somewhat in committee, but Thomas Jefferson (1743–1826) was the principal author and guiding spirit behind its formulation. His deistic views were not shared by all the revolutionary leaders, and still less by the American public at large. As a result, the abstract "natural rights" rhetoric of the Declaration tended to fade into the background in later phases of the revolution. Nevertheless, the document of 1776 remained a hallowed text for the emerging United States of America and has remained so ever since.

Revolutionary movements elsewhere, from the French of 1789 to Asians and Africans after World War II, have also found the language of the Declaration of Independence useful as justifying their various efforts at overturning established political authority.

THE DECLARATION OF INDEPENDENCE JULY 4, 1776

The Unanimous Declaration of the Thirteen United States of America

When in the course of human events, it becomes necessary for one people to dissolve the political bands which have connected them with another, and to assume among the powers of the earth the separate and equal station to which the Laws of Nature and of Nature's God entitle them, a decent respect to the opinions of mankind requires that they should declare the causes which impel them to the separation.

We hold these truths to be self-evident, that all men are created equal, that they are endowed by their Creator with certain unalienable rights, that among these are life, liberty, and the pursuit of happiness. That to secure these rights, governments are instituted among men, deriving their just powers from the consent of the governed. That whenever any form of government becomes destructive of these ends, it is the right of the people to alter or to abolish it, and to institute new government, laying its foundations on such principles and organizing its powers in such form, as to them shall seem most likely to effect their safety and happiness. Prudence, indeed, will dictate that governments long established should not be changed for light and transient causes; and accordingly all experience hath shown, that mankind are more disposed to suffer, while evils are sufferable, than to right themselves by abolishing the forms to which they are accustomed. But when a long train of abuses and usurpations, pursuing invariably the same object evinces a design to reduce them under absolute despotism, it is their right, it is their duty, to throw off such government, and to provide new guards for their future security. Such has been the patient sufferance of these Colonies; and such is now the

From *Messages and Papers of the Presidents*, Vol. I, edited by James B. Richardson (New York, 1897), pp. 1-2, 5.

necessity which constrains them to alter their former systems of government. The history of the present King of Great Britain is a history of repeated injuries and usurpations, all having in direct object the establishment of an absolute tyranny over these States. To prove this, let facts be submitted to a candid world. . . .

[A list of specific grievances follows.]

We, therefore, the Representatives of the United States of America, in General Congress assembled, appealing to the Supreme Judge of the world for the rectitude of our intentions, do, in the name, and by authority of the good people of these Colonies, solemnly publish and declare, That these United Colonies are, and of right ought to be Free and Independent States; that they are absolved from all allegiance to the British Crown, and that all political connection between them and the State of Great Britain is and ought to be totally dissolved; and that as Free and Independent States they have full power to levy war, conclude peace, contract alliances, establish commerce, and to do all other acts and things which independent States may of right do. And for the support of this declaration, with a firm reliance on the protection of Divine Providence, we mutually pledge to each other our lives, our fortunes and our sacred honor.

Democratic Demands in France

Louis XVI, King of France from 1774 to 1792, inherited a financial crisis that was the product of several generations of mismanagement and neglect. He and his ministers attempted to reform the tax system and increase revenues, but their efforts were blocked repeatedly by high administrative courts, the Parlements. The judges of these Parlements were ennobled; they feared that any taxation of aristocratic fortunes would damage their own interests. In August of 1788, this aristocratic resistance persuaded the King's principal minister, Lomenie de Brienne, to call a meeting of the Estates General. The

Estates General was the traditional French representative assembly; it had not met since 1614.

By custom, the Estates General consisted of three groups of deputies: the First Estate, or clergy, the Second Estate, the nobility, and the Third Estate, composed mainly of land-owning commoners. Each estate had only one vote in the general sessions; each met as a separate body to determine by simple majority how its vote would be cast on any issue. But most of the higher clergy (and their deputies to the Estates General) were members of noble families and thus would vote with the nobility; an alliance of First and Second Estates could always prevail against the single vote of the Third. Antiaristocratic political leaders, therefore, demanded a new method of voting for the coming session of the Estates General, a method which would increase the relative power of the Third Estate.

The Abbé Emmanuel Sieyès (1748–1836) wrote *What Is the Third Estate?* in November 1788, in the midst of this debate. Sieyès was an anticlerical churchman, a financial administrator of the cathedral at Chartres. His parents had pushed him against his will into an ecclesiastical career; he disliked the sentiment and superstition of the Church, but endured without complaint the economic and social security it offered him. He represented the clergy in the estates of his province, and likewise spent much time in Paris attending to cathedral business.

When Brienne issued the call for a meeting of the Estates General, he also issued a call for the "thinkers" of France to submit their advice and schemes for governmental reform. Sieyès responded with three anonymous pamphlets, of which the second was *What Is the Third Estate?*; approximately one-half of the work appears below. It became popular immediately and went through four printings within a year.

Sieyès, who had never published anything prior to the pamphlets, gained immediate fame as a leader of the Third Estate. He served in all of the revolutionary governments from 1789 to 1799; in the latter year he helped to engineer the *coup d'état* which brought Napoleon to power. Napoleon made Sieyès a count of the empire and a senator. When Napoleon was overthrown in 1815, Sieyès went into exile in England; he returned to France in 1830 and died six years later.

ABBÉ EMMANUEL SIEYÈS: WHAT IS THE THIRD ESTATE?

The outline of this essay is quite simple. We must ask ourselves three questions:

1) What is the Third Estate? Everything.
2) What has it been hitherto in politics? Nothing.
3) What does it ask? To become something.

We will see whether these answers are correct. We will examine the methods which have been tried, and then those which ought to be used, in order for the Third Estate to become, in effect, *something*. Thus we shall say:

4) What the ministers have attempted, and what the privileged orders themselves *propose* in favor of the Third Estate.
5) What *ought* to have been done.
6) Finally, what remains to be done for the Third Estate to take the place to which it is entitled.

Chapter I
The Third Estate is a Complete Nation

What is needed for a nation to exist and to prosper? Private activity and public services.

All private activity can be divided into four categories: (1) Because earth and water supply the basic needs of man, the first category will be that of all the families occupied in agriculture. (2) From the time of the first sale of goods to that of their consumption or use, manufacturing processes, more or less complicated, increase the value of these goods. Human industry thus manages to perfect the bounties of nature, and the product tends to increase twice, ten times or a hundred times in value. This is the second category of individual activ-

Translated by Elizabeth D. McNeill from Abbé Sieyès, *Qu'est-ce que le Tiers Etat?* (Paris: Société de l'histoire de la Revolution française, 1888), pp. 27-50, 92-93. Reprinted by permission of University of Chicago Press.

ity. (3) Between production and consumption, just as between the different stages of production, there are established a horde of intermediary agents, just as useful to the producer as to the consumer; these are the merchants and traders. . . . This type of occupation constitutes the third category. (4) Besides these three categories of laboring and useful citizens who concern themselves with the actual *things* to be consumed or used, society must also have a multitude of special services *directly* useful or agreeable to the *person*. This fourth category includes everything from the most distinguished liberal and scientific professions down to the least respected of domestic services.

Such are the labors which uphold society. Who supports them? The Third Estate.

Public functions can equally, in the existing State, be arranged into four known classifications: the Sword, the Robe,[1] the Church and the Administration. It would be superfluous to describe them in detail, in order to show that the Third Estate constitutes nineteen-twentieths of the nation (with this distinction, that it is burdened with all that is truly painful, with all the chores which the privileged class refuses to undertake). The lucrative and honorific posts alone are filled by members of the privileged orders. Shall we construe this as praiseworthy on their part? For that, either the Third Estate would have to refuse to fill these posts, or it would have to be less capable of exercising their functions. The real facts are known; nevertheless, the Third Estate has been stricken by a ban which says, "No matter what your services or your talents may be, you will go just so far; you will not pass beyond that point. It is not good that you should be honored." The rare exceptions to this rule are properly felt to be a mere derision, and the language the privileged orders allow themselves on these rare occasions is only an added insult. If this ban is a social crime against the Third Estate, might it not be said at least that it is useful to the public? Piffle! Are the effects of monopoly not known? If it discourages those whom it excludes, is it not known that it

1. The Sword means nobles who owed their titles to military service; the Robe refers to those who owed their rank to judicial service, i.e., in the Parlements.

debilitates those whom it favors? Is it not known that all work from which free competition has been eliminated is done more expensively and done worse? . . .

It suffices here to have shown that the pretended usefulness of a privileged class for public service is but a chimera; that everything unpleasant in this service is carried out by the Third Estate; that without it, the higher offices would be infinitely better filled; that they ought naturally to be the rewards for recognized talents and services; and that, if the privileged classes have managed to usurp all the lucrative and honorific posts, it is an odious iniquity for the mass of the citizens as well as a betrayal of the public trust.

Who then would dare to say that the Third Estate does not include everything necessary to the formation of a complete nation? It is like a strong and robust man with one arm still chained. If the privileged class were dispensed with, the nation would not be anything less than it is, but rather something more. Thus, what is the Third Estate? Everything, but a hobbled and oppressed everything. What would it be without the privileged classes? Everything—but a free and flourishing everything. Nothing can function without the Third Estate; everything would work infinitely better without the other estates.

It is not enough to have shown that the privileged classes, far from being useful to the nation, can only enfeeble and hinder it; it must still be proven that the nobles are not a part of the social organization; that while they may be a charge on the nation, they cannot learn how to become a part of it.

First of all, it is not possible, among the basic components of a nation, to find where to place the caste of nobles. I know that there are individuals, in too large number, whose infirmities, incapacities, incurable laziness or multiplicity of evil habits make them strangers to socially useful activities. Every law has exceptions and abuses, especially in a great state. But at least we can agree that the fewer there are of these abuses, the better regulated the state will seem. The worst regulated of all would be that state where not only isolated individuals, but an entire class of citizens would glory in remaining idle in the midst of general activity, and would consume the greater part of production, without having done a thing toward producing it. Such a class is assuredly foreign to the nation by reason of its laziness.

The noble class is no less foreign to us, by reason of its civil and public prerogatives.

What is a nation? A body of associates living under a common law and represented by the same legislature.

Is it not too clear that the noble class has privileges, dispensations, even separate rights distinct from those of the main body of citizens? It is thus outside the common order, the common law. So its civil rights already make of it a people separate from the nation. It is truly *imperium in imperio*.[2]

Concerning its public rights, these too are exercised separately. It has its own representatives, who are in no respect representatives of the people. The body of its deputies sits apart; and even if it should gather in the same hall with the deputies of simple citizens, it is no less true that its representation is essentially distinct and separate: representatives of the nobles are foreign to the nation in principle, since their commission does not come from the people; and in purpose, since this consists of defending, not the general interest, but special class interests.

The Third Estate therefore includes all that which belongs to the nation; and all that which is not the Third Estate cannot consider itself as being of the nation. What is the Third Estate? Everything.

Chapter II
What Has the Third Estate Been Hitherto? Nothing

We shall not examine the state of servitude in which the people has languished for so long, nor the state of constraint and humiliation in which it is still held. Its civil condition has changed; it must change further; it is clearly impossible for the nation in a body, or even any particular section of it, to become free, if the Third Estate is not free. One is not free be-

2. Latin: "A state within a state."

cause of one's privileges but because of the rights belonging to all. . . .

We must understand by the term Third Estate the totality of citizens who belong to the common order. All who are privileged by law, no matter how, lie outside the common order, are exceptions to the common order, and therefore do not belong to the Third Estate. As we have said before, what makes a nation is a common law and common representation. It is only too true that in France one is nothing when one has only the protection of the common law; if one holds no privilege, one must resolve to endure being despised, insulted, and vexed in every way. In order to avoid being completely crushed, the unfortunate non-privileged individual can only resort to attaching himself to a noble's train by some means, however base. Only in this way can he manage, and then only in some cases, to become somebody.

But it is less in its civil state than in its relation to the constitution that we shall here consider the Third Estate. Let's see what there is to the Estates General.

Who were the so-called representatives of the Third Estate? Either recently ennobled or temporarily privileged persons. These false deputies have not always even been freely elected by the people. Sometimes in the Estates General, and almost always in the Provincial Estates, representation of the people is looked upon as the prerogative of certain officials.

The old nobility will not admit the new nobles to its ranks. It does not permit them to sit with it unless they can prove four generations and a hundred years of noble ancestry. So the old nobility pushes the newcomers back into the ranks of the Third Estate, to which quite obviously they no longer belong. Nevertheless, in the eyes of the law, all nobles are equal, and the noble of yesterday is considered the same as the noble who succeeds in concealing his origin or his usurpation. All have the same privileges. Opinion alone distinguishes between them. But if the Third Estate is compelled to suffer discrimination sanctioned by law, there is no reason why it should endure a discrimination contrary to the letter of the law.

Let them make all the new nobles they want to; it is sure

that the moment a citizen acquires privileges contrary to the common right, he ceases to belong to the common order. His new interest is opposed to the general interest; he is incapable of voting on behalf of the people. . . .

People sometimes seem astonished at hearing complaints of a triple aristocracy, the Church, the Sword and the Robe. They would like to think that this is only a manner of speaking. But the expression must be taken in all literalness. If the Estates General is the interpreter of the General Will and consequently has legislative powers, and if it is only a clerical-noble-judicial assembly, is it not certain that we have a veritable aristocracy?

Add to this frightful truth the fact that in one way or another, all the branches of the executive power have also fallen into the hands of the caste which constitutes the Church, the Robe and the Sword. A kind of spirit of confraternity makes the nobles prefer one another to the rest of the nation. The usurpation is complete; veritably they reign.

Read history with the intention of determining whether the facts are in conformity with or contrary to this assertion, and you will be assured, as I have been by this means, that it is a great mistake to believe that France is subjected to a monarchic regime.

Remove from our annals a few years under Louis XI and under Richelieu, and a few moments under Louis XIV, in which one sees only unadulterated despotism, and you would think you were reading the history of a court aristocracy. It is not the monarch who reigns but his courtiers. The court makes and unmakes, summons and sends away the ministers; it creates and distributes offices, etc. And what is the court, if not the head of that immense aristocracy which reaches into all parts of France, which through its members touches everything and exercises everywhere all essential powers in all parts of the public domain? Moreover, the public in its whisperings has become accustomed to distinguishing between the monarch and the true wielders of power. It has always regarded the King as a man so certainly mistaken and so defenceless in the midst of an active and all-powerful court, that it has never thought to hold him responsible for all the evil which has been perpetrated in his name.

To sum up: the Third Estate has not, up to the present, had real representatives in the Estates General. Thus its political rights are nil.

Chapter III
What Does the Third Estate Demand? To Become Something

One must not judge the demands of the Third Estate by the isolated observations of a few authors more or less well-informed about the Rights of Man. The order of the Third Estate is still very backward in this respect; I do not say this only on the authority of those who have studied the social order, but also on the authority of the mass of common ideas which make up public opinion. One can only appreciate the true wishes of this order by the authentic petitions which the large municipalities of the kingdom have addressed to the government. What does one see? That the people want to be *something*, but in truth a very modest *something*. They want to have real representatives in the Estates General, that is to say, deputies chosen from among their own ranks, who will be adept at interpreting their wishes and defending their interests. But what good would it do the people to take part in the Estates General if interests contrary to their own predominate? They would only sanction by their presence the oppression whose eternal victim they would be. Thus, it is sure that the people cannot come and vote in the Estates General unless they can have influence at least equal to that of the two other orders together. Finally, this equality in representation would become completely illusory if each order had a separate vote. The Third Estate therefore demands that votes be counted by head and not by order. The claims of the Third Estate reduce simply to this, yet these demands seem to have alarmed the privileged orders because they believe that this by itself would make the reform of abuses unavoidable. The real intention of the Third Estate is to have in the Estates General an influence equal to that of the privileged orders. I repeat, can it ask for less? And is it not clear that if its influence is anything less than equal, it cannot hope to emerge from its political nullity and become *something*? . . .

THE FIRST DEMAND

That the representatives of the Third Estate be chosen only from among those citizens who really belong to the Third.

We have already explained that, in order really to belong to the Third Estate, one must not be tainted by any sort of privilege.

The gentlemen of the Robe, having reached nobility through a door which they closed behind them, no one knows why, now strenuously want to be part of the Estates General. They said to themselves: "The nobility[3] does not want us; we don't want the Third Estate; if it were possible for us to form a particular class, that would suit us admirably; but we can't do it. So what is to be done? There only remains for us to maintain the old abuses whereby the Third Estate drew its deputies from among us; that way we shall satisfy our desires without abandoning our pretensions." All the newly-made nobles, no matter what their origin, made haste to repeat in the same spirit: "It is necessary that the Third Estate should be able to choose gentlemen as their representatives." The ancient nobility, which considers itself the good nobility, does not have the same interest in preserving this abuse; but it does know how to count. It said: "We shall put our children in the Chambre de Communes, and, altogether, it is an excellent idea for us to take over the representation of the Third Estate."

Once an intention has been thoroughly determined, reasons are never lacking. One must, it was said, preserve ancient usage —excellent usage, which in order to represent the Third Estate, had until this moment positively excluded it from any representation whatsoever!

But the Third Estate has its political rights, just as it has its civil rights; it must exercise them itself, one as much as another. What an idea, to make a distinction between the orders when it is to the benefit of the first two and damages the Third, and to break down barriers between the orders, the moment that it suits the first two, and obstructs the nation! What a practice to uphold, one by which the ecclesiastics and nobles could take over

3. I.e., the nobility of the Sword, whose members regarded their titles of nobility to be superior to titles flaunted by nobles of the Robe.

the chamber of the Third Estate! In good faith, would they believe themselves represented if the Third Estate could invade the delegations of their order? . . .

One might object that it is a hindrance to the liberty of the voters to limit them in their choice: I have two answers to this pretended difficulty. The first is that it is advanced in bad faith, and I will prove it. The dominion of the seigneurs over the peasants and other country dwellers is well-known; the accustomed or possible manoeuvres of their numerous agents, including officers of justice, are equally well-known. Therefore, every lord who wishes to influence the primary election is, in general, assured of becoming the elector for the district, where he will bestir himself to choose only from among the nobles themselves or from among those who have won the deepest confidence of the nobles. Is it on behalf of the liberty of the people that one manipulates things in such a way as to destroy the people's confidence? It is shocking to hear the sacred name of liberty profaned to hide designs which are utterly contrary. Doubtless, one must leave the voters all their freedom, and it is for that very reason that it is necessary to exclude from the delegation of the Third Estate all privileged persons who are too imperiously accustomed to dominating the people.

My second answer is direct. There cannot be any form of liberty or any kind of right without limit. In all countries, the law has fixed certain qualifications, without which one can be neither a voter nor eligible for election. Thus, for instance, the law must determine an age beneath which one would be incapable of representing one's fellow citizens. Women are everywhere, for good or bad, deprived of this sort of representation. It is axiomatic that vagabonds or beggars cannot be charged with the political confidence of the people. Ought a servant, anyone who is dependent on a master, or a non-naturalized foreigner, be allowed to figure among the representatives of the nation? Political liberty thus has its limits, like civil liberty. We are concerned only with knowing whether the exclusion, which the Third Estate demands, is not just as essential as all those I have just indicated. Moreover, the comparison is all in its favor; for a beggar, or a foreigner, might conceivably have no interest opposed to that of the Third Estate. Instead of which, the nobles and the ecclesiastics are, by reason of their position, friends of the privileges they profit from. Thus, the condition demanded by the Third Estate is for it the most important of all those which the law, in accord with equity and the nature of things, must set for the choice of representatives.

To bring out this reasoning more clearly, I will make a hypothesis. I will suppose that France is at war with England and everything connected with the hostilities is conducted, at home, by a Directory composed of national representatives. In such a case, I ask you, would one permit the provinces, under the pretext of not infringing upon their liberty, to choose as their deputies to the Directory members of the English cabinet?

Certainly the privileged order proves itself no less the enemy of the common people than the English are of the French in time of war.

As a consequence of these principles, one cannot permit those members of the Third Estate who really belong exclusively among the two first orders, to be entrusted with the confidence of the communes. . . .

It is to the odious remains of this barbarous feudal regime that we owe the still existing enmity, so unfortunate for France, between the three orders. Everything would be lost if the agents of the nobility came to usurp the representation of the Third Estate. Who does not know that servants will behave more avidly and more boldly in the interest of their masters than the masters themselves? . . .

It has been objected that the Third Estate does not have members famous enough and courageous enough to represent it, and that it must fall back upon the leadership of the nobility. This strange assertion is not worthy of a reply. Consider the classes at the disposal of the Third Estate, and I mean those whom relatively easy circumstances have allowerd to receive a liberal education, to cultivate their reason and to interest themselves in public affairs. These classes have no interest other than that of the rest of the people. See if they do not contain enough educated and honest citizens, worthy in all respects to represent the nation.

But what if a district is obstinate and does not want to give its Third Estate vote to anyone but a noble or an ecclesiastic? What if it only has confidence in one of them?

I have already said that there cannot be unlimited liberty and that, among all the conditions to be imposed on eligibility for election, those which the Third Estate demands are the most necessary of all. But more to the point, suppose that a district wants to obstruct its own progress, should it therefore have the right to obstruct that of others? If I alone were interested in the activities of my legal representative, he could say to me: "That's just too bad; why did you choose so badly?" But the deputies of a district are not only the representatives of the place from which they are elected; they are also called to represent the general public and to vote for all the kingdom. It is necessary then to have common rules and conditions which can reassure the whole of the nation against the caprice of a few of the voters, even though it may displease some of them.

SECOND DEMAND OF THE THIRD ESTATE

That its deputies be equal in number to those of the two privileged orders.

I cannot avoid repeating: the timid insufficiency of this demand is a reflection of former times. The cities of the kingdom have not sufficiently considered the progress of enlightenment and of public opinion. At one time they would not have encountered any difficulty in asking for two votes instead of one, and perhaps the government might even have hastened to grant them this equality against which it now fights with such vigor.

Besides, when one wants to decide a question such as this, one must not be content, as is so often the case, with giving as arguments one's desires, wishes or mere precedent; one must revert to principles. Political, like civil right, must inhere in the status of citizen. This legal right is the same for everyone, without regard to the amount of property from which each individual makes his fortune or his living. Every citizen who meets the conditions prescribed for voting has the right to be represented, and his representation cannot be less than that of another. This right is indivisible; all exercise it equally, just as all are protected equally by the law which they have united to establish. How can one maintain, on the one hand that the law is the expression of the General Will—that is to say of the majority—and on the other pretend at the same time that the will of ten nobles can balance that of a thousand commoners? Does that not permit the making of the law by a minority, which is self-evidently contrary to the nature of things?

If these principles, logically certain though they be, go a bit beyond commonly accepted ideas, I will remind the reader of a comparison which lies right before his eyes.

Is it not true that it seems just to everyone . . . that the immense district of Poitou should have more representatives in the Estates General than the little district of Gex? Why is this? Because, it is said, the population and the taxes of Poitou are much greater than those of Gex. One thus admits principles according to which one may determine the proportion of representatives. Should tax-paying then decide? But although we do not have accurate information concerning the exact assessment of the various orders, it is at once obvious that the Third Estate pays more than half.

With regard to population, we see the immense superiority of the Third Estate over the two first. I, as everyone else, am ignorant of the exact figures; but like everyone else, I shall indulge in my own calculations.

The clergy. First of all for the clergy. We will count 40,000 parishes, including annexes; right away we have the number of curés[4] 40,000

One can allow one vicar for every four parishes, on an average, thus 10,000

The number of cathedrals is the same as the number of dioceses (140), and 20 canons on an average, along with the bishops and archbishops 2,800

One may suppose, taking the country as a whole, that collegiate canons number twice this 5,600

Beyond that, one must not believe that there are as many more clergy as there are benefices, abbeys, priories and chapels.

4. Parish priests.

Plurality of benefices is not unknown in France. The bishops and the canons are at the same time abbés, priors and chaplains. In order not to count them twice I estimate at 3,000 the holders of benefices not already counted in the figures given above 3,000

Then I estimate about 2,000 ecclesiastics, established members of sacred orders, who have no sort of benefice 2,000

There remain the monks and nuns, whose numbers have diminished in the last thirty years at an accelerating rate. I do not believe that today there are more than 17,000

Total number of clergy 80,400

The nobility. I know only one way to estimate the number of individuals in this order. That is to take the province where the number is best known and then compare this with the rest of France. Brittany is this province; and I remark in advance that it breeds more nobles than the others, either because nobles there do not debauch themselves or because of the local privileges which families retain, etc. There are in Brittany 1,800 noble families. I will allow 2,000, however, because there are some who no longer take part in the provincial assembly.

Estimating every family at five persons, there are in Brittany 10,000 nobles—man, woman and child. Its total population is 2,300,000. This is an eleventh of the total population of France. Thus if one multiplies 10,000 by eleven, one will have 110,000 nobles as a maximum for the whole kingdom.

So, altogether, there are not quite 200,000 privileged persons in the first two orders. Compare this number with the twenty-five or twenty-six million total population of France and then judge! . . .

When, several years from now, all the difficulties which faced the over-modest demands of the Third Estate are remembered, people will be amazed at the triviality of the pretexts, but even more at the iniquitous boldness which dared to discover such pretexts.

Those same persons who invoke the authority of facts against the Third Estate could read in them, if they were of good faith, the proper rule for their conduct. Under Philip the Fair, the existence of a small number of towns sufficed to form a chamber of the commons in the Estates General.

Since that time, feudal servitude has disappeared, and the countryside has produced a numerous population of *new citizens*. Cities have multiplied and increased. Commerce and the arts have created, so to speak, a multitude of new classes among which there are a large number of wealthy families and of well-educated men who are interested in public affairs. Why has not this double increase, in country and town, (far more important than the towns formerly were in the national balance) won the right to create two new chambers to represent the Third Estate? Equity and sound politics combine to demand it.

No one dares to show himself as irrational concerning another sort of growth which has come to France—I mean the new provinces which have been added since the last Estates General. No one dares to say that these new provinces should not be represented in addition to those which were represented in the Estates of 1614. Since the growth of the Third Estate is comparable with territorial expansion (because, like new territory, factories and the arts supply new riches, new taxes and new population) why then, I ask, should one refuse to give them representation over and above that which they had in the Estates of 1614?

But I avoid reasoning with men who only know how to listen to their own interests. They can be touched only by other considerations; and here is one which I offer. Does it become the nobility today to retain the language and the attitudes which it had during the Gothic centuries? And does it become the Third Estate to retain at the end of the Eighteenth Century the sad and cowardly customs of ancient servitude? If the Third Estate knows and respects itself, then the others will respect it also. Consider how the old relations between the orders were gradually modified on both sides. The Third Estate, which had been reduced to nothing, has reacquired, through its industry, a part of what the injustice of the stronger had taken from it. Instead of demanding the restoration of its rights, it consented to pay for them. The nobles did not restore them; they sold them. But in the end, in one way or another, the Third Estate was able to regain possession of its rights. One must not forget that the Third Estate is today the real nation, while before it was only a shadow; and that during this gradual change, the nobility has ceased to be the monstrous feudal reality which could oppress the people with impunity. The nobility is in its turn no more than a shadow and this shadow will vainly try to thwart the entire nation.

THIRD AND LAST DEMAND OF THE THIRD ESTATE THAT THE ESTATES GENERAL VOTE NOT BY ORDERS BUT BY HEAD.

One may look at this question in three ways: in the spirit of the Third Estate; according to the interests of the privileged estates; or according to sound principles. In connection with the first point of view, it would be useless to add anything to what we have already said. It is clear that for the Third Estate this demand is a necessary consequence of the two others.

The privileged fear the equal influence of the Third Estate and they declare it to be unconstitutional. This conduct is all the more striking inasmuch as they have up to the present been two against one and have found nothing unconstitutional in this unjust superiority. They feel an urgent necessity for keeping a veto over anything which could possibly be contrary to their interests. I will not repeat the reasoning which twenty writers have used to support this pretension, or the arguments for the old forms. I have only one observation to make. There are certainly abuses in France, and these abuses work for somebody's profit. It is scarcely to the Third Estate that they are advantageous, but it is certainly true that they hurt the Third Estate especially. But I ask, given this state of things, is it possible to destroy a single abuse, if a veto is left in the hands of those who profit from abuses? All justice would be without force; it would be necessary to depend on the pure generosity of the privileged classes. Is this your idea of a proper social order?

If we wish actually to consider the same subject according to enlightened principles (that is to say, according to the principles of social science) independent of all particular interests, we will see this question assume a new form. One may not accept either the demand of the Third Estate or the defense of the privileged classes without overthrowing the most positive principles. I certainly do not accuse the cities of the kingdom of having such an intention. They merely wanted to approximate their rights by claiming at least a balance between the two influences. They have, moreover, professed some sound principles: for it is sure that the veto of one order over the others would be a right to paralyze everything in a country where interests are so divided. It is certain that by not voting by head one would be in danger of disregarding the true majority; this would be of the greatest impropriety, since it would nullify the law at its very root. These truths are indisputable. But can the three orders, as they are constituted, combine to vote by head? That is the real question. No! In the light of true principles, they cannot vote together, either by head or by order. Whatever proportion you may establish between them, they cannot achieve the objective which has been agreed upon—that is, to bind the whole body of representatives by a single common will. This assertion doubtless needs elaboration and proof, which I will however postpone to the sixth chapter. I do not wish to displease those moderate persons who always fear that the truth will be embarrassing. One must first force them to admit that the present situation is such, through the sole fault of the privileged classes, that it is time to take sides and to state categorically what is true and just without the slightest reservation.

. . . .

Moderate persons, to whom I address these reflections, would cease to fear the sort of truths which they call premature if they did not obstinately confuse the measured and prudent conduct of the administrator (who would spoil everything if he did not consider frictions and obstacles) with the free élan of the philosopher who is only the more excited by the existence of difficulties, and who is called to present sound social principles all the more strongly because the people's minds are encrusted with feudal barbarism.

But, one may say, if the privileged classes have no right to interest the common will in their privileges, at least they ought to enjoy, as citizens, along with the rest of society, their political rights of representation.

I have already said that, in clothing themselves with privileges, they have become the real enemies of the common interest. They cannot then be allowed any participation. I add that they are always free to re-enter the social order when they so desire. Thus it is entirely by their own will that they are excluded from the exercise of political rights. Their true rights, those which can be the object of a national assembly, are held in common with the deputies; and they can console themselves with the thought that these deputies would be hurting themselves if they should try to touch these rights.

It is thus certain that the non-privileged classes alone are capable of being voters for and deputies in the National Assembly. The wishes of the Third Estate will always be good for the great mass of citizens; the wishes of the privileged classes will always be bad for them, unless, neglecting their special interests, they are willing to vote as ordinary citizens—that is to say, like the Third Estate itself. Thus the Third Estate suffices to accomplish everything that can be hoped from a National Assembly. It alone is capable of securing all the advantages some hope for from the Estates General.

Perhaps some people may think that the privileged classes may, as a last resort, consider themselves a separate nation, and demand a separate and independent representation. I have already replied to this claim in the first chapter of this work, when I proved that the privileged orders never have been and cannot be a separate people. They exist and can only exist at the expense of the real nation. Who would voluntarily consent to such an alliance?

Meanwhile, it is impossible to say what place the two privileged orders ought to occupy in the social order. It is like asking what place one wants to accord, in a sick body, to the malignant tumor which threatens and torments it. It is necessary to neutralize it. It is necessary to re-establish health and co-ordinate all the internal organs so well that they no longer form morbid combinations capable of vitiating the principles most essential for life.

Natural Rights and Revolution in France

When the Estates General convened at Versailles in May 1789, the deputies of the Third Estate acted upon the demands voiced by such men as Sieyès. Faced with strong opposition to reform, they simply refused to meet under the old rules, and reorganized themselves as a National Assembly. Noble and clerical representatives eventually joined the National Assembly, and this new body set about drawing up a constitution for the government of France. On July 11 the Marquis de Lafayette, who had served with Washington in the American Revolution, made a motion in the Assembly to adopt a declaration of basic human rights as a preamble to the new constitution. At the same time, he presented a preliminary list of such rights. The Assembly adopted the motion and appointed a committee to draft the declaration. Besides Lafayette's proposed version, the committee collected some twenty others. The final document, adopted on August 20, was a distillation of these.

The Declaration resembles statements of rights attached to the constitutions of several American states—most especially the Bill of Rights of Virginia. Copies of these constitutions had been translated and printed in France after 1776. Further, Thomas Jefferson (1743–1826), who chaired the committee which wrote the American Declaration of Independence, was Minister to Paris from 1785 to 1789. Several of the men who drafted the French Declaration knew Jefferson and his democratic theories well. Thus the evidence is strong, if circumstantial, that the authors of the *Declaration of the Rights of Man* were influenced by American constitutional models.

DECLARATION OF THE RIGHTS OF MAN AND OF THE CITIZEN

The representatives of the French people, organized in national assembly, considering that ignorance, forgetfulness, or contempt of the rights of man are the sole causes of the public miseries

Translated by Margaret Maddox from *Les Constitutions de la France*, edited by F. A. Helie (Paris: A. Marescq, ainé, 1879), pp. 268-71. Reprinted by permission of University of Chicago Press.

and of the corruption of governments, have resolved to set forth a solemn declaration of the natural, inalienable, and sacred rights of man, in order that this declaration, being ever present to all members of society, may constantly remind them of their rights and their duties in order that the acts of the legislative power and those of the executive power may be at each moment compared with the purpose of every political institution and thereby may be more respected; and in order that the demands of the citizens, grounded henceforth on simple and incontestable principles, may always be directed to the maintenance of the constitution and to the welfare of all.

In consequence, the National Assembly recognizes and declares, in the presence and under the auspices of the Supreme Being, the following rights of man and the citizen:

Art. 1. Men are born and remain free and equal in rights. Social distinctions can be based only on public utility.

Art. 2. The aim of every political association is the preservation of the natural and imprescriptible rights of man. These rights are liberty, property, security, and resistance to oppression.

Art. 3. The source of all sovereignty is essentially in the nation. No body, no individual can exercise authority that does not plainly proceed from it.

Art. 4. Liberty consists in the power to do anything that does not injure others. Accordingly, the exercise of the natural rights of each man is limited only by those that assure to the other members of society the enjoyment of the same rights. These limits can be determined only by law.

Art. 5. The law has the right to forbid only such actions as are injurious to society. Nothing can be forbidden that is not interdicted by law, and no one can be constrained to do what it does not order.

Art. 6. The law is the expression of the general will. All citizens have the right to participate personally or by their representatives in its formation. It must be the same for all, whether it protects, or whether it punishes. All citizens, being equal in its eyes, are equally eligible to all public dignities, places, and employments, according to their capacities, and without other distinction than that of their virtues and their talents.

Art. 7. No man can be accused, arrested, or detained except in the cases determined by law and according to the forms it prescribes. Those who procure, expedite, execute, or cause to be executed arbitrary orders ought to be punished; but every citizen summoned or seized in conformity with the law ought to obey at once; he makes himself guilty by resistance.

Art. 8. The law ought to establish only penalties that are strictly and obviously necessary, and one ought to be punished only in conformity with a law established and promulgated prior to the offense and legally applied.

Art. 9. Every man is presumed to be innocent until he has been declared guilty; if it is thought indispensable to arrest him, all severity that may not be necessary to secure his person ought to be strictly forbidden by law.

Art. 10. No one ought to be disturbed because of his opinions, even religious, provided their manifestation does not disturb the public order established by law.

Art. 11. The free communication of thought and opinions is one of the most precious rights of men: every citizen then can freely speak, write, and print, subject to responsibility for the abuse of this freedom in the cases determined by law.

Art. 12. The guarantee of the rights of man and the citizen requires a public force; this force then is instituted for the benefit of all, and not for the personal benefit of those to whom it is entrusted.

Art. 13. For the maintenance of the public force and for the expenses of administration a general tax is indispensable, it ought to be distributed equally among all the citizens according to their means.

Art. 14. All citizens have the right to ascertain, by themselves or by their representatives, the necessity of the public tax, to consent to it freely, to follow the employment of it, and to determine the quota, the assessment, the collection, and the duration of it.

Art. 15. Society has the right to demand an accounting of his administration from every public agent.

Art. 16. Any society in which the guarantee of rights is not secured or the separation of powers is not determined has no constitution at all.

Art. 17. Property being an inviolable and sacred right, no one can be deprived of it, unless legally established public necessity obviously demands it, and upon condition of a just and prior indemnity.

Virtue Through Terror, if Need Be

Maximilien Robespierre (1758–94) began his career as a lawyer in the small provincial city of Arras, in France. He was intelligent and well educated, with a good professional and social reputation, and was elected to the Estates General in 1789 as a deputy for the Third Estate.

While serving in the National Assembly (1789–1791), Robespierre became a member of the Jacobin Club, and he helped to make that society into a radical party caucus. He was elected from Paris to the National Convention (1792) and used his position within the Jacobin Club to become one of the Convention's most influential members.

In July 1793 the Jacobins gained control of the Committee of Public Safety, the executive body which directed France's defense and internal security. Of the twelve members of the Committee, Robespierre, by virtue of his political skills and strong popular support, was the most prominent. The *Report on the Principles of Public Morality*, of which one-third appears below, is the text of a speech he made to the Jacobins on February 5, 1794. In it he attempted to steer between two factions—one which urged massive terror against the counter-revolutionaries, and another, more moderate, which demanded a curtailment of political executions.

Robespierre, unwilling to renounce terror as a tactic, ultimately became its victim. In July 1794, he implied in a speech that several of his colleagues on the Committee of Public Safety were politically unreliable and should be removed. His colleagues removed him instead; he was executed, along with some ninety of his supporters, at the end of July, known in the revolutionary calendar as Thermidor. General reaction against revolutionary extremism ensued, though the men who overthrew Robespierre had no such intention.

MAXIMILIEN ROBESPIERRE: REPORT UPON THE PRINCIPLES OF POLITICAL MORALITY

Citizens, Representatives of the People:

Some time since we laid before you the principles of our exterior political system, we now come to develop the principles of political morality which are to govern the interior. After having long pursued the path which chance pointed out, carried away in a manner by the efforts of contending factions, the Representatives of the People at length acquired a character and produced a form of government. A sudden change in the success of the nation announced to Europe the regeneration which was operated in the national representation. But to this point of time, even now that I address you, it must be allowed that we have been impelled thro' the tempest of a revolution, rather by a love of right and a feeling of the wants of our country, than by an exact theory, and precise rules of conduct, which we had not even leisure to sketch.

It is time to designate clearly the purposes of the revolution and the point which we wish to attain: It is time we should examine ourselves the obstacles which yet are between us and our wishes, and the means most proper to realize them: A consideration simple and important which appears not yet to have been contemplated. Indeed, how could a base and corrupt government have dared to view themselves in the mirror of political rectitude? A king, a proud senate, a Caesar, a Cromwell; of these the first care was to cover their dark designs under the cloak of religion, to covenant with every vice, caress every party, destroy men of probity, oppress and deceive the people in order to attain the end of their perfidious ambition. If we had not had a task of the first magnitude to accomplish; if all our concern had been to raise a party or create a new aristocracy, we might have believed, as certain writers more ignorant than wicked asserted, that the plan of the French revolution was to be found written in the works of Tacitus and of Machiavel; we might have sought

From Maximilien Robespierre, *Report upon the Principles of Public Morality Which Are To Form the Basis of the Administration of the Interior Concerns of the Republic* (Philadelphia, 1794).

the duties of the representatives of the people in the history of Augustus, of Tiberius, or of Vespasian, or even in that of certain French legislators; for tyrants are substantially alike and only differ by trifling shades of perfidy and cruelty.

For our part we now come to make the whole world partake in your political secrets, in order that all friends of their country may rally at the voice of reason and public interest, and that the French nation and her representatives be respected in all countries which may attain a knowledge of their true principles; and that intriguers who always seek to supplant other intriguers may be judged by public opinion upon settled and plain principles.

Every precaution must early be used to place the interests of freedom in the hands of truth, which is eternal, rather than in those of men who change; so that if the government forgets the interests of the people or falls into the hands of men corrupted, according to the natural course of things, the light of acknowledged principles should unmask their treasons, and that every new faction may read its death in the very thought of a crime.

Happy the people that attains this end; for, whatever new machinations are plotted against their liberty, what resources does not public reason present when guaranteeing freedom!

What is the end of our revolution? The tranquil enjoyment of liberty and equality; the reign of that eternal justice, the laws of which are graven, not on marble or stone, but in the hearts of men, even in the heart of the slave who has forgotten them, and in that of the tyrant who disowns them.

We wish that order of things where all the low and cruel passions are enchained, all the beneficient and generous passions awakened by the laws; where ambition subsists in a desire to deserve glory and serve the country; where distinctions grow out of the system of equality, where the citizen submits to the authority of the magistrate, the magistrate obeys that of the people, and the people are governed by a love of justice; where the country secures the comfort of each individual, and where each individual prides himself on the prosperity and glory of his country; where every soul expands by a free communication of republican sentiments, and by the necessity of deserving the esteem of a great people; where the arts serve to embellish that liberty which gives them value and support, and commerce is a source of public wealth and not merely of immense riches to a few individuals.

We wish in our country that morality may be substituted for egotism, probity for false honour, principles for usages, duties for good manners, the empire of reason for the tyranny of fashion, a contempt of vice for a contempt of misfortune, pride for insolence, magnanimity for vanity, the love of glory for the love of money, good people for good company, merit for intrigue, genius for wit, truth for tinsel show, the attractions of happiness for the ennui of sensuality, the grandeur of man for the littleness of the great, a people magnanimous, powerful, happy, for a people amiable, frivolous and miserable; in a word, all the virtues and miracles of a Republic, instead of all the vices and absurdities of a Monarchy.

We wish, in a word, to fulfil the intentions of nature and the destiny of man, realize the promises of philosophy, and acquit providence of a long reign of crime and tyranny. That France, once illustrious among enslaved nations, may, by eclipsing the glory of all free countries that ever existed, become a model to nations, a terror to oppressors, a consolation to the oppressed, an ornament of the universe, and that, by sealing the work with our blood, we may at least witness the dawn of the bright day of universal happiness. This is our ambition,—this is the end of our efforts.

What kind of government can realize these prodigies? A democratic or republican government only: These two terms are synonimous notwithstanding the abuse of common language; for aristocracy is no more republic than monarchy is. A democracy is not where the people, always assembled, regulate themselves public affairs; much less is it where one hundred thousand portions of the people, by measures insulated, precipitate and contradictory, should decide the fate of the whole nation: Such a government has never existed except to bring back the people under the yoke of despotism.

A democratic government is that in which the sovereign people, guided by laws of their own enacting, do themselves all that they can do well, and by means of delegates all which they cannot do themselves. It is therefore in the principles of a democratic government that you are to seek the rules of your political conduct.

But, in order to found and consolidate among us democracy, to reach the peaceful reign of constitutional laws, we must terminate the war of liberty against tyranny, and weather successfully the tempests of the revolution: This is the end of the revolutionary government you have framed. You should therefore yet regulate your conduct by the tempestuous circumstances in which the republic exists, and the plan of your administration should be the result of the spirit of the revolutionary government combined with the general principles of democracy.

And what is the fundamental principle of a democratic or popular government—I mean, what is the primary spring which supports and gives it motion? It is virtue; I speak of public virtue, that which produced so many prodigies in Greece and Rome, and which ought to produce prodigies yet more wonderful in republican France; of that virtue which is nothing else than a love of country and of its laws.

But as equality is the essence of republicanism or democracy, it follows, that the love of country necessarily includes the love of equality.

Again, it is true that this sublime passion supposes a preference of the public interest over all private considerations; whence there results that the love of country supposes or produces all virtues: for what are they but a strength of mind which commands such sacrifices? And how could the slave of avarice and ambition, for example, immolate his idol to his country's weal?

Not only virtue is the soul of democracy, but it can exist in no other government. In a monarchy I know but one individual who can love his country, and who for this indeed needs no virtue; it is the monarch. The reason is, that of all the inhabitants of his dominions the monarch alone has a country.—Is he not sovereign at least in fact? Does he not assume the prerogative of the people? And what is our country but where we are citizens and partake in the sovereignty?

By a natural consequence of this principle, in aristocratical governments the word *patrie* (country) means nothing for any but the *patrician* families who usurp the sovereignty.

It is only in democracies that all citizens find truly a country, and where that country can reckon as many zealous defenders of its cause as there are citizens. This is the source of the superiority of free people over all others. If Athens and Sparta triumphed over the tyrants of Asia, and the Swiss over the tyrants of Spain and Austria, this is the only cause.

But the French are the first people in the world that have established democracy in its purity, by holding out to all men equality and a full enjoyment of the rights of the citizen; and this is, in my opinion, the true reason why all the tyrants leagued against the republic will be vanquished.

If virtue be the spring of a popular government in times of peace, the spring of that government during a revolution is virtue combined with terror: virtue, without which terror is destructive; terror, without which virtue is impotent. Terror is only justice prompt, severe and inflexible; it is then an emanation of virtue; it is less a distinct principle than a natural consequence of the general principle of democracy, applied to the most pressing wants of the country.

. . . .

The protection of government is only due to peaceable citizens; and all citizens in the republic are republicans. The royalists, the conspirators, are strangers, or rather enemies. Is not this dreadful contest, which liberty maintains against tyranny, indivisible? Are not the internal enemies the allies of those in the exterior? The assassins who lay waste the interior; the intriguers who purchase the consciences of the delegates of the people; the traitors who sell them; the mercenary libellists paid to dishonor the cause of the people, to smother public virtue, to fan the flame of civil discord, and bring about a political counter revolution by means of a moral one: all these men, are they less culpable or less dangerous than the tyrants whom they serve? All those who interpose their parricidious lenity between these villains and the avenging sword of national justice are as culpable as those who would throw themselves between the satellites of tyrants and bayonets of our soldiers, all the transports of their false sensibility appear to me nothing but sighs for the success of England and Austria.

V

The Industrial Revolution

How To Be Successful in Business While Still in Your Teens
Robert Owen: Autobiography

How Capitalism Is Its Own Gravedigger
Karl Marx and Friedrich Engels: The Communist Manifesto

How To Head off Proletarian Revolution
Otto von Bismarck: Speech on Social Insurance

How To Be Successful in Business While Still in Your Teens

Robert Owen (1771–1858) became a successful businessman while still in his teens, taking advantage both of the technical changes that came to cotton-spinning in the last decades of the eighteenth century and of his own shrewd self-assertiveness and managerial talents. He became skeptical of Christian teachings while still on the way up; but after he had made a substantial fortune as a cotton spinner, he decided to try to better the lives of others, beginning with the living and working conditions of his own employees at New Lanark. Losing interest in this form of benevolence, Owen tried to establish a completely new society in America at New Harmony, Indiana. That failed to work out; and in 1828 he returned to Britain and became a leader of an effort to organize the workingmen of Great Britain into a Grand National Consolidated Trades Union (1833–34). The movement grew very fast and collapsed as rapidly. Thereafter, until the end of his life Robert Owen continued to agitate on behalf of his ideas of how to make society over through education, cooperation, and good will. He had a powerful influence on the growth of socialism in Great Britain, although Karl Marx scornfully classed him among the "Utopian socialists."

His autobiography dates from the very end of his life, having been completed in 1857, the year before he died. The extract published below describes Owen's first steps in the cotton business in 1790, when the new technology of machine spinning and weaving was transforming production and making the earliest really large-scale factories economically feasible.

ROBERT OWEN:
THE LIFE OF ROBERT OWEN

To return to my narrative. On leaving Messrs. Flint and Palmer's,[1] I went to reside with Mr. Satterfield in Manchester. His establishent was then the first in his line in the retail department, but not much to boast of as a wholesale warehouse. It was upon the whole pretty well managed. Mr. Satterfield was an indifferent buyer of goods for his trade, but an excellent salesman. Mr. McGuffog[2] was an extremely good buyer, and when goods are well and judiciously purchased for a local trade, they almost sell themselves, and give little trouble to the seller; while if they are not bought with judgment, the trouble of sale is greatly increased. The good buyer also is almost sure to gain success to his business;—while indifferent buyers scarcely ever succeed in accumulating independence. Hence Mr. McGuffog retired from business with what, in those days, was considered a good fortune for a retail tradesman, leaving his widow upwards of one thousand a year, besides other gifts; while Mr. Satterfield, with a larger business, and with great toil and labour, and much anxiety, could only during his life clear his way, unable to purchase except on credit. His son, I understood, who succeeded to his business, was more fortunate. Here also, however, I was very comfortable, and gained new experience in another class in society. Mr. Satterfield's customers were generally of the upper middle-class—the well-to-do manufacturers' and merchants' wives and families—a class intermediate between Mr. McGuffog's and Messrs. Flint and Palmer's,—and I thus became acquainted with the ideas and habits of this class.

Our living was good, our treatment kind, and the young persons assistants in the business were generally from respectable families and well behaved, and none were over-taxed with occupation in their respective departments. I therefore soon be-

From *The Life of Robert Owen by Himself* (New York: Alfred A. Knopf, 1920), pp. 31-44. Reprinted by permission of Alfred A. Knopf, Inc.

1. Sellers of cotton cloth for whom Owen had worked as a store clerk.
2. The storekeeper to whom Owen had been apprenticed.

came reconciled to the change which my friend had made for me, and with forty pounds a year, over my board, lodging, and washing, I deemed myself overflowing with wealth, having more than my temperate habits required, for I had never accustomed myself to strong liquors of any kind, and my eating was always moderate and of the most simple and easily digested quality. I thus continued until I was eighteen years of age. Among other articles which we sold were wires for the foundation or frame of ladies' bonnets. The manufacturer of these wire bonnet-frames was a mechanic with some small inventive powers and a very active mind. When he brought his weekly supply of wire frames, I had to receive them from him, and he began to tell me about great and extraordinary discoveries that were beginning to be introduced into Manchester for spinning cotton by new and curious machinery. He said he was endeavouring to see and to get a knowledge of them, and that if he could succeed he could make a very good business of it. This kind of conversation was frequently renewed by the wire manufacturer, whose name was Jones. At length he told me he had succeeded in seeing these machines at work, and he was sure he could make them and work them. He had, however, no capital, and he could not begin without some. He said that with one hundred pounds he could commence and soon accumulate capital sufficient to proceed; and he ended by saying that if I would advance one hundred pounds, I should have one half of the great profits that were to result if I would join him in partnership. He made me believe that he had obtained a great secret, and that if assisted as he stated, he could soon make a good business. I wrote to my brother William in London, to ask him if he could conveniently advance me the sum required, and he immediately sent me the hundred pounds. I had now to give notice to Mr. Satterfield according to our engagement, and that because I was going into a new business for myself. He was, I believe, disappointed, for I had by this time become a useful and steady assistant, and a favourite server with his principal customers. During the time between my giving notice and finally leaving Mr. Satterfield's establishment, Jones and I had agreed with a builder that he should erect and let to us a large machine workshop, with rooms also for some cotton spinners, and the building was finished by the time I left Mr. Satterfield. We had shortly about forty men at work to make machines, and we obtained wood, iron, and brass, for their construction, upon credit.

I soon found however that Jones was a mere working mechanic, without any idea how to manage workmen, or how to conduct business on the scale on which he had commenced.

I had not the slightest knowledge of this new machinery—had never seen it at work. I was totally ignorant of what was required; but as there were so many men engaged to work for us, I knew that their wages must be paid, and that if they were not well looked after, our business must soon cease and end in our ruin. Jones knew little about book-keeping, finance matters, or the superintendence of men. I therefore undertook to keep the accounts—pay and receive all; and I was the first and last in the manufactory. I looked very wisely at the men in their different departments, although I really knew nothing. But by intensely observing everything, I maintained order and regularity throughout the establishment, which proceeded under such circumstances far better than I had anticipated. We made what are technically called "mules" for spinning cotton, sold them, and appeared to be carrying on a good business; while, having discovered the want of business capacity in my partner, I proceeded with fear and trembling.

We had not been in business many months, when a capitalist with moderate means, thinking the prospects of the establishment very good, applied to Jones to be allowed to join him with increased means, on the supposition that Jones was the efficient man of business, and that if I could be induced to leave it, he (the applicant, whose name I have forgotten) could easily do what I did. They hesitated to break their intentions to me, under the impression that I should be very unwilling to leave a business holding out so fair a prospect of future success. They at once offered me terms, which, if I had declined to accept, they would, I afterwards found, have increased, in order to secure to themselves this, as they considered, thriving business, and which with continued good looking after and good management might have become so. But I was too happy to separate from Jones, to hesitate to accept their proposal. They offered to give me for my share of the business six mule machines such as we were making for sale, a reel, and a making up machine, with which to pack the yarn when finished in skeins into bundles for sale. I had now, when about nineteen years of age, to begin the world on my own account, having the promise of the machinery named to commence with.

. . . .

. . . When I separated from Jones and the machine making business, I took a large newly-erected building, or factory, as such places were then beginning to be called. It was situated in Ancoats Lane. I rented it from a builder of the name of Woodruff, with whom I afterwards went to board and lodge. From Jones and his new partner I received *three* out of *six* mule machines which were promised, with the reel and making up machine; and with this stock I commenced business for myself in a small part of one of the large rooms in this large building.

The machines were set to work, and I engaged three men to work them—that is, to spin cotton yarn or thread upon them from a previous preparation called rovings. When the yarn was spun, it was in the cop form, from which it was to be made upon the reel into hanks, each one hundred and forty yards in length. This operation I performed, and then made these hanks into bundles of five pounds weight each, and in this state, wrapped neatly up in paper, I sold them to a Mr. Mitchell, an agent from some mercantile manufacturing houses in Glasgow, who sold the yarn to muslin weavers, or manufactured it themselves. The manufacture of British muslins was but in its infancy. The first British muslins were made when I was an apprentice with Mr. McGuffog, by a Mr. Oldknow at Stockport in Cheshire, about seven miles from Manchester, who must have commenced this branch about the year 1780, 1781, or 1782; and it is curious to trace the history of this manufacture.

When I first went to Mr. McGuffog, there were no other muslins for sale, except those made in the East Indies, and known as East India muslins; but while I was with him, Mr. Oldknow began to manufacture a fabric which he called, by way of distinction, British Mull Muslin. It was a new article in the market, less than yard wide, for which he charged to Mr. McGuffog 9s. or 9s. 6d., and which Mr. McGuffog resold to his customers at half a guinea[3] per yard. It was eagerly sought for, and rapidly bought up by the nobility at that price,—and Mr. McGuffog could not obtain from Mr. Oldknow a supply equal to his demand. He was obliged to beg and pray of Mr. Oldknow to add a piece or two more to his weekly order for them, but frequently without success. Such is the all-powerful influence of fashion and its absurdities under the present disorder of the human intellects, that the parties who were then so earger to buy this new fabric at 10s. 6d. the yard, would not now look at it; and a much better quality may be at this time purchased by the poor at *two pence* the yard.

I have said that my three spinners were spinning the cotton yarn on my three mules from *rovings*. I had no machinery to make rovings, and was obliged to purchase them,—they were the half-made materials to be spun into thread. I had become acquainted with two young industrious Scotchmen, of the names of McConnell and Kennedy, who had also commenced about the same time as myself to make cotton machinery upon a small scale, and they had now proceeded so far as to make some of the machinery for preparing the cotton for the mule spinning machinery so far as to enable them to make the rovings, which they sold in that state to the spinners at a good profit. I was one of their first and most regular customers, giving them, as I recollect, 12s. per pound for rovings, which, when spun into thread, and made up into the five pound bundles, I sold to Mr. Mitchell at 22s. per pound. This was in the year 1790.

Such was the commencement of Messrs. McConnell and Kennedy's successful career as cotton spinners,—such the foundation of those palace-like buildings which were afterwards erected by this firm,—of the princely fortunes which they made by them, and of my own proceedings in Manchester and in New Lanark in Scotland. *They* could then only make the *rovings*, without finishing the thread; and I could only *finish* the thread, without being competent to make the *rovings*.

These are the kind of circumstances which, without our

3. A guinea equaled 21 shillings; half a guinea was, therefore, 10s. 6d.

knowledge or control, from small beginning produce very different results to any anticipated by us when we commence.

Jones and his new partner, as I foresaw, were getting rapidly into confusion and pecuniary difficulties. They informed me they could not make good their engagement with me, and I never received the three remaining mule machines. I believe they ultimately stopped payment, and that Jones returned to his wire bonnet-frame making.

Seeing that I was not likely to obtain more machinery from my former partner, I made up my mind to do as well as I could with that amount which I had obtained. With the three men spinning for me, reeling, and making up that which they spun, and by selling it weekly to Mr. Mitchell, I made on the average about six pounds of profit each week, and deemed myself doing well for a young beginner,—for I had let the remainder of the large building which I occupied, to tenants who paid my whole rent, and I retained my portion of it by these means free of cost.

About this period cotton spinning was so profitable that it began to engage the attention of many parties with capitals. Mr. Arkwright, the introducer, if not the inventor of the new cotton spinning machinery, had had a cotton spinning mill erected in Manchester, under a manager of the name of Simpson; and a Mr. Drinkwater, a rich Manchester manufacturer and foreign merchant, had built a mill for finer spinning, and was beginning to fill it with machinery under the superintendence of a Mr. George Lee, a very superior scientific person in those days. Mr., afterwards Sir George Philips, was desirous of building a large mill in Salford, and he, unknown to Mr. Drinkwater, formed a partnership with Mr. George Lee, afterwards known for many years as a leading firm in Manchester, as Philips and Lee. Mr. Lee had given Mr. Drinkwater notice that he must leave him, having formed this new partnership. Mr. Drinkwater being totally ignorant of everything connected with cotton spinning, although a good fustian manufacturer and a first-rate foreign merchant, and by this time become very wealthy, was greatly nonplussed by Mr. Lee thus abandoning the establishment, which, except with the expectation of Mr. Lee's permanent services, he would not have commenced.

Under this to him very untoward circumstance he had to advertise for a manager to undertake the superintendence of this mill, now in progress; and his advertisement appeared on a Saturday in the Manchester papers, but I had not seen or heard of it until I went to my factory on the Monday morning following, when, as I entered the room where my spinning machines were, one of the spinners said—"Mr. Lee has left Mr. Drinkwater, and he has advertised for a manager." I merely said—"what will he do?" and passed on to my own occupation. But (and how such an idea could enter my head I know not), without saying a word, I put on my hat and proceeded straight to Mr. Drinkwater's counting-house, and boy, and inexperienced, as I was, I asked him for the situation for which he had advertised. The circumstances which now occurred made a lasting impression upon me, because they led to important future consequences. He said immediately—"You are too young,"—and at that time being fresh coloured I looked younger than I was. I said, "That was an objection made to me four or five years ago, but I did not expect it would be made to me now." "How old are you?" "Twenty in May this year"—was my reply. "How often do you get drunk in the week?" (This was a common habit with almost all persons in Manchester and Lancashire at that period.) "I was never," I said, "drunk in my life"—blushing scarlet at this unexpected question. My answer and the manner of it made, I suppose, a favourable impression; for the next question was—"What salary do you ask?" "Three hundred a year"—was my reply. "What?" Mr. Drinkwater said, with some surprise, repeating the words—"Three hundred a year! I have had this morning I know not how many seeking the situation, and I do not think that all their askings together would amount to what you require." "I cannot be governed by what others ask," said I, "and I cannot take less. I am now making that sum by my own business." "Can you prove that to me?" "Yes, I will show you the business and my books." "Then I will go with you, and let me see them," said Mr. Drinkwater. We went to my factory. I explained the nature of my business, opened the book, and proved my statement to his satisfaction. He then said—"What reference as to past character can you give?" I referred him to

Mr. Satterfield, Messrs. Flint and Palmer, and Mr. McGuffog. "Come to me on such a day, and you shall have my answer." This was to give him time to make the inquiries.

I called upon him at the time appointed. He said, "I will give you the three hundred a year, as you ask, and I will take all your machinery at its cost price, and I shall require you to take the management of the mill and of the workpeople, about 500, immediately." I accordingly made my arrangements. Mr. Drinkwater knew nothing about the mill; but so far as the business had proceeded he had supplied the capital as it was wanted, and had received the money when the produce was sold and paid for. Mr. Lee had left the day before I was sent for to take his place, and I entered it without the slightest instruction or explanation about anything. When I arrived at the mill, which was in another part of the town from Mr. Drinkwater's place of business, I found myself at once in the midst of five hundred men, women, and children, who were busily occupied with machinery, much of which I had scarcely seen, and never in regular connection to manufacture from the cotton to the finished thread. I said to myself, with feelings I shall never forget,—"How came I here? and how is it possible I can manage these people and this business?" To this period I had been a thoughtful, retiring character, extremely sensitive, and could seldom speak to a stranger without blushing, especially to one of the other sex, except in the ordinary routine of serving in the departments of business through which I had passed; and I was diffident of my own powers, knowing what a very imperfect and deficient education I had received. I was therefore greatly surprised at myself, that, without thought or reflection, on the impulse of the moment, I had solicited this situation. But I had no idea of the task which I had to perform, in many respects entirely new to me, or I should never have made the attempt to perform it. My only experience had been in serving in a retail shop, except during the few months I had been in partnership with Jones, which short time was spent in keeping wages' accounts, and in seeing that the men were at work, and in working on a capital of one hundred pounds. Had I seen the establishment before I applied to manage it, I should never have thought of doing an act so truly presumptuous. Mr. Lee had left the mill the day before I undertook it,—Mr. Drinkwater did not come with me to introduce me to any of the people,—and thus, uninstructed, I had to take the management of the concern. I had to purchase the raw material,—to make the machines, for the mill was not nearly filled with machinery,—to manufacture the cotton into yarn,—to sell it,—and to keep the accounts,—pay the wages,—and, in fact, to take the whole responsibility of the first fine cotton spinning establishment by machinery that had ever been erected, commenced by one of the most scientific men of his day, and who was considered a man of very superior attainments, having been highly educated, and being a finished mathematician. Such was the concern I had to manage when not yet twenty years of age, and such the person I had to succeed.

When it was known in Manchester that Mr. Drinkwater had engaged me, a mere boy without experience, to take the entire direction of his new mill, which was then considered almost one of the wonders of the mechanical and manufacturing world, the leading people, as I learned afterwards, thought he had lost his senses, and they predicted a failure and great disappointment. Well—there I was, to undertake this task, and no one to give me any assistance. I at once determined to do the best I could, and began to examine the outline and detail of what was in progress. I looked grave,—inspected everything very minutely,—examined the drawings and calculations of the machinery, as left by Mr. Lee, and these were of great use to me. I was with the first in the morning, and I locked up the premises at night, taking the keys with me. I continued this silent inspection and superintendence day by day for six weeks, saying merely yes or no to the questions of what was to be done or otherwise, and during that period I did not give one direct order about anything. But at the end of that time I felt myself so much master of my position, as to be ready to give directions in every department. My previous habits had prepared me for great nicety and exactness of action, and for a degree of perfection in operations to which parties then employed in cotton spinning were little accustomed. I soon perceived the defects in the various processes, and in the correctness which was required in making certain parts of the machinery—all yet in a rude state, compared with the advances which have been made from that time to the present. This factory or cotton mill was built on purpose to manufacture the finest yarns or thread, and Mr. Lee had attained what was then considered an extraordinary degree of fineness, having succeeded in producing what was technically known as *one hundred and twenty* hanks in the pound. But it was of very indifferent quality. By my acquired faculty under Mr. McGuffog's discipline, of great exactness and nicety in handling and keeping fine and expensive articles, I soon improved the quality of our manufacture. There was a large stock of yarn upon hand unsold, manufactured under Mr. Lee's management, of various degrees of fineness, from seventy to one hundred and twenty.

Mr. Drinkwater lived in his country house in the summer, and in his town house in the winter. He was now living in the country, and came to his counting-house and warehouse, adjoining his winter residence, twice a week. He never came to the mill, but almost always desired to see me at his counting-house on the days he attended there, and that I should bring specimens of the manufacture week by week. He found the quality gradually to improve, and the customers for it to prefer the new-made to the old stock. He found also that the people employed were, according to reports made to him by others, well disciplined, and yet well satisfied with the rules, regulations, and mode of management which I had adopted; and he became week by week more satisfied with the boy he had taken in opposition to public opinion to manage his new factory. The advantages which I possessed to counteract my ignorance and inexperience arose from my early training with Mr. McGuffog, amidst fine and superior fabrics, and a knowledge acquired of human nature by having early overcome the prejudices of religion.

I had by this period perceived the constant influence of circumstances over my own proceedings and those of others, and by comparison with myself and others I became conscious of the created differences in our original organizations. Relieved from religious prejudices and their obstructive influences to the attainment of common sense, my mind became simple in its new arrangement of ideas, and gradually came to the conclusion that man could not make his own organization, or any one of its qualities, and that these qualities were, according to their nature, more or less influenced by the circumstances which occurred in the life of each, over which the individual had no other control than these combined circumstances gave him, but over which society had an overwhelming influence; and I therefore viewed human nature in my fellow-creatures through a medium different from others, and with far more charity. Knowing that they did not make themselves, or the circumstances or conditions in which they were involved, and that these conditions combined necessarily forced them to be that which they became,—I was obliged to consider my fellow-men as beings made by circumstances before and after their birth, not under their own control, except as previously stated and to a limited extent,—and therefore to have illimitable charity for their feelings, thoughts, and actions. This knowledge of our common nature gave me the early habit of considering man the necessary result of his organization and the conditions by which nature and society surrounded him, and of looking upon and acting towards all in the spirit which this knowledge created. My mind, in consequence, gradually became calm and serene, and anger and ill-will died within me.

This knowledge of human nature gave me for a long period an unconscious advantage over others. My treatment of all with whom I came into communication was so natural, that it generally gained their confidence, and drew forth only their good qualities to me; and I was often much surprised to discover how much more easily I accomplished my objects than others whose educated acquirements were much superior to mine. Very generally I had the good will of all; and,—except when I afterwards opposed in public all the religions of the world, and the past and present system of society, and thus aroused the oldest prejudices of all against my new views of society,—I was generally a favourite with both sexes and all classes.

In consequence of this to me unconscious power over others—I had produced such effects over the workpeople in the factory in the first six months of my management, that I had the most complete influence over them, and their order and discipline exceeded that of any other in or near Manchester; and for regularity and sobriety they were an example which none could then imitate; for the workpeople earned at that period higher wages, and were far more independent than they have ever been since.

The factory also I had re-arranged, and always had it kept in superior order, so that at all times it was in a state to be inspected by any parties.

But at this period cotton mills were closed against all strangers, and no one was admitted. They were kept with great jealousy against all intruders; the outer doors being always locked. Mr. Drinkwater himself had not yet entered the mill since I took charge of it, and he came only three times during the four years I retained the management of it. . . .

Mr. Drinkwater, who from some source knew, no doubt, the particulars of my management, and the progress and change I had made in the factory, at the end of the first six months sent for me to his country residence, having something which he wished to communicate to me.

I was yet but an ill-educated awkward youth, strongly sensitive to my defects of education, speaking ungrammatically, a kind of Welsh English, in consequence of the imperfect language spoken in Newtown,[4] which was an imperfect mixture of both languages; and I had yet only had the society attainable by a retail assistant. I was also so sensitive as among strangers to feel and to act awkwardly, and I was never satisfied with my own speaking and acting, and was subject painfully to blushing, which, with all my strongest efforts, I could not prevent. In fact, I felt the possession of ideas superior to my power of expressing them, and this always embarrassed me with strangers, and especially when in the company of those who had been systematically well educated, according to existing notions of education. I had not yet been in Mr. Drinkwater's house in Manchester, and therefore when I was requested to go to him at his country house, I was at a loss to conjecture what was the object of this new proceeding, and I felt uncertain and somewhat uncomfortable as to the result. When, however, I had arrived, and was taken into Mr. Drinkwater's room of business, he said,—"Mr.

4. Robert Owen's birthplace, a town in Wales.

Owen, I have sent for you to propose a matter of business important to you and me. I have watched your proceedings, and know them well, since you came into my service, and I am well pleased with all you have done. I now wish you to make up your mind to remain permanently with me. I have agreed to give you three hundred pounds for this year; and if you will consent to remain with me, I will give you four hundred for the next year,—five hundred for the third year,—and I have two sons growing up, and the fourth year you shall join them in partnership with me, and you shall have a fourth of the profits, and you know now what they are likely to be. What do you say to this proposal?" I said, "I think it most liberal, and willingly agree to it."

"Then," he replied, "the agreement shall be made out while you are here, and you shall take a copy of it home with you." When this was done, and both agreements were signed, I returned home well pleased with my visit.

I was now placed in an independent position for one not yet twenty years of age. I was born in 1771, as previously stated, and this event occurred early in 1790. I had also given to me full power to take my own course in what I should deem beneficial to promote the interests of the establishment.

How Capitalism Is Its Own Gravedigger

Karl Marx's father was a prosperous lawyer and civil servant in the small German city of Trier. In 1835 he sent his son to study law at the University of Bonn, where Karl (1818–83) joined a drinking club and led a boistrous social life. In 1836, however, Marx transferred to the more demanding University of Berlin, where he settled down to his law studies and developed a passionate interest in philosophy. After graduation he edited a newspaper in Cologne; when the Prussian government suppressed the paper in 1843 because of its anti-Russian editorials, Marx moved to Paris. He returned to Cologne at the outbreak of the Revolution of 1848 (he had just completed the Communist Manifesto) and again took over a newspaper. But the Prussians again suppressed the paper, and Marx went into permanent exile.

Marx's collaborator, Friedrich Engels (1820–95) was likewise a German who settled in England. He was the third generation of a wealthy family of textile manufacturers; they owned mills both in the Rhineland and in Manchester. Engels spent the year 1841 in Berlin and met some of the same philosophy students and teachers who had so stimulated Marx. The two did not meet, however, until 1842, when Engels began to contribute articles to Marx's paper. Each discovered that the other shared a radical dissatisfaction with capitalism and its effect on factory laborers; jointly, they developed their critique of industrial society and their proposals for solving its abuses. They wrote the *Communist Manifesto,* of which three-fourths appear below, in 1847 as a program for the Communist League, a small and secret German workingman's organization.

After the failure of the revolutions of 1848, Marx moved to England where he spent the rest of his life working at a vast exposition of his social and economic ideas, *Das Kapital.* In addition, he conducted a vigorous polemic against fellow socialists who differed from him on points of doctrine or tactics; and he tried to organize an international association of socialist parties to prepare for the proletarian revolution whose coming he had predicted.

Marx's ideas found wide acceptance in Germany in the 1880's where the Social Democratic party became more or less Marxian. From Germany, Marxian ideas spread to other European countries, among them Russia, where in the 1890's they inspired the young Lenin to embark upon his revolutionary career. Communist movements all around the world since 1917 claim that they derived their principles from Karl Marx. Needless to say, new strands and emphases wove their way into Marxianism as it spread and made converts; Engels himself toward the end of his life changed tone in some of his remarks. But the youthful pamphlet *The Communist Manifesto,* published in 1848, always remained the most eloquent as well as the most concise statement of Marxian doctrine.

KARL MARX AND FRIEDRICH ENGELS: MANIFESTO OF THE COMMUNIST PARTY

A spectre is haunting Europe—the spectre of communism. All the powers of old Europe have entered into a holy alliance to

From *The Essential Left* (New York: Harper & Row/Barnes and Noble, 1961; George Allen & Unwin, Ltd.), pp. 14-36, 42-47. Reprinted by permission of the publishers.

exorcise this spectre: Pope and Tsar, Metternich[1] and Guizot,[2] French Radicals and German police-spies.

Where is the party in opposition that has not been decried as communistic by its opponents in power? Where is the opposition that has not hurled back the branding reproach of communism, against the more advanced opposition parties, as well as against its reactionary adversaries?

Two things result from this fact:

I. Communism is already acknowledged by all European powers to be itself a power.

II. It is high time that Communists should openly, in the face of the whole world, publish their views, their aims, their tendencies, and meet this nursery tale of the spectre of communism with a manifesto of the party itself.

To this end, Communists of various nationalities have assembled in London and sketched the following manifesto, to be published in the English, French, German, Italian, Flemish and Danish languages.

I. Bourgeois and Proletarians

The history of all hitherto existing society is the history of class struggles.

Freeman and slave, patrician and plebeian, lord and serf, guild-master[3] and journeyman, in a word, oppressor and oppressed, stood in constant opposition to one another, carried on an uninterrupted, now hidden, now open fight, a fight that each time ended, either in a revolutionary reconstitution of society at large, or in the common ruin of the contending classes.

In the earlier epochs of history, we find almost everywhere a complicated arrangement of society into various orders, a manifold gradation of social rank. In ancient Rome we have patricians, knights, plebeians, slaves; in the Middle Ages, feudal

1. Prince Clemens von Metternich (1773-1859) Chancellor of the Hapsburg monarchy and major upholder of the existing order in Europe, 1815-48.

2. François Guizot (1787-1874) historian and chief minister to King Louis Phillipe of France, 1840-48.

3. Guild-master, that is a full member of a guild, a master within, not a head of a guild. [K. M.]

lords, vassals, guild-masters, journeymen, apprentices, serfs; in almost all of these classes, again, subordinate gradations.

The modern bourgeois society that has sprouted from the ruins of feudal society has not done away with class antagonisms. It has but established new classes, new conditions of oppression, new forms of struggle in place of the old ones.

Our epoch, the epoch of the bourgeoisie, possesses, however, this distinctive feature: It has simplified the class antagonisms. Society as a whole is more and more splitting up into two great hostile camps, into two great classes directly facing each other—bourgeoisie and proletariat.

From the serfs of the Middle Ages sprang the chartered burghers of the earliest towns. From these burgesses the first elements of the bourgeoisie were developed.

The discovery of America, the rounding of the Cape, opened up fresh ground for the rising bourgeoisie. The East-Indian and Chinese markets, the colonization of America, trade with the colonies, the increase in the means of exchange and in commodities generally, gave to commerce, to navigation, to industry, an impulse never before known, and thereby, to the revolutionary element in the tottering feudal society, a rapid development.

The feudal system of industry, in which industrial production was monopolized by closed guilds, now no longer sufficed for the growing wants of the new markets. The manufacturing system took its place. The guild-masters were pushed aside by the manufacturing middle class; division of labour between the different corporate guilds vanished in the face of division of labour in each single workshop.

Meantime the markets kept ever growing, the demand ever rising. Even manufacture no longer sufficed. Thereupon, steam and machinery revolutionized industrial production. The place of manufacture was taken by the giant, modern industry, the place of the industrial middle class by industrial millionaires, the leaders of whole industrial armies, the modern bourgeois.

Modern industry has established the world market, for which the discovery of America paved the way. This market has given an immense development to commerce, to navigation, to communication by land. This development has, in its turn, reacted on the extension of industry; and in proportion as industry, commerce, navigation, railways extended, in the same proportion the bourgeoisie developed, increased its capital, and pushed into the background every class handed down from the Middle Ages.

We see, therefore, how the modern bourgeoisie is itself the product of a long course of development, of a series of revolutions in the modes of production and of exchange.

Each step in the development of the bourgeoisie was accompanied by a corresponding political advance of that class. An oppressed class under the sway of the feudal nobility, an armed and self-governing association in the medieval commune;[4] here independent urban republic (as in Italy and Germany), there taxable "third estate" of the monarchy (as in France); afterwards, in the period of manufacture proper, serving either the semifeudal or the absolute monarchy as a counterpoise against the nobility, and, in fact, cornerstone of the great monarchies in general—the bourgeoisie has at last, since the establishment of modern industry and of the world market, conquered for itself, in the modern representative state, exclusive political sway. The executive of the modern state is but a committee for managing the common affairs of the whole bourgeoisie.

The bourgeoisie, historically, has played a most revolutionary part.

The bourgeoisie, wherever it has got the upper hand, has put an end to all feudal, patriarchal, idyllic relations. It has pitilessly torn asunder the motley feudal ties that bound man to his "natural superiors," and has left no other nexus between man and man than naked self-interest, than callous "cash payment." It has drowned the most heavenly ecstasies of religious fervour, of chivalrous enthusiasm, of philistine sentimentalism, in the icy water of egotistical calculation. It has resolved personal worth into exchange value, and in place of the numberless indefeasible chartered freedoms, has set up that single, unconscionable free-

4. "Commune" was the name taken in France by the nascent towns even before they had conquered from their feudal lords and masters local self-government and political rights as the "Third Estate." Generally speaking, for the economical development of the bourgeoisie, England is here taken as the typical country, for its political development, France. [K. M.]

dom—Free Trade. In one word, for exploitation, veiled by religious and political illusions, it has substituted naked, shameless, direct, brutal exploitation.

The bourgeoisie has stripped of its halo every occupation hitherto honoured and looked up to with reverent awe. It has converted the physician, the lawyer, the priest, the poet, the man of science, into its paid wage labourers.

The bourgeoisie has torn away from the family its sentimental veil, and has reduced the family relation to a mere money relation.

The bourgeoisie has disclosed how it came to pass that the brutal display of vigour in the Middle Ages, which reactionaries so much admire, found its fitting complement in the most slothful indolence. It has been the first to show what man's activity can bring about. It has accomplished wonders far surpassing Egyptian pyramids, Roman aqueducts, and Gothic cathedrals; it has conducted expeditions that put in the shade all former exoduses of nations and crusades.

The bourgeoisie cannot exist without constantly revolutionizing the instruments of production, and thereby the relations of production, and with them the whole relations of society. Conservation of the old modes of production in unaltered form, was, on the contrary, the first condition of existence for all earlier industrial classes. Constant revolutionizing of production, uninterrupted disturbance of all social conditions, everlasting uncertainty and agitation distinguish the bourgeois epoch from all earlier ones. All fixed, fast frozen relations, with their train of ancient and removable prejudices and opinions, are swept away, all new-formed ones become antiquated before they can ossify. All that is solid melts into air, all that is holy is profaned, and man is at last compelled to face with sober senses his real conditions of life and his relations with his kind.

The need of a constantly expanding market for its products chases the bourgeoisie over the whole surface of the globe. It must nestle everywhere, settle everywhere, establish connections everywhere.

The bourgeoisie has through its exploitation of the world market given a cosmopolitan character to production and consumption in every country. To the great chagrin of reactionaries, it has drawn from under the feet of industry the national ground on which it stood. All old-established national industries have been destroyed or are daily being destroyed. They are dislodged by new industries, whose introduction becomes a life and death question for all civilized nations, by industries that no longer work up indigenous raw material, but raw material drawn from the remotest zones; industries whose products are consumed, not only at home, but in every quarter of the globe. In place of the old wants, satisfied by the production of the country, we find new wants, requiring for their satisfaction the products of distant lands and climes. In place of the old local and national seclusion and self-sufficiency, we have intercourse in every direction, universal inter-dependence of nations. And as in material, so also in intellectual production. The intellectual creations of individual nations become common property. National one-sidedness and narrow-mindedness become more and more impossible, and from the numerous national and local literatures there arises a world literature.

The bourgeoisie, by the rapid improvement of all instruments of production, by the immensely facilitated means of communication, draws all, even the most barbarian, nations into civilization. The cheap prices of its commodities are the heavy artillery with which it batters down all Chinese walls, with which it forces the barbarians' intensely obstinate hatred of foreigners to capitulate. It compels all nations, on pain of extinction, to adopt the bourgeois mode of production; it compels them to introduce what it calls civilization into their midst, i.e. to become bourgeois themselves. In one word, it creates a world after its own image.

The bourgeois has subjected the country to the rule of the towns. It has created enormous cities, has greatly increased the urban population as compared with the rural, and has thus rescued a considerable part of the population from the idiocy of rural life. Just as it has made the country dependent on the towns, so it has made barbarian and semi-barbarian countries dependent on the civilized ones, nations of peasants on nations of bourgeois, the East on the West.

The bourgeoisie keeps more and more doing away with the scattered state of the population, of the means of production, and of property. It has agglomerated population, centralized means of production, and has concentrated property in a few hands. The necessary consequences of this was political centralization. Independent, or but loosely connected provinces, with separate interests, laws, governments, and systems of taxation, became lumped together into one nation, with one government, one code of laws, one national class interest, one frontier and one customs tariff.

The bourgeoisie, during its rule of scarce one hundred years, has created more massive and more colossal productive forces than have all preceding generations together. Subjection of nature's forces to man, machinery, application of chemistry to industry and agriculture, steam navigation, railways, electric telegraphs, clearing of whole continents for cultivation, canalization of rivers, whole populations conjured out of the ground—what earlier century had even a presentiment that such productive forces slumbered in the lap of social labour?

We see then: the means of production and of exchange, on whose foundation the bourgeoisie built itself up, were generated in feudal society. At a certain stage in the development of these means of production and of exchange, the conditions under which feudal society produced and exchanged, the feudal organization of agriculture and manufacturing industry, in one word, the feudal relations of property became no longer compatible with the already developed productive forces; they became so many fetters. They had to be burst asunder; they were burst asunder.

Into their place stepped free competition, accompanied by a social and political constitution adapted to it, and by the economic and political sway of the bourgeois class.

A similar movement is going on before our own eyes. Modern bourgeois society with its relations of production, of exchange and of property, a society that has conjured up such gigantic means of production and of exchange, is like the sorcerer who is no longer able to control the powers of the nether world whom he has called up by his spells. For many a decade past the history of industry and commerce is but the history of the revolt of modern productive forces against modern conditions of production, against the property relations that are the conditions for the existence of the bourgeoisie and of its rule. It is enough to mention the commercial crises that by their periodical return put the existence of the entire bourgeois society on its trial, each time more threateningly. In these crises a great part not only of the existing products, but also of the previously created productive forces, are periodically destroyed. In these crises there breaks out an epidemic that, in all earlier epochs, would have seemed an absurdity—the epidemic of over-production. Society suddenly finds itself put back into a state of momentary barbarism; it appears as if a famine, a universal war of devastation had cut off the supply of every means of subsistence; industry and commerce seem to be destroyed. And why? Because there is too much civilization, too much means of subsistence, too much industry, too much commerce. The productive forces at the disposal of society no longer tend to further the development of the conditions of bourgeois property; on the contrary, they have become too powerful for these conditions, by which they are fettered, and so soon as they overcome these fetters, they bring disorder into the whole of bourgeois society, endanger the existence of bourgeois property. The conditions of bourgeois society are too narrow to comprise the wealth created by them. And how does the bourgeoisie get over these crises? On the one hand, by enforced destruction of a mass of productive forces; on the other, by the conquest of new markets, and by the more thorough exploitation of the old ones. That is to say, by paving the way for more extensive and more destructive crises, and by diminishing the means whereby crises are prevented.

The weapons with which the bourgeoisie felled feudalism to the ground are now turned against the bourgeoisie itself.

But not only has the bourgeoisie forged the weapons that bring death to itself; it has also called into existence the men who are to wield those weapons—the modern working class—the proletarians.

In proportion as the bourgeoisie, i.e. capital, is developed, in the same proportion is the proletariat, the modern working class, developed—a class of labourers, who live only so long as they find work, and who find work only so long as their labour increases capital. These labourers, who must sell themselves piecemeal, are a commodity, like every other article of commerce, and are consequently exposed to all the vicissitudes of competition, to all the fluctuations of the market.

Owing to the extensive use of machinery and to division of labour, the work of the proletarians has lost all individual character, and, consequently, all charm for the workman. He becomes an appendage of the machine, and it is only the most simple, most monotonous, and most easily acquired knack, that is required of him. Hence, the cost of production of a workman is restricted, almost entirely, to the means of subsistence that he requires for his maintenance, and for the propagation of his race. But the price of a commodity, and therefore also of labour, is equal to its cost of production. In proportion, therefore, as the repulsiveness of the work increases, the wage decreases. Nay more, in proportion as the use of machinery and division of labour increases, in the same proportion the burden of toil also increases, whether by prolongation of the working hours, by increase of the work exacted in a given time, or by increased speed of the machinery, etc.

Modern industry has converted the little workshop of the patriarchal master into the great factory of the industrial capitalist. Masses of labourers, crowded into the factory, are organized like soldiers. As privates of the industrial army they are placed under the command of a perfect hierarchy of officers and sergeants. Not only are they slaves of the bourgeois class, and of the bourgeois state, they are daily and hourly enslaved by the machine, by the overlooker, and, above all, by the individual bourgeois manufacturer himself. The more openly this despotism proclaims gain to be its end and aim, the more petty, the more hateful and the more embittering it is.

The less the skill and exertion of strength implied in manual labour, in other words, the more modern industry becomes developed, the more is the labour of men superseded by that of women. Differences of age and sex have no longer any distinctive social validity for the working class. All are instruments of labour, more or less expensive to use, according to their age and sex.

No sooner is the exploitation of the labourer by the manufacturer, so far at an end, that he receives his wages in cash, than he is set upon by the other portions of the bourgeoisie, the landlord, the shopkeeper, the pawnbroker, etc.

The lower strata of the middle class—the small tradespeople, shopkeepers, and retired tradesmen generally, the handicraftsmen and peasants—all these sink gradually into the proletariat, partly because their diminutive capital does not suffice for the scale on which modern industry is carried on, and is swamped in the competition with the large capitalists, partly because their specialized skill is rendered worthless by new methods of production. Thus the proletariat is recruited from all classes of the population.

The proletariat goes through various stages of development. With its birth begins its struggle with the bourgeoisie. At first the contest is carried on by individual labourers, then by the work people of a factory, then by the operatives of one trade, in one locality, against the individual bourgeois who directly exploits them. They direct their attacks not against the bourgeois conditions of production, but against the instruments of production themselves; they destroy imported wares that compete with their labour, they smash to pieces machinery, they set factories ablaze, they seek to restore by force the vanished status of the workman of the Middle Ages.

At this stage the labourers still form an incoherent mass scattered over the whole country, and broken up by their mutual competition. If anywhere they unite to form more compact bodies, this is not yet the consequence of their own active union, but of the union of the bourgeoisie, which class, in order to attain its own political ends, is compelled to set the whole proletariat in motion, and is moreover yet, for a time, able to do so. At this stage, therefore, the proletarians do not fight their enemies, but the enemies of their enemies, the remnants of absolute monarchy, the landowners, the non-industrial bourgeois, the petty bourgeoisie. Thus the whole historical movement is concentrated in the hands of the bourgeoisie; every victory so obtained is a victory for the bourgeoisie.

But with the development of industry the proletariat not only increases in number; it becomes concentrated in greater masses, its strength grows, and it feels that strength more. The various interests and conditions of life within the ranks of the proletariat are more and more equalized, in proportion as machinery obliterates all distinctions of labour, and nearly everywhere reduces wages to the same low level. The growing competition among the bourgeois, and the resulting commercial crises, make the wages of the workers ever more fluctuating. The unceasing improvement of machinery, ever more rapidly developing, makes their livelihood more and more precarious; the collisions between individual workmen and individual bourgeois take more and more the character of collisions between two classes. Thereupon the workers begin to form combinations (trade unions) against the bourgeois; they club together in order to keep up the rate of wages; they found permanent associations in order to make provisions beforehand for these occasional revolts. Here and there the contest breaks out into riots.

Now and then the workers are victorious, but only for a time. The real fruit of their battles lies, not in the immediate result, but in the ever expanding union of the workers. This union is helped on by the improved means of communication that are created by modern industry, and that place the workers of different localities in contact with another. It was just this contact that was needed to centralize the numerous local struggles, all of the same character, into one national struggle between classes. But every class struggle is a political struggle. And that union, to attain which the burghers of the Middle Ages, with their miserable highways, required centuries, the modern proletarians, thanks to railways, achieve in a few years.

This organization of the proletarians into a class, and consequently into a political party, is continually being upset again by the competition between the workers themselves. But it ever rises up again, stronger, firmer, mightier. It compels legislative recognition of particular interests of the workers, by taking advantage of the divisions among the bourgeoisie itself. Thus the Ten-Hours Bill in England was carried.

Altogether, collisions between the classes of the old society further in many ways the course of development of the proletariat. The bourgeoisie finds itself involved in a constant battle. At first with the aristocracy; later on, with those portions of the bourgeoisie itself, whose interests have become antagonistic to the progress of industry; at all times with the bourgeoisie of foreign countries. In all these battles it sees itself compelled to appeal to the proletariat, to ask for its help, and thus, to drag it into the political arena. The bourgeoisie itself, therefore, supplies the proletariat with its own elements of political and general education, in other words, it furnishes the proletariat with weapons for fighting the bourgeoisie.

Further, as we have already seen, entire sections of the ruling classes are, by the advance of industry, precipitated into the proletariat, or are at least threatened in their conditions of existence. These also supply the proletariat with fresh elements of enlightenment and progress.

Finally, in times when the class struggle nears the decisive hour, the process of dissolution going on within the ruling class, in fact within the whole range of old society, assumes such a violent, glaring character, that a small section of the ruling class cuts itself adrift, and joins the revolutionary class, the class that holds the future in its hands. Just as, therefore, at an earlier period, a section of the nobility went over to the bourgeoisie, so now a portion of the bourgeoisie goes over to the proletariat, and in particular, a portion of the bourgeois ideologists, who have raised themselves to the level of comprehending theoretically the historical movement as a whole.

Of all the classes that stand face to face with the bourgeoisie today, the proletariat alone is a really revolutionary class. The other classes decay and finally disappear in the face of modern industry; the proletariat is its special and essential product.

The lower middle class, the small manufacturer, the shopkeeper, the artisan, the peasant, all these fight against the bourgeoisie, to save from extinction their existence as fractions of the middle class. They are therefore not revolutionary, but conservative. Nay, more, they are reactionary, for they try to roll back the wheel of history. If by chance they are revolutionary, they are so only in view of their impending transfer into the proletariat; they thus defend not their present, but their future interests; they desert their own standpoint to place themselves at that of the proletariat.

The "dangerous class," the social scum, that passively rotting mass thrown off by the lowest layers of old society, may, here and there, be swept into the movement by a proletarian revolution; its conditions of life, however, prepare it far more for the part of a bribed tool of reactionary intrigue.

In the conditions of the proletariat, those of old society at large are already virtually swamped. The proletarian is without property; his relation to his wife and children has no longer anything in common with the bourgeois family relations; modern industrial labour, modern subjection to capital, the same in England as in France, in America as in Germany, has stripped him of every trace of national character. Law, morality, religion, are to him so many bourgeois prejudices, behind which lurk in ambush just as many bourgeois interests.

All the preceding classes that got the upper hand, sought to fortify their already acquired status by subjecting society at large to their conditions of appropriation. The proletarians cannot become masters of the productive forces of society, except by abolishing their own previous mode of appropriation, and thereby also every other previous mode of appropriation. They have nothing of their own to secure and to fortify; their mission is to destroy all previous securities for, and insurances of, individual property.

All previous historical movements were movements of minorities, or in the interest of minorities. The proletarian movement is the self-conscious, independent movement of the immense majority, in the interest of the immense majority. The proletariat, the lowest stratum of our present society, cannot stir, cannot raise itself up, without the whole superincumbent strata of official society being sprung into the air.

Though not in substance, yet in form, the struggle of the proletariat with the bourgeoisie is at first a national struggle. The proletariat of each country must, of course, first of all settle matters with its own bourgeoisie.

In depicting the most general phases of the development of the proletariat, we traced the more or less veiled civil war, raging within existing society, up to the point where that war breaks out into open revolution, and where the violent overthrow of the bourgeoisie lays the foundation for the sway of the proletariat.

Hitherto, every form of society has been based, as we have already seen, on the antagonism of oppressing and oppressed classes. But in order to oppress a class, certain conditions must be assured to it under which it can, at least, continue its slavish existence. The serf, in the period of serfdom, raised himself to membership in the commune, just as the petty bourgeois, under the yoke of feudal absolutism, managed to develop into a bourgeois. The modern labourer, on the contrary, instead of rising with the progress of industry, sinks deeper and deeper below the conditions of existence of his own class. He becomes a pauper, and pauperism develops more rapidly than population and wealth. And here it becomes evident that the bourgeoisie is unfit any longer to be the ruling class in society, and to impose its conditions of existence upon society as an overriding law. It is unfit to rule because it is incompetent to assure an existence to its slave within his slavery, because it cannot help letting him sink into such a state, that it has to feed him, instead of being fed by him. Society can no longer live under this bourgeoisie, in other words, its existence is no longer compatible with society.

The essential condition for the existence and for the sway of the bourgeois class is the formation and augmentation of capital; the condition for capital is wage labour. Wage labour rests exclusively on competition between the labourers. The advance of industry, whose involuntary promoter is the bourgeoisie, replaces the isolation of the labourers, due to competition, by their revolutionary combination, due to association. The development of modern industry, therefore, cuts from under its feet the very foundation on which the bourgeoisie produces and appropriates products. What the bourgeoisie therefore produces, above all, are its own grave-diggers. Its fall and the victory of the proletariat are equally inevitable.

II. Proletarians and Communists

In what relation do the Communists stand to the proletarians as a whole?

The Communists do not form a separate party opposed to other working-class parties.

They have no interests separate and apart from those of the proletariat as a whole.

They do not set up any sectarian principles of their own, by which to shape and mould the proletarian movement.

The Communists are distinguished from the other working-class parties by this only: (1) In the national struggles of the proletarians of the different countries, they point out and bring to the front the common interests of the entire proletariat, independently of all nationality. (2) In the various stages of development which the struggle of the working class against the bourgeoisie has to pass through, they always and everywhere represent the interests of the movement as a whole.

The Communists, therefore, are on the one hand, practically, the most advanced and resolute section of the working-class parties of every country, that section which pushes forward all others; on the other hand, theoretically, they have over the great mass of the proletariat the advantage of clearly understanding the lines of march, the conditions, and the ultimate general results of the proletarian movement.

The immediate aim of the Communists is the same as that of all other proletarian parties: Formation of the proletariat into a class, overthrow of the bourgeois supremacy, conquest of political power by the proletariat.

The theoretical conclusions of the Communists are in no way based on ideas or principles that have been invented, or discovered, by this or that would-be universal reformer.

They merely express, in general terms, actual relations springing from an existing class struggle, from a historical movement going on under our very eyes. The abolition of existing property relations is not at all a distinctive feature of communism.

All property relations in the past have continually been subject to historical change consequent upon the change in historical conditions.

The French Revolution, for example, abolished feudal property in favour of bourgeois property.

The distinguishing feature of communism is not the abolition of property generally, but the abolition of bourgeois property. But modern bourgeois private property is the final and most complete expression of the system of producing and appropriating products that is based on class antagonisms, on the exploitation of the many by the few.

In this sense, the theory of the Communists may be summed up in the single sentence: Abolition of private property.

We Communists have been reproached with the desire of abolishing the right of personally acquiring property as the fruit of a man's own labour, which property is alleged to be the groundwork of all personal freedom, activity and independence.

Hard-won, self-acquired, self-earned property! Do you mean the property of the petty artisan and of the small peasant, a form of property that preceded the bourgeois form? There is no need to abolish that; the development of industry has to a great extent already destroyed it, and is still destroying it daily.

Or do you mean modern bourgeois private property?

But does wage labour create any property for the labourer? Not a bit. It creates capital, i.e. that kind of property which exploits wage labour, and which cannot increase except upon conditions of begetting a new supply of wage labour for fresh exploitation. Property, in its present form, is based on the antagonism of capital and wage labour. Let us examine both sides of this antagonism.

To be a capitalist is to have not only a purely personal, but a social, *status* in production. Capital is a collective product, and only by the united action of many members, nay, in the last resort, only by the united action of all members of society, can it be set in motion.

Capital is therefore not a personal, it is a social power.

When, therefore, capital is converted into common property, into the property of all members of society, personal property is not thereby transformed into social property. It is only the social character of the property that is changed. It loses its class character.

Let us now take wage labour.

The average price of wage labour is the minimum wage, i.e. that quantum of the means of subsistence which is absolutely requisite to keep the labourer in bare existence as a labourer. What, therefore, the wage labourer appropriates by means of his labour, merely suffices to prolong and reproduce a bare existence. We by no means intend to abolish this personal appropriation of the products of labour, an appropriation that is made for the maintenance and reproduction of human life, and that leaves no surplus wherewith to command the labour of others. All that we want to do away with is the miserable character of this appropriation, under which the labourer lives merely to increase capital, and is allowed to live only in so far as the interest of the ruling class requires it.

In bourgeois society, living labour is but a means to increase accumulated labour. In communist society, accumulated labour is but a means to widen, to enrich, to promote the existence of the labourer.

In bourgeois society, therefore, the past dominates the present; in communist society, the present dominates the past. In bourgeois society capital is independent and has individuality, while the living person is dependent and has no individuality.

And the abolition of this state of things is called by the bourgeois, abolition of individuality and freedom! And rightly so. The abolition of bourgeois individuality, bourgeois independence, and bourgeois freedom is undoubtedly aimed at.

By freedom is meant, under the present bourgeois conditions of production, free trade, free selling and buying.

But if selling and buying disappears, free selling and buying disappears also. This talk about free selling and buying, and all the other "brave words" of our bourgeoisie about freedom in general, have a meaning, if any, only in contrast with restricted selling and buying, with the fettered traders of the Middle Ages, but have no meaning when opposed to the communist abolition of buying and selling, of the bourgeois conditions of production, and of the bourgeoisie itself.

You are horrified at our intending to do away with private property. But in your existing society, private property is already done away with for nine-tenths of the population; its existence for the few is solely due to its non-existence in the hands of those nine-tenths. You reproach us, therefore, with intending to do away with a form of property, the necessary condition for whose existence is the non-existence of any property for the immense majority of society.

In one word, you reproach us with intending to do away with your property. Precisely so; that is just what we intend.

From the moment when labour can no longer be converted into capital, money or rent, into a social power capable of being monopolized, i.e. from the moment when individual property can no longer be transformed into bourgeois property, into capital, from that moment, you say, individuality vanishes.

You must, therefore, confess that by "individual" you mean no other person than the bourgeois, than the middle-class owner of property. This person must, indeed, be swept out of the way, and made impossible.

Communism deprives no man of the power to appropriate the products of society; all that it does is to deprive him of the power to subjugate the labour of others by means of such appropriation.

It has been objected, that upon the abolition of private property all work will cease, and universal laziness will overtake us.

According to this, bourgeois society ought long ago to have gone to the dogs through sheer idleness; for those of its members who work acquire nothing, and those who acquire anything do not work. The whole of this objection is but another expression of the tautology: There can no longer be any wage labour when there is no longer any capital.

All objections urged against the communistic mode of producing and appropriating material products, have, in the same way, been urged against the communistic modes of producing and appropriating intellectual products. Just as to the bourgeois, the disappearance of class property is the disappearance of production itself, so the disappearance of class culture is to him identical with the disappearance of all culture.

That culture, the loss of which he laments, is, for the enormous majority, a mere training to act as a machine.

But don't wrangle with us so long as you apply, to our intended abolition of bourgeois property, the standard of your bourgeois notions of freedom, culture, law, etc. Your very ideas are but the outgrowth of the conditions of your bourgeois production and bourgeois property, just as your jurisprudence is but the will of your class made into a law for all, a will whose essential character and direction are determined by the economical conditions of existence of your class.

The selfish misconception that induces you to transform into eternal laws of nature and of reason, the social forms springing from your present mode of production and form of property—historical relations that rise and disappear in the progress of production—this misconception you share with every ruling class that has preceded you. What you see clearly in the case of ancient property, what you admit in the case of feudal property, you are of course forbidden to admit in the case of your own bourgeois form of property.

Abolition of the family! Even the most radical flare up at this infamous proposal of the Communists.

On what foundation is the present family, the bourgeois family, based? On capital, on private gain. In its completely developed form this family exists only among the bourgeoisie. But this state of things finds its complement in the practical absence of the family among proletarians, and in public prostitution.

The bourgeois family will vanish as a matter of course when its complement vanishes, and both will vanish with the vanishing of capital.

Do you charge us with wanting to stop the exploitation of children by their parents? To this crime we plead guilty.

But, you will say, we destroy the most hallowed of relations, when we replace home education by social.

And your education! Is not that also social, and determined by the social conditions under which you educate, by the intervention direct or indirect, of society, by means of schools, etc.? The

Communists have not invented the intervention of society in education; they do but seek to alter the character of that intervention, and to rescue education from the influence of the ruling class.

The bourgeois claptrap about the family and education, about the hallowed correlation of parent and child, becomes all the more disgusting, the more, by the action of modern industry, all family ties among the proletarians are torn asunder, and their children transformed into simple articles of commerce and instruments of labour.

But you Communists would introduce community of women, screams the whole bourgeoisie in chorus.

The bourgeois sees in his wife a mere instrument of production. He hears that the instruments of production are to be exploited in common, and, naturally, can come to no other conclusion than that the lot of being common to all will likewise fall to the women.

He has not even a suspicion that the real point aimed at is to do away with the status of women as mere instruments of production.

For the rest, nothing is more ridiculous than the virtuous indignation of our bourgeois at the community of women which, they pretend, is to be openly and officially established by the Communists. The Communists have no need to introduce community of women; it has existed almost from time immemorial.

Our bourgeois, not content with having wives and daughters of their proletarians at their disposal, not to speak of common prostitutes, take the greatest pleasure in seducing each other's wives.

Bourgeois marriage is in reality a system of wives in common and thus, at the most, what the Communists might possibly be reproached with is that they desire to introduce, in substitution for a hypocritically concealed, an openly legalized community of women. For the rest, it is self-evident that the abolition of the present system of production must bring with it the abolition of the community of women springing from that system, i.e. of prostitution both public and private.

The Communists are further reproached with desiring to abolish countries and nationality.

The working men have no country. We cannot take from them what they have not got. Since the proletariat must first of all acquire political supremacy, must rise to be the leading class of the nation, must constitute itself the nation, it is, so far, itself national, though not in the bourgeois sense of the word.

National differences and antagonism between peoples are daily more and more vanishing, owing to the development of the bourgeoisie, to freedom of commerce, to the world market, to uniformity in the mode of production and in the conditions of life corresponding thereto.

The supremacy of the proletariat will cause them to vanish still faster. United action of the leading civilized countries at least, is one of the first conditions for the emancipation of the proletariat.

In proportion as the exploitation of one individual by another is put an end to, the exploitation of one nation by another will also be put an end to. In proportion as the antagonism between classes within the nation vanishes, the hostility of one nation to another will come to an end.

The charges against communism made from a religious, a philosophical and, generally, from an ideological standpoint, are not deserving of serious examination.

Does it require deep intuition to comprehend that man's ideas, views, and conceptions, in one word, man's consciousness, changes with every change in the conditions of his material existence, in his social relations and in his social life?

What else does the history of ideas prove, than that intellectual production changes its character in proportion as material production is changed? The ruling ideas of each age have ever been the ideas of its ruling class.

When people speak of ideas that revolutionize society, they do but express the fact that within the old society the elements of a new one have been created, and that the dissolution of the old ideas keeps even pace with the dissolution of the old conditions of existence.

When the ancient world was in its last throes, the ancient religions were overcome by Christianity. When Christian ideas succumbed in the eighteenth century to rationalist ideas, feudal society fought its death battle with the then revolutionary bourgeoisie. The ideas of religious liberty and freedom of conscience, merely gave expression to the sway of free competition within the domain of knowledge.

"Undoubtedly," it will be said, "religious, moral, philosophical and juridical ideas have been modified in the course of historical development. But religion, morality, philosophy, political science, and law, constantly survived this change."

"There are, besides, eternal truths, such as Freedom, Justice, etc., that are common to all states of society. But communism abolishes eternal truths, it abolishes all religion, and all morality, instead of constituting them on a new basis; it therefore acts in contradiction to all past historical experience."

What does this accusation reduce itself to? The history of all past society has consisted in the development of class antagonisms, antagonisms that assumed different forms at different epochs.

But whatever form they may have taken, one fact is common to all past ages, viz., the exploitation of one part of society by the other. No wonder, then, that the social consciousness of past ages, despite all the multiplicity and variety it displays, moves within certain common forms, or general ideas, which cannot completely vanish except with the total disappearance of class antagonisms.

The communist revolution is the most radical rupture with traditional relations; no wonder that its development involves the most radical rupture with traditional ideas.

But let us have done with the bourgeois objections to communism.

We have seen above that the first step in the revolution by the working class is to raise the proletariat to the position of ruling class to win the battle of democracy.

The proletariat will use its political supremacy to wrest, by degrees, all capital from the bourgeoisie, to centralize all instruments of production in the hands of the state, i.e. of the proletariat organized as the ruling class; and to increase the total of productive forces as rapidly as possible.

Of course, in the beginning, this cannot be effected except by means of despotic inroads on the rights of property, and on the conditions of bourgeois production; by means of measures, therefore, which appear economically insufficient and untenable, but which, in the course of the movement, outstrip themselves, necessitate further inroads upon the old order, and are unavoidable as a means of entirely revolutionizing the mode of production.

These measures will of course be different in different countries.

Nevertheless, in the most advanced countries, the following will be pretty generally applicable.

1. Abolition of property in land and application of all rents of land to public purposes.

2. A heavy progressive or graduated income tax.

3. Abolition of all right of inheritance.

4. Confiscation of the property of all emigrants and rebels.

5. Centralization of credit in the hands of the state, by means of a national bank with state capital and an exclusive monopoly.

6. Centralization of the means of communication and transport in the hands of the state.

7. Extension of factories and instruments of production owned by the state; the bringing into cultivation of waste lands, and the improvement of the soil generally in accordance with a common plan.

8. Equal obligation of all to work. Establishment of industrial armies, especially for agriculture.

9. Combination of agriculture with manufacturing industries; gradual abolition of all the distinction between town and country by a more equable distribution of the population over the country.

10. Free education for all children in public schools. Abolition of children's factory labour in its present form. Combination of education with industrial production, etc.

When, in the course of development, class distinctions have disappeared, and all production has been concentrated in the hands of a vast association of the whole nation, the public power will lose its political character. Political power, properly so called, is merely the organized power of one class for oppressing another. If the proletariat during its contest with the bourgeoisie is compelled, by the force of circumstances, to organize itself as a class; if, by means of a revolution, it makes itself the ruling class, and, as such, sweeps away by force the old conditions of production, then it will, along with these conditions, have swept away the conditions for the existence of class antagonisms and of classes generally, and will thereby have abolished its own supremacy as a class.

In place of the old bourgeois society, with its classes and class antagonisms, we shall have an association in which the free development of each is the condition for the free development of all.

[Part III, omitted here, criticizes other radical movements of the day.]

IV. Position of the Communist in Relation To the Various Existing Opposition Parties

. . . .

The Communists fight for the attainment of the immediate aims, for the enforcement of the momentary interests of the working class; but in the movement of the present they also represent and take care of the future of that movement. In France the Communists ally themselves with the Social-Democrats[5] against the conservative and radical bourgeoisie, reserving, however, the right to take up a critical position in regard to phrases and illusions traditionally handed down from the Great Revolution.

In Switzerland they support the Radicals, without losing sight of the fact that this party consists of antagonistic elements, partly of Democratic Socialists, in the French sense, partly of radical bourgeois.

In Poland they support the party that insists on an agrarian revolution as the prime condition for national emancipation,

5. The party then represented in Parliament by Ledru-Rollin, in literature by Louis Blanc (1811-82), in the daily press by the *Réforme*. The name of Social-Democracy signifies, with these its inventors, a section of the Democratic or Republican Party more or less tinged with socialism. [K. M.]

that party which fomented the insurrection of Cracow in 1846.

In Germany they fight with the bourgeoisie whenever it acts in a revolutionary way, against the absolute monarchy, the feudal squirearchy, and the petty-bourgeoisie.

But they never cease, for a single instant, to instil into the working class the clearest possible recognition of the hostile antagonism between bourgeoisie and proletariat, in order that the German workers may straightway use, as so many weapons against the bourgeoisie, the social and political conditions that the bourgeoisie must necessarily introduce along with its supremacy, and in order that, after the fall of the reactionary classes in Germany, the fight against the bourgeoisie itself may immediately begin.

The Communists turn their attention chiefly to Germany, because that country is on the eve of a bourgeois revolution that is bound to be carried out under more advanced conditions of European civilization and with a much more developed proletariat than that of England in the seventeenth, and of France in the eighteenth century, and because the bourgeois revolution in Germany will be but the prelude to an immediately following proletarian revolution.[6]

In short, the Communists everywhere support every revolutionary movement against the existing social and political order of things.

In all these movements they bring to the front, as the leading question in each, the property question, no matter what its degree of development at the time.

Finally, they labour everywhere for the union and agreement of the democratic parties of all countries.

The Communists disdain to conceal their views and aims. They openly declare that their ends can be attained only by the forcible overthrow of all existing social conditions. Let the ruling classes tremble at a communist revolution. The proletarians have nothing to lose but their chains. They have a world to win.

Working men of all countries, unite!

6. Revolution did break out in Germany a few weeks after *The Communist Manifesto* was written; but the revolutionaries failed to attain their goals and proletarian revolution did not ensue.

How To Head Off Proletarian Revolution

Otto von Bismarck (1815–98) was the principal maker of late nineteenth-century Germany. Born to a noble family, the young Bismarck entered the Prussian diplomatic service. In 1862 he became President of the Prussian cabinet when the King could not get a parliamentary majority to support an increase in appropriations for the army. Bismarck defied the constitution, and disregarded the parliamentary majority. At the same time he skilfully angled for popular support and achieved an overwhelming success when, through two short, victorious wars, he made Prussia the core of a new German empire, formed in 1871 by a federation among all the remaining German states (except Austria).

As Chancellor of the new German Empire and as President of the Prussian Council of Ministers, Bismarck continued to dominate German political affairs until 1890. Many of the Liberals who had opposed him in 1862–66 later came around to support his method of uniting Germany; but in 1879 he broke with them again. This time the issue was economic. Bismarck, together with landowners in eastern Germany and some industrialists in western Germany, wished to establish a protective tariff; his Liberal opponents rejected this step on grounds of economic theory and political principle.

To rally support, Bismarck came to terms with the Catholic "Center" party, and used an attempted assassination of the Emperor to push through a series of laws against the Socialists, who were beginning to win considerable support among German workmen employed in the mines and factories that were rising very rapidly as Germany industrialized. Many Liberals were fearful of the Socialists, who from 1875 adopted a more or less Marxian program. Hence in attacking the Socialists, Bismarck expected to weaken Liberal opposition to his tariff and other policies.

It was against this general background that the government introduced a law in 1884 proposing to make insurance against sickness and accident compulsory for factory workers. The state was to be the insuring agency, collecting premiums and paying out benefits. This ran counter to Liberal principles favoring private enterprise and economic freedom. Socialists (who in spite of the Socialist laws were able to elect representatives to the Imperial Parliament) also were critical, arguing that the proposed law was too little to really help the workers very much.

Toward the end of the debate on March 15, 1884, Bismarck appeared before the Parliament to defend the proposal his government was making. The following selection translates approximately two-thirds of his remarks.

The law did in fact pass, and Germany became the first European state to institute a system of compulsory workingman's insurance against sickness and accident. Long-standing "Cameralist" traditions that viewed the state and its officials as custodians of the welfare of the entire nation made it easier for Bismarck, conservative though he was, to put through this "Socialist" legislation.

OTTO VON BISMARCK: SPEECH ON THE LAW FOR WORKMEN'S COMPENSATION INSURANCE, 1884

If in the general debate I speak about the matter under discussion, it cannot be my intention to enter into exhaustive discourse about the whole of the subject which concerns us, and even less to anticipate in any way the special debate over the great number of items which the proposal contains. I consider it necessary, however, to say a few words concerning the position of the united governments[1] with respect to the genesis of the present proposal and to the intentions which unite them to the bill. Indeed, I shall connect my remarks to a discussion of those objections which were made in the previous debate against the principle of the law in general in order to find a guide.

I turn first to the remarks of the speaker, Representative v. Vollmar,[2] . . .

Representative v. Vollmar avowed a certain satisfaction,

Translated by John W. Boyer from *Verhandlingen der Reichstages* IV Session 1884, Vol. LXXV (Berlin, 1884), pp. 72-8. Reprinted by permission of translator.

1. I.e., the government of Prussia and the government of the German empire. Bismarck was chief minister of both.

2. Georg Heinrich von Vollmar (1850-1922), German Social Democratic leader.

which was not free from malicious pleasure, that the ambitious socialist intentions which may have been the basis of the first version of this proposal had disappeared. Yes, gentlemen, but this is only seemingly the case . . . that which we refrain today from presenting has not been consigned to the fire, but only put back in reserve. We have to explore a *terra incognita*. This field of legislation was first entered by Germany in 1871 with the law on liability. . . . At that time we finally convinced ourselves that difficulties become greater with the widening of the front on which we appear, while attempting to march through the narrow gate of your consent. We have limited ourselves—and to be sure on my own motion, and therefore, I believe it my duty to comment on this matter—to the most restricted, necessary scope . . . we do not lend ourselves to the intention of discarding and not considering the remaining occupational groups, but we wish only to be on guard against those dangers to which the proverb alludes, that the better is the enemy of the good. When one attempts too much at one time, one runs the danger of achieving nothing. I wish that we and the present Reichstag might have the honour at least to do something, and at least make a first beginning in this area and thereby take the lead among European states. Restraint is justified by the consideration that the wider and more comprehensive the proposal is, so much more are diverse interests affected, . . . so that the acceptance of the law becomes that much the more difficult. . . .

Representative v. Vollmar has expressed his astonishment that . . . we are making new and different proposals. Gentlemen, that is not our fault. Yesterday Representative Bamberger[3] compared the business of government with that of a cobbler who measures shoes, which he thereupon examines as to whether they are suitable for him or not and accordingly accepts or rejects them. I am by no means dissatisfied with this humble comparison, by which you place the united governments in the perspective of a shoemaker taking measurements for Herr Bamberger. The profession of government in the sense of Frederick the Great is to serve the people, and may it be also as a cobbler; the

3. Ludwig Bamberger (1823-99), banker and co-founder of the Liberal Party.

opposite is to dominate the people. We want to serve the people. But I make the demand on Herr Bamberger that he act as my co-shoemaker in order to make sure that no member of the public goes barefoot, and to create a suitable shoe for the people.

(Bravo!)

Up to now I find that lacking.

Representative v. Vollmar then proceeded to the connection in which he brings our proposal with the Socialist Law.[4] It is not correct, as he conceives it, that we made the proposal in order to win more support for the Socialist Law. There is, indeed, a connection, but it is quite different. At the time of the submission of the Socialist Law the government and particularly His Majesty the Emperor and, if I am not in error, also the majority of the Reichstag, underwrote certain promissory notes for the future and gave assurances that as a corollary to this Socialist Law a serious effort for the betterment of the fate of the workers should go hand in hand. In my opinion that is the complement to the Socialist Law; and if you have decided persistently not to improve the situation of the workers, then I understand that you reject the Socialist Law. For it is an injustice on the one hand to hinder the self-defense of a numerous class of our fellow citizens and on the other hand not to offer them aid for the redress of that which causes the dissatisfaction. That the Social Democratic leaders wish no advantage for this law, that I understand; they need dissatisfied workers. They are committed to taking power, and the necessary prerequisite for that is a countless dissatisfied class. They must oppose naturally any attempt of the government, however well intentioned it may be, to remedy this situation, if they do not wish to lose control over the masses they mislead.

Therefore, on the objections which come from the leaders of the Social Democrats I place no value; on the objections which come from the workers in general, I would put a very high value. Our workers, God be praised, are not all Social Democrats and are not by and large unreceptive to the efforts of the united

4. A law passed 1878 which made the Social Democratic party illegal, though this did not prevent members of the party from being elected to the Reichstag.

governments to help them. Perhaps also they note the difficulties which these efforts meet in the sphere of the Parliament. The Parliament had indeed the right to prevent any progress on our legislation; you have the absolute veto with regard to legislation and through the uncontrolled exercise of this veto, you can certainly paralyse legislation, whether it be because you oppose the government on principle, or whether you do so only tactically, but regularly in each individual case. . . . The parliamentary element, if it is used only as an obstacle, if proof is provided to the people that it refuses its cooperation to the benevolent intentions of the government, that it has only a simple "No," that it makes no attempt to help the government—that must of course to a high degree prove self-destructive and self-diminishing. This I would consider a great misfortune, since I don't know how we could compensate for that. I in no way support an absolutist government. I believe properly exercised parliamentary cooperation to be as necessary and as useful as I consider parliamentary control damaging and impossible.

(Bravo, from the Right)

Parliament should be capable of preventing evil; it should be able to set its veto against the dangers which can be associated with a monarchist government. It must oppose wastefulness, bureaucratic narrowness, the complications of red tape, and systems of protection. . . . It should be able to prevent bad laws from being passed, it should be capable of hindering the squandering of money; but rule, gentlemen, that it cannot do. I do not wish to enter into particulars over this; there will be another opportunity to give a lecture on fundamental conceptions in this connection.

I do not know what one would set in the place of the parliament in order to guard against the dangers which would surround a non-parliamentary government, without any publicity or freedom of the press. I suggest that in complete seriousness. . . .

[The real question is] whether the State—by State I always mean the Empire—whether the State has the right to abandon to chance the performance of a responsibility of the State, namely, to protect the worker from accidents and need when he is injured or becomes old, in order to permit private companies to take premiums from the workers and the employers so as to make a profit as high as they can possibly achieve. . . . As soon as the State concerns itself, however, with these matters at all—and I believe that it is the State's duty to concern itself—it must strive for the cheapest form and must for its own part take no advantage from this, and never lose sight of the benefit of the poor and the needy above all. Otherwise one ought to relinquish the fulfillment of definite State duties, such as care of the poor, in the widest sense of the word, as well as schools and national defense . . . to private stock companies. . . . In the same way one can continue to believe that the whole of the State's responsibility must be relinquished to the voluntary formation of stock companies. The whole problem is established in the question: does the State have the responsibility to care for its destitute fellow citizens, or does it not? I maintain that it does have this duty, and to be sure, not simply the Christian State, as I once permitted myself to allude to with the words "practical Christianity," but rather every State by its very nature. It would be madness for a corporate body or a commonality to take charge of those objectives which the individual can accomplish; but those goals which the community can fulfill with justice and profit should be relinquished to the community. There are objectives which only the State in its totality can fulfill. . . . Among the last mentioned objectives of the State belong the national defense, and the general system of transportation. . . . To these belongs also the help of persons in distress and the prevention of such justified complaints as in fact provide excellent material for exploitation by the Social Democrats. That is the responsibility of the State from which the State will not be able to withdraw in the long run.

If one argues against my position that this is socialism, then I do not fear that at all. The question is, where do the justifiable limits of State Socialism lie? Without such a boundary we could not manage our affairs. Each law for poor relief is socialism. There are states, which hold themselves so far from socialism, that poor laws do not exist at all. I remind you of France. From these conditions in France the theories of the remarkable social politician, Léon Say,[5] whom Herr Bamberger referred to, are completely accounted for. This man expresses the French view that every French citizen has the right to starve, and that the State has no responsibility to hinder him in the exercise of his right.

(Hear, hear! on the Right).

You see also that for many years, ever since the government of the July Monarchy,[6] social conditions in France have been unsettled, and I believe that France will not be able in the long run to avoid promoting somewhat more state socialism than it has up to now. Was not also, for example, the Stein–Hardenberg legislation[7] of glorious memory state socialism, the constitutional justification and appropriateness of which today no one doubts anymore? Is there a stronger state socialism than when the law declares: I take away from the property owner a definite part of his real estate and transfer it to tenant farmers, whom he had on the property up to that point? . . . Whoever censures state socialism completely must also repudiate the Stein–Hardenberg legislation. He must refuse the State the right, whenever law and privilege bind as a chain and . . . hinder our free breathing, to cut with the knife of the surgeon, in order to create healthy conditions. . . .

I can pass over in general to the comments of Representative Bamberger because he has summed up the preceding speakers and can therefore serve as a guide. The Representative mentioned in the introduction to his speech that "yesterday—once again as a prelude to the day's agenda the danger and reprehensibleness of any opposition was indicated." Gentlemen, it is not correct to so characterize my position towards the matter as if I had treated any opposition as contemptible. I have only refused on my part to cooperate with the goals of the opposition; my whole speech at that time can be summarized in the sentence: I do not wish to allow myself to be harnessed to the triumphant wagon of the opposition. I myself have been in the opposition during

5. Jean Baptiste Léon Say (1826-96), French Liberal; Finance Minister in four cabinets between 1872 and 1882.

6. Established 1830.

7. Laws abolishing serfdom in Prussia, 1807-8.

my life under other ministries. . . . In my opinion, a primary reason for the success which the leaders of the real Social Democracy have had with their never clearly defined future goals lies in the fact that the State does not sponsor enough state socialism; it allows a vacuum to form in a place where it should be active, and this is filled by others, by agitators who trespass on the State's property. . . . Representative v. Vollmar has for his own part admitted, . . . that the ideals of Social Democracy could not be implemented in one individual state, but rather would only be attainable, if a general, international foundation existed. I believe that also, and therefore I believe them to be impossible, since this international basis will never exist; but even if internationalism comes some day, the interim period might be long enough to make it worth finding a *modus vivendi* which is somewhat more bearable and pleasant for the oppressed and suffering among us. We cannot be satisfied with promises which perhaps are not even payable in the next century; we must provide something which holds good for tomorrow or the next day. . . .

Representative Bamberger has objected that the proposed organization is not compatible with the word "free" and with the concept of freedom; there would be too much compulsion therein and a motto for the whole law would be: "If you aren't willing, I'll use force!" Gentlemen, freedom is a vague concept; no one has a use for the freedom to starve. But here freedom is in my opinion also not at all limited and not in contradiction with itself. The proposal desires a freedom in the organization, but it makes the accomplishment obligatory. . . .

The expression: "If you aren't willing, I'll force you" is totally unjustified. There scarcely exists nowadays a word with which more abuse is committed than with the word "free." . . .

According to my experience everyone understands by "freedom" only the freedom for oneself and not for others, as well as the responsibility of others to refrain absolutely from any limitation of the self. In short, they mean by "freedom" actually "domination"; by "freedom of speech" they understand the predominant and preponderant influence of editorial offices and of newspapers. Indeed, gentlemen,— . . . very frequently under "freedom of the Church" the domination of the priests is understood— . . . That is more strikingly illustrated in our own history than in any other. In the centuries of the decay of the German Empire, German freedom was always sharply accentuated. What was meant by that? The freedom of the princes from the Emperor, and the domination of the nobles over the serfs! For their own sakes they wanted to be free; that means "to be free" was for them and also for others identical with the concept "to dominate." They did not feel themselves to be free unless they dominated. Therefore, this word makes me suspicious whenever I read "free."

Representative Bamberger expressed subsequently his regret concerning the "socialist fad"—It is, however, a harsh expression, when one characterizes as a "socialist fad" the careful decision of the united governments in Germany, weighed for three years, which they again, for the third time, propose to you in the hope finally to obtain your approval. Perhaps the whole institution of the State is a socialist fad. If everyone could live on their own, perhaps everyone would be much more free, but also much less protected and guarded. If the Representative calls the proposal a socialist whim, I reply simply that it is untrue, and my assertion is as justified as his.

He uses further the expression that the old age and disability care were "chimerical plans!" . . . The gentlemen may excuse my expression—in that lay an arrogance of judgment. There is nothing about our proposal which is chimerical. Our proposals are completely genuine; they are the result of an existing need. . . . The fulfillment of a State responsibility is never a chimera, and as such I recognize it as a duty for legislation. It is in fact not a joyful vocation to dedicate a State cobbler service to a customer like Representative Bamberger, who treats us with contempt, and ingratitude in the face of real exertions, and who characterizes the proposal which is prepared in order to make it acceptable to you as a "whim" and a "chimera." I would like to recommend in general that we were somewhat more mild in the expressions with which we characterize our mutual efforts. . . .

When Representative Bamberger refers to the fact that for the sake of a socialist whim [the existing] system of insurance in the Empire is to be abolished, I reply: if the State occupies itself at all with accident insurance, then the present system is just too expensive. If it were strengthened, who would pay the cost? It would be at the cost of the suffering poor and at the cost of industry, whose export capability is reduced by the burdens laid upon it by [private] insurance. We, for our part, want to lighten these burdens by means of a general and, therefore, beneficent arrangement.

I believe that I have arrived at the end of the thread provided by the preceding speaker, and I have only to add the request, that you gentlemen meet the united governments half-way and serve as pathfinders in an unknown land, which we are entering. The entry into this realm we believe to be a responsibility of the State. As leaders, according to your experience and opinion, do not doubt that we are acting honorably to strengthen the inner peace of society, and particularly the peace between worker and employer. Thereby we hope we will be in the position to renounce on the part of the State a continuance of this emergency law, which we refer to as a Socialist Law, without exposing the commonwealth to new dangers.

VI

World Wars I and II

The Shock of Trench Warfare
Wilfred Owen: Poems

The Russian Recipe for Peace
Bolshevik Proclamation on Peace

The American Recipe for Peace
Woodrow Wilson: Speech

The Nation as Refuge for the Lost Soul
Benito Mussolini: The Doctrine of Fascism

The Race as Refuge for the Lost Soul
Adolf Hitler: Mein Kampf

Freedom as Cure for the World's Ills
Franklin D. Roosevelt: State of the Union, 1941

The Shock of Trench Warfare

European elites suffered a profound shock between 1914 and 1918. World War I seemed more brutal, more senseless, and more futile than any recorded war in the past; and all the nineteenth century's confidence in progress and certainty that European civilization was superior to anything that had ever been seen among men before came under more and more severe scrutiny.

A cluster of English soldier-poets voiced the somber mood created by World War I. The most accomplished of them was Wilfred Owen, born in 1893, enlisted 1915, killed in action November 4, 1918, precisely one week before the armistice ended the long slaughter. The four poems reproduced below constitute about a quarter of his published work.

WILFRED OWEN: POEMS FROM WORLD WAR I

Strange Meeting

Earth's wheels run oiled with blood. Forget we that.
Let us lie down and dig ourselves in thought.
Beauty is yours and you have mastery,
Wisdom is mine, and I have mystery.
We two will stay behind and keep our troth.
Let us forego men's minds that are brute's natures,
Let us not sup the blood which some say nurtures,
Be we not swift with swiftness of the tigress.

Let us break ranks from those who trek from progress.
Miss we the march of this retreating world
Into old citadels that are not walled.
Let us lie out and hold the open truth.
Then when their blood hath clogged the chariot wheels
We will go up and wash them from deep wells.
What though we sink from men as pitchers falling
Many shall raise us up to be their filling
Even from wells we sunk too deep for war
And filled by brows that bled where no wounds were.

The Show

My soul looked down from a vague height with Death,
As unremembering how I rose or why,
And saw a sad land, weak with sweats of dearth,
Gray, cratered like the moon with hollow woe,
And fitted with great pocks and scabs of plaques.

Across its beard, that horror of harsh wire,
There moved thin caterpillars, slowly uncoiled.
It seemed they pushed themselves to be as plugs
Of ditches, where they writhed and shrivelled, killed.

By them had slimy paths been trailed and scraped
Round myriad warts that might be little hills.

From gloom's last dregs these long-strung creatures crept,
And vanished out of dawn down hidden holes.

(And smell came up from those foul openings
As out of mouths, or deep wounds deepening.)

On dithering feet upgathered, more and more,
Brown strings towards strings of gray, with bristling spines,
All migrants from green fields, intent on mire.

Those that were gray, of more abundant spawns,
Ramped on the rest and ate them and were eaten.

I saw their bitten backs curve, loop, and straighten,
I watched those agonies curl, lift, and flatten.

Whereat, in terror what that sight might mean,
I reeled and shivered earthward like a feather.

And Death fell with me, like a deepening moan.

And He, picking a manner of worm, which half had hid

Its bruises in the earth, but crawled no further,
Showed me its feet, the feet of many men,
And the fresh-severed head of it, my head.

Insensibility

I

Happy are men who yet before they are killed
Can let their veins run cold.
Whom no compassion fleers
Or makes their feet
Sore on the alleys cobbled with their brothers.
The front line withers,
But they are troops who fade, not flowers
For poets' tearful fooling:
Men, gaps for filling
Losses who might have fought
Longer; but no one bothers.

II

And some cease feeling
Even themselves or for themselves.
Dullness best solves
The tease and doubt of shelling,
And Chance's strange arithmetic
Comes simpler than the reckoning of their shilling.
They keep no check on Armies' decimation.

III

Happy are these who lose imagination:
They have enough to carry with ammunition.
Their spirit drags no pack.
Their old wounds save with cold can not more ache.
Having seen all things red,
Their eyes are rid
Of the hurt of the colour of blood for ever.
And terror's first constriction over,
Their hearts remain small drawn.
Their senses in some scorching cautery of battle
Now long since ironed,
Can laugh among the dying, unconcerned.

IV

Happy the soldier home, with not a notion
How somewhere, every dawn, some men attack,
And many sighs are drained.
Happy the lad whose mind was never trained:
His days are worth forgetting more than not.
He sings along the march
Which we march taciturn, because of dusk,
The long, forlorn, relentless trend
From larger day to huger night.

V

We wise, who with a thought besmirch
Blood over all our soul,
How should we see our task
But through his blunt and lashless eyes?
Alive, he is not vital overmuch;
Dying, not mortal overmuch;
Nor sad, nor proud,
Nor curious at all.
He cannot tell
Old men's placidity from his.

VI

But cursed are dullards whom no cannon stuns,
That they should be as stones.
Wretched are they, and mean
With paucity that never was simplicity.
By choice they made themselves immune
To pity and whatever mourns in man
Before the last sea and the hapless stars;
Whatever mourns when many leave these shores;
Whatever shares
The eternal reciprocity of tears.

Dulce Et Decorum Est

Bent double, like old beggars under sacks,
Knock-kneed, coughing like hags, we cursed through sludge,
Till on the haunting flares we turned our backs,
And towards our distant rest began to trudge.
Men marched asleep. Many had lost their boots,

But limped on, blood-shod. All went lame, all blind;
Drunk with fatigue; deaf even to the hoots
Of gas-shells dropping softly behind.

Gas! GAS! Quick, boys!—An ecstasy of fumbling
Fitting the clumsy helmets just in time,
But someone still was yelling out and stumbling
And flound'ring like a man in fire or lime.—
Dim through the misty panes and thick green light,
As under a green sea, I saw him drowning.

In all my dreams before my helpless sight
He plunges at me, guttering, choking, drowning.

If in some smothering dreams, you too could pace
Behind the wagon that we flung him in,
And watch the white eyes writhing in his face,
His hanging face, like a devil's sick of sin,
If you could hear, at every jolt, the blood
Come gargling from the froth-corrupted lungs
Bitten as the cud
Of vile, incurable sores on innocent tongues,—
My friend, you would not tell with such high zest
To children ardent for some desperate glory,
The old Lie: *Dulce et decorum est*
Pro patria mori.[1]

1. Latin: "Sweet and proper it is to die for one's fatherland."

The Russian Recipe for Peace

Tsar Nicholas II's government proved incapable of waging a prolonged mass war of the sort that descended on Europe in 1914. Supplies of every kind soon ran short for the home front as well as for the soldiers; administrative inefficiency made things worse; and suspicion of treason in high places began to undermine morale in the Russian armies. In March 1917 revolution brought the Provisional government to power. Its members hoped to establish a democratic regime in Russia. At the same time, however, the Provisional government wished to carry the war through to victory and in collaboration with the French and British governments.

The difficulty with such a plan was that none of the shortcomings that had brought such deep discredit upon the Tsars's government had been removed by the March revolution. Supplies became even shorter; administrative efficiency continued to decay; morale in the army cracked as soldiers began to form councils (soviets) where they discussed what orders to obey. Vladimir Ilyich Ulyanov (1870–1924), better known by his pseudonym, Lenin, took full advantage of this situation to advance the cause of the party he headed. Lenin's party was called "Bolshevik," (meaning "majority" of the tiny Social Democratic party) and was committed to Marxian revolutionary ideals. When the war began in 1914, Lenin was in Switzerland. He arrived in Russia in April 1917, having been allowed to cross Germany in a sealed train because German authorities figured that his brand of revolutionary socialism would hurt the Russian war effort and improve the chances for German victory.

On his arrival in the Russian capital, Lenin quickly devised a tellingly effective slogan for the Bolsheviks: "Peace, Land, Bread." Peace appealed to almost every Russian and especially to the soldiers; land meant land for the peasants, who constituted the overwhelming majority of the Russian population as well as of the Russian army; bread meant food for the cities and especially for the poor who as proletarians were the special target of Bolshevik propaganda. This slogan had enormous appeal; even the accusation that Lenin was a German agent did not do much to check the growth of his following in the major cities of Russia and in the ranks of the army.

The authority of the Provisional government decayed as Lenin's power grew, so that when the Bolsheviks decided to organize a popular uprising, they met with very little resistance. Accordingly, on the night of November 6–7, 1917, Lenin's party took power. They did so in the name of the Soviets of Workers' and Soldiers' Deputies. These were informal councils that had arisen more or less spontaneously in factories and military units as discontent mounted against the way the war was being waged. These soviets were modeled on much older village ways of responding to emergencies by calling a meeting of all heads of households at which consensus as to what should be done emerged from highly informal procedures. The wartime soviets followed similar informal procedures, and aimed, always, at unanimity after listening to a series of self-appointed speakers. This type of organization allowed the very small number of experienced Bolshevik revolutionaries to spread their point of view among workers and soldiers very effectively—as long, at least, as the Bolshevik party line appealed to the common wishes of the delegates to the soviets.

On taking power Lenin and his fellow revolutionaries had to act on their program without delay, lest they lose the confidence of their supporters in the soviets. The Proclamation on Peace, translated below, was therefore passed on the night of November 8, within twenty-four hours of the formal seizure of power. A parallel decree on land, abolishing all private ownership of large estates without compensation, was passed at the same session of the Congress of Soviets. In this way, the Bolsheviks met the popular wish for prompt, decisive action.

Lenin and his fellow revolutionaries rejected the customary procedures of international diplomacy by bringing this proclamation before the Congress of Soviets and publicizing it in every way at their command. A profound ambiguity nevertheless remained. Obviously, the new Russian government had to deal with other constituted governments if an armistice and peace were to be secured quickly. Yet Lenin's revolutionary principles required him to do all he could to help trigger proletarian revolution against those same constituted governments. To try to achieve both peace and revolution at the same time was bound to be awkward. The text that follows, drawn up as it was in great haste and under conditions of intense excitement, does little to disguise this awkwardness.

BOLSHEVIK PROCLAMATION ON PEACE

Proclamation

The Workers' and Peasants' Government, created by the revolution of November 6-7, and drawing its strength from the Soviets of Workers', Soldiers', and Peasants' Deputies, proposes to all warring peoples and their governments to begin at once negotiations leading to a just democratic peace.

From *The Bolshevik Revolution 1917-1918: Documents and Materials*, edited by James Bunyan and H. H. Fisher (Stanford: Stanford University Press, 1934).

A just and democratic peace for which the great majority of wearied, tormented, and war-exhausted toilers and laboring classes of all belligerent countries are thirsting, a peace which the Russian workers and peasants have so loudly and insistently demanded since the overthrow of the Tsar's monarchy, such a peace the government considers to be an immediate peace without annexations (i.e., without the seizing of foreign territory and the forcible annexation of foreign nationalities) and without indemnities.

The Russian Government proposes to all warring peoples that this kind of peace be concluded at once; it also expresses its readiness to take immediately, without the least delay, all decisive steps pending the final confirmation of all the terms of such a peace by the plenipotentiary assemblies of all countries and all nations.

By annexation or seizure of foreign territory the government, in accordance with the legal concepts of democracy in general and of the working class in particular, understands any incorporation of a small and weak nationality by a large and powerful state without a clear, definite, and voluntary expression of agreement and desire by the weak nationality, regardless of the time when such forcible incorporation took place, regardless also of how developed or how backward is the nation forcibly attached or forcibly detained within the frontiers of the [larger] state, and, finally, regardless whether or not this large nation is located in Europe or in distant lands beyond the seas.

If any nation whatsoever is detained by force within the boundaries of a certain state, and if [that nation], contrary to its expressed desire—whether such desire is made manifest in the press, national assemblies, party relations, or in protests and uprisings against national oppression—is not given the right to determine the form of its state life by free voting and completely free from the presence of the troops of the annexing or stronger state and without the least pressure, then the adjoining of that nation by the stronger state is annexation, i.e., seizure by force and violence.

The government considers that to continue this war simply to decide how to divide the weak nationalities among the powerful and rich nations which had seized them would be the greatest crime against humanity, and it solemnly announces its readiness to sign at once the terms of peace which will end this war on the indicated conditions, equally just for all nationalities without exception.

At the same time the government declares that it does not regard the conditions of peace mentioned above as an ultimatum; that is, it is ready to consider any other conditions, insisting, however, that such be proposed by any of the belligerents as soon as possible, and that they be expressed in the clearest terms, without ambiguity or secrecy.

The government abolishes secret diplomacy, expressing, for its part, the firm determination to carry on all negotiations absolutely openly and in view of all the people. It will proceed at once to publish all secret treaties ratified or concluded by the government of landlords and capitalists from March to November 7, 1917. All the provisions of these secret treaties, in so far as they have for their object the securing of benefits and privileges to the Russian landlords and capitalists—which was true in a majority of cases—and retaining or increasing the annexation by the Great Russians, the government declares absolutely and immediately annulled.

While addressing to the governments and peoples of all countries the proposal to begin at once open peace negotiations, the government, for its part, expresses its readiness to carry on these negotiations by written communications, by telegraph, by parleys of the representatives of different countries, or at a conference of such representatives. To facilitate such negotiations the government appoints its plenipotentiary representative to neutral countries.

The government proposes to all governments and peoples of all belligerent countries to conclude an armistice at once; at the same time it considers it desirable that this armistice should be concluded for a period of not less than three months—that is, a period during which it would be entirely possible to complete the negotiations for peace with the participation of representatives of all peoples and nationalities which were drawn into the war or forced to take part in it, as well as to call the plenipotentiary assemblies of people's representatives in every country for the final ratification of the peace terms.

In making these peace proposals to the government and peoples of all warring countries, the Provisional Government of Workers and Peasants of Russia appeals particularly to the class-conscious workers of the three most advanced nations of mankind, who are also the largest states participating in the present war—England, France, and Germany. The workers of these countries have rendered the greatest possible service to the cause of progress and socialism by the great example of the Chartist movement in England, several revolutions of universal historic significance accomplished by the French proletariat, and, finally, the heroic struggle against the Law of Exceptions in Germany, a struggle which was prolonged, stubborn, and disciplined, which could be held up as an example for the workers of the whole world, and which aimed at the creation of proletarian mass organizations in Germany. All these examples of proletarian heroism and historic achievement serve us as a guaranty that the workers of these three countries will understand the tasks which lie before them by way of liberating humanity from the horrors of war and its consequences, and that by their resolute, unselfishly energetic efforts in various directions these workers will help us to bring to a successful end the cause of peace, and, together with this, the cause of the liberation of the toiling and exploited masses from all forms of slavery and all exploitation.

The Workers' and Peasants' Government created by the revolution of November 6-7 and drawing its strength from the Soviets of Workers', Soldiers', and Peasants' Deputies must begin peace negotiations at once. Our appeal must be directed to the governments as well as to the peoples. We cannot ignore the governments, because this would delay the conclusion of peace, a thing which a people's government does not dare to do, but at the same time we have no right not to appeal to the peoples. Everywhere governments and peoples are at arm's length; we must, therefore, help the peoples to take a hand in [settling] the question of peace and war. We shall of course stand by our program of peace without annexations and without indemnities.

We shall not relinquish [that program], but we must deprive our enemies of the possibility of saying that their conditions are different and that they do not wish, therefore, to enter into negotiations with us. No, we must dislodge them from that advantageous position by not presenting them our conditions in the form of an ultimatum. For this reason we have included a statement to the effect that we are ready to consider any condition of peace, in fact, every proposal. Consideration, of course, does not necessarily mean acceptance. We shall submit [the proposals] for consideration to the Constituent Assembly, which will then decide, officially, what can and what cannot be granted. We have to fight against the hypocrisy of the governments, which, while talking about peace and justice, actually carry on wars of conquest and plunder. Not one single government will tell you what it really means. But we are opposed to secret diplomacy and can afford to act openly before all people. We do not now close nor have we ever closed our eyes to the difficulties. Wars cannot be ended by a refusal [to fight]; they cannot be ended by one side alone. We are proposing an armistice for three months —though we are not rejecting a shorter period—[in the hope] that this will give the suffering army at least a breathing spell and will make possible the calling of popular meetings in all civilized countries to discuss the conditions [of peace].

The American Recipe for Peace

Thomas Woodrow Wilson (1856–1924) was elected President of the United States in 1912 and re-elected in 1916 for a second term. In his first administration, President Wilson carried through an extensive reform program at home by using the powers of his office and his personal persuasiveness to get Congress to pass a series of important laws. After the outbreak of World War I in 1914, President Wilson had to face a new problem in defining United States' policy toward the warring states of Europe. Until 1917 President Wilson maintained official neutrality but allowed private firms to supply the

Allies with munitions of war while the British Navy prevented deliveries to Germany.

Controversy developed over American rights on the high seas, and when the German government announced that U-boats would sink ships without warning within a broad portion of the Atlantic, Wilson and the U.S. Congress reacted by declaring war against Germany on April 6, 1917. Many factors besides the official controversy over neutral rights on the seas entered into this decision. One important factor was the weakening of Russia after the March revolution of 1917. Decay of Russia's capacity to wage war seemed to presage German victory in the west over France and Great Britain; and the prospect of German victory, putting most of Europe at the Kaiser's feet, displeased or frightened many influential Americans.

It took time for United States' manpower and military resources to reach the battlefields of France. In the meanwhile, a second revolution in Russia brought the Bolsheviks to power in November 1917. Lenin, the Bolshevik leader, immediately proposed peace, and negotiations with representatives of the Central Powers began at Brest-Litovsk on December 3, 1917. Peace negotiations were broken off on December 28 to permit the Russians to invite the western powers to join the conference, hoping, in the meantime, that revolution would break out in Europe. Neither of these moves had concrete results, and on January 9, 1918, peace negotiations between the Germans and Austrians on the one hand and the Russians on the other began anew.

This was the situation when President Wilson came before the United States Congress on January 8, 1918, and delivered the address reproduced below. His purpose was to outline terms of peace that accorded with a sense of law and justice which he and many other Americans shared. In addition, Wilson was bidding against the Bolsheviks for the support of European peoples, and trying at the same time to force the hands of his British and French governments, which were not ready to endorse all the terms and principles President Wilson here set forth.

The Fourteen Points were widely publicized in the months that followed, and when the German government initiated the negotiations that led to armistice on November 11, 1918, thus ending World War I, the German Imperial Chancellor did so by declaring, "The German government accepts the program set forth by the President of the United States in his message to Congress of January 8, 1918 . . . as a basis for peace negotiations." One of the grievances Germans nursed in the 1920's and 1930's was that Wilson's Fourteen Points were not, in fact, the basis of the Versailles Peace Treaty, although many of Wilson's ideas, as set forth here, were realized in the peace treaties that ended World War I.

WOODROW WILSON: SPEECH ON THE FOURTEEN POINTS

Gentlemen of the Congress, once more, as repeatedly before, the spokesmen of the Central Empires have indicated their desire to discuss the objects of the war and the possible bases of a general peace. Parleys have been in progress at Brest-Litovsk between Russian representatives and representatives of the Central Powers, to which the attention of all the belligerents has been invited for the purpose of ascertaining whether it may be possible to extend these parleys into a general conference with regard to terms of peace and settlement. The Russian representatives presented not only a perfectly definite statement of the principles upon which they would be willing to conclude peace, but also an equally definite programme of the concrete application of those principles. The representatives of the Central Powers, on their part, presented an outline of settlement which, if much less definite, seemed susceptible of liberal interpretation until their specific programme of practical terms was added. That programme proposed no concessions at all either to the sovereignty of Russia or to the preferences of the populations with whose fortunes it dealt, but meant, in a word, that the Central Empires were to keep every foot of territory their armed forces had occupied.—every province, every city, every point of vantage,—as a permanent addition to their territories and their power. It is a reasonable conjecture that the general principles of settlement which they at first suggested originated with the more liberal statesmen of Germany and Austria, the men who have begun to feel the force of their own peoples' thought and purpose, while the

From the *Congressional Record*, 65th Congress, Second Session, pp. 680-81.

concrete terms of actual settlement came from the military leaders who have no thought but to keep what they have got. The negotiations have been broken off. The Russian representatives were sincere and in earnest. They cannot entertain such proposals of conquest and domination.

The whole incident is full of significance. It is also full of perplexity. With whom are the Russian representatives dealing? For whom are the representatives of the Central Empires speaking? Are they speaking for the majorities of their respective parliaments or for the minority parties, that military and imperialistic minority which has so far dominated their whole policy and controlled the affairs of Turkey and of the Balkan states which have felt obliged to become their associates in the war? The Russian representatives have insisted, very justly, very wisely, and in the true spirit of modern democracy, that the conferences they have been holding with the Teutonic and Turkish statesmen should be held within open, not closed, doors, and all the world has been audience, as was desired. To whom have we been listening, then? To those who speak the spirit and intention of the Resolutions of the German Reichstag of the ninth of July last, the spirit and intention of the liberal leaders and parties of Germany, or to those who resist and defy that spirit and intention and insist upon conquest and subjugation? Or are we listening, in fact, to both, unreconciled and in open and hopeless contradiction? These are very serious and pregnant questions. Upon the answer to them depends the peace of the world.

But whatever the results of the parleys at Brest-Litovsk, whatever the confusions of counsel and of purpose in the utterances of the spokesmen of the Central Empires, they have again attempted to acquaint the world with their objects in the war and have again challenged their adversaries to say what their objects are and what sort of settlement they would deem just and satisfactory. There is no good reason why that challenge should not be responded to, and responded to with the utmost candor. We did not wait for it. Not once, but again and again, we have laid our whole thought and purpose before the world, not in general terms only, but each time with sufficient definition to make it clear what sort of definitive terms of settlement must necessarily spring out of them. Within the last week Mr. Lloyd George[1] has spoken with admirable candor and in admirable spirit for the people and Government of Great Britain. There is no confusion of counsel among the adversaries of the Central Powers, no uncertainty of principle, no vagueness of detail. The only secrecy of counsel, the only lack of fearless frankness, the only failure to make definite statement of the objects of the war, lies with Germany and her Allies. The issues of life and death hang upon these definitions. No statesman who has the least conception of his responsibility ought for a moment to permit himself to continue this tragical and appalling outpouring of blood and treasure unless he is sure beyond a peradventure that the objects of the vital sacrifice are part and parcel of the very life of Society, and that the people for whom he speaks think them right and imperative as he does.

There is, moreover, a voice calling for these definitions of principle and of purpose which is, it seems to me, more thrilling and more compelling than any of the many moving voices with which the troubled air of the world is filled. It is the voice of the Russian people. They are prostrate and all but helpless, it would seem, before the grim power of Germany, which has hitherto known no relenting and no pity. Their power, apparently, is shattered. And yet their soul is not subservient. They will not yield either in principle or in action. Their conception of what is right, of what it is humane and honorable for them to accept, has been stated with a frankness, a largeness of view, a generosity of spirit, and a universal human sympathy which must challenge the admiration of every friend of mankind; and they have refused to compound their ideals or desert others that they themselves may be safe. They call to us to say what it is that we desire, in what, if in anything, our purpose and our spirit differ from theirs; and I believe that the people of the United States would wish me to respond, with utter simplicity and frankness. Whether their present leaders believe it or not, it is our heartfelt desire and hope that same way may be opened whereby we may be privileged to assist the people of Russia to attain their utmost hope of liberty and ordered peace.

1. Prime Minister of Great Britain, 1916-22.

It will be our wish and purpose that the processes of peace, when they are begun, shall be absolutely open and that they shall involve and permit henceforth no secret understandings of any kind. The day of conquest and aggrandizement is gone by; so is also the day of secret covenants entered into in the interest of particular governments and likely at some unlooked-for moment to upset the peace of the world. It is this happy fact, now clear to the view of every public man whose thoughts do not still linger in an age that is dead and gone, which makes it possible for every nation whose purposes are consistent with justice and the peace of the world to avow now or at any other time the objects it has in view.

We entered this war because violations of right had occurred which touched us to the quick and made the life of our own people impossible unless they were corrected and the world secured once for all against their recurrence. What we demand in this war, therefore, is nothing peculiar to ourselves. It is that the world be made fit and safe to live in; and particularly that it be made safe for every peace-loving nation which, like our own, wishes to live its own life, determine its own institutions, be assured of justice and fair dealing by the other peoples of the world as against force and selfish aggression. All the peoples of the world are in effect partners in this interest, and for our own part we see very clearly that unless justice be done to others it will not be done to us. The programme of the world's peace, therefore, is our programme; and that programme, the only possible programme, as we see it, is this:

I. Open covenants of peace, openly arrived at, after which there shall be no private international understandings of any kind but diplomacy shall proceed always frankly and in the public view.

II. Absolute freedom of navigation upon the seas, outside territorial waters, alike in peace and in war, except as the seas may be closed in whole or in part by international action for the enforcement of international covenants.

III. The removal, so far as possible, of all economic barriers and the establishment of an equality of trade conditions among all the nations consenting to the peace and associating themselves for its maintenance.

IV. Adequate guarantees given and taken that national armaments will be reduced to the lowest point consistent with domestic safety.

V. A free, open-minded, and absolutely impartial adjustment of all colonial claims, based upon a strict observance of the principle that in determining all such questions of sovereignty the interests of the populations concerned must have equal weight with the equitable claims of the government whose title is to be determined.

VI. The evacuation of all Russian territory and such a settlement of all questions affecting Russia as will secure the best and freest cooperation of the other nations of the world in obtaining for her an unhampered and unembarrassed opportunity for the independent determination of her own political development and national policy and assure her of a sincere welcome into the society of free nations under institutions of her own choosing; and, more than a welcome, assistance also of every kind that she may need and may herself desire. The treatment accorded Russia by her sister nations in the months to come will be the acid test of their good will, of their comprehension of her needs as distinguished from their own interests, and of their intelligent and unselfish sympathy.

VII. Belgium, the whole world will agree, must be evacuated and restored, without any attempt to limit the sovereignty which she enjoys in common with all other free nations. No other single act will serve as this will serve to restore confidence among the nations in the laws which they have themselves set and determined for the government of their relations with one another. Without this healing act the whole structure and validity of international law is forever impaired.

VIII. All French territory should be freed and the invaded portions restored, and the wrong done to France by Prussia in 1871 in the matter of Alsace-Lorraine, which has unsettled the peace of the world for nearly fifty years, should be righted, in order that peace may once more be made secure in the interest of all.

IX. A readjustment of the frontiers of Italy should be effected along clearly recognizable lines of nationality.

X. The peoples of Austria-Hungary, whose place among the

nations we wish to see safeguarded and assured, should be accorded the freest opportunity of autonomous development.

XI. Rumania, Serbia, and Montenegro should be evacuated; occupied territories restored; Serbia accorded free and secure access to the sea; and the relations of the several Balkan states to one another determined by friendly counsel along historically established lines of allegiance and nationality; and international guarantees of the political and economic independence and territorial integrity of the several Balkan states should be entered into.

XII. The Turkish portions of the present Ottoman Empire should be assured a secure sovereignty, but the other nationalities which are now under Turkish rule should be assured an undoubted security of life and an absolutely unmolested opportunity of autonomous development, and the Dardanelles should be permanently opened as a free passage to the ships and commerce of all nations under international guarantees.

XIII. An independent Polish state should be erected which should include the territories inhabited by indisputably Polish populations, which should be assured a free and secure access to the sea, and whose political and economic independence and territorial integrity should be guaranteed by international covenant.

XIV. A general association of nations must be formed under specific covenants for the purpose of affording mutual guarantees of political independence and territorial integrity to great and small states alike.

In regard to these essential rectifications of wrong and assertions of right we feel ourselves to be intimate partners of all the governments and peoples associated together against the Imperialists. We cannot be separate in interest or divided in purpose. We stand together until the end.

For such arrangements and covenants we are willing to fight and to continue to fight until they are achieved; but only because we wish the right to prevail and desire a just and stable peace such as can be secured only by removing the chief provocations to war, which this programme does remove. We have no jealousy of German greatness, and there is nothing in this programme that impairs it. We grudge her no achievement or distinction of learning or of pacific enterprise such as have made her record very bright and very enviable. We do not wish to injure her or to block in any way her legitimate influence or power. We do not wish to fight her either with arms or with hostile arrangements of trade if she is willing to associate herself with us and the other peace-loving nations of the world in covenants of justice and law and fair dealing. We wish her only to accept a place of equality among the peoples of the world,—the new world in which we now live,—instead of a place of mastery.

Neither do we presume to suggest to her any alteration or modification of her institutions. But it is necessary, we must frankly say, and necessary as a preliminary to any intelligent dealings with her on our part, that we should know whom her spokesmen speak for when they speak to us, whether for the Reichstag majority or for the military party and the men whose creed is imperial domination.

We have spoken now, surely, in terms too concrete to admit of any further doubt or question. An evident principle runs through the whole programme I have outlined. It is the principle of justice to all peoples and nationalities, and their right to live on equal terms of liberty and safety with one another, whether they be strong or weak. Unless this principle be made its foundation no part of the structure of international justice can stand. The people of the United States could act upon no other principle; and to the vindication of this principle they are ready to devote their lives, their honor, and everything that they possess. The moral climax of this the culminating and final war for human liberty has come, and they are ready to put their own strength, their own highest purpose, their own integrity and devotion to the test.

The Nation As Refuge for a Lost Soul

Benito Mussolini (1883–1945) was a successful socialist politician and journalist before World War I, a leader of the more radical wing of the party. As such he was a violent pacifist, and when war broke out in 1914, threatened that there would be proletarian revolution if the bourgeois parties took Italy into the conflict. Soon, however, Mussolini gave up his belligerent pacifism in favor of a no less belligerent advocacy of intervention on the French and British side. This meant a break with most of his socialist colleagues, who remained pacifist internationalists. Mussolini attacked them for disregarding Italian national feelings and claimed to be a truer socialist than they because he was now a flaming nationalist. Some combination of these two ideals lay at the heart of all later fascist movements, as the name of the most famous of them all, Hitler's National Socialism, demonstrated.

When Italy joined the allies in the war, Mussolini was called up to serve as a private. After being wounded in a training accident, he was discharged and resumed his journalistic career. In 1919, after the war had ended, unsatisfactorily from an Italian nationalistic point of view, Mussolini launched a new political movement, the *Fasci di Combattimento.* Street-fighting became a way of life for Mussolini's *Fasci*; meanwhile the older Italian political parties fumbled about, unable to form a stable government or to cope with the effervescent violence fomented by Mussolini and his Fascists on the one hand and by revolutionary Communists, Socialists, and anarchists on the other.

In 1922 Mussolini proclaimed a March on Rome. As trainloads of his followers converged on the capital city, he was rewarded by being offered the post of Prime Minister by King Victor Emmanuel III. At first most of the members of Mussolini's cabinet were not Fascists, but represented various conservative and nationalist parties that hoped to use Mussolini as he hoped to use them. Only after 1926 did a Fascist monopoly of power end the old Parliamentary pattern of government. In the years that followed, Mussolini tried to set up the "corporative state"; that is, arrange for various corporate interest groups to elect representatives to a Chamber that exercised some of the functions formerly assigned to Parliament. In addition, all political parties except the Fascist party were prohibited.

In 1932 as these "revolutionary" changes were being worked out in practice (the corporative organization of Italian society was never entirely completed) the article reproduced below appeared over Mussolini's signature. It was first published in an Italian encyclopedia, and many critics, then and since, believe that the first part came from the pen of Giovanni Gentile, a professor of philosophy and apologist for the Fascist regime, who was also editor of the encyclopedia. The more personal, rambling and occasionally reminiscent style of the later portions of the article certainly differ sharply from the rigorous abstraction of the initial pages. Very likely Mussolini revised and then added some thoughts of his own to an article Gentile had prepared and then signed his name to the end result.

Whatever lies behind its published form, this text quickly came to be accepted as the most authentic and official formulation of Fascist theory. Mussolini's government used it as a kind of high level propaganda for intellectuals and arranged for its translation into foreign languages. The text that follows was therefore semiofficial, aimed, of course, at attracting sympathizers in the English-speaking world.

BENITO MUSSOLINI: THE DOCTRINE OF FASCISM

Like all sound political systems, Fascism has a practical as well as a theoretical aspect; the practical side embodies the theory, and the theory springs from certain historical forces in which it is engrafted and within which it works. Fascism therefore has an aspect due to circumstances of time and place; but it also includes ideals which are the expression of truths of the highest philosophical importance. The human will cannot exercise a spiritual influence in the world by dominating the will of others, unless man has a clear idea of the transitory and permanent reality upon which that action is to be exercised, and of the lasting and universal reality in which transitory things dwell and exist. In order to know men one must know man; and to know man one must be acquainted with reality and its laws. There can be no conception of the State which is not fundamentally a conception of life: philosophy or intuition, a system of ideas evolving within the limits of logic or concentrated in a vision or

From Benito Mussolini, *The Doctrine of Fascism*, trans. by E. Cope (Florence: Vallecchi Publisher, 1937), pp. 9-19, 22-28, 30, 33-38, 39-42.

a creed, but always at least potentially, an organic conception of the world.

Thus many of the practical expressions of Fascism, such as party organisation, educational systems, discipline, can only be understood when considered in relation to its general attitude towards life. Fascism does not see in the world only those superficial, material aspects in which man appears as a self-centred individual, standing alone, subject to natural laws and instincts which urge him towards a life of selfish momentary pleasure; it does not only see the individual, but also the nation and the country; individuals and generations bound together by a moral law, moral traditions and a mission which, repressing the instinct for life enclosed in a brief circle of pleasure, builds up a higher life founded on duty, a life free from the limitations of time and space, in which the individual may achieve that purely spiritual existence in which his worth as a man consists, by self-sacrifice, the renunciation of self-interest, by death itself.

The idea is therefore a spiritual one, and arises from a general reaction of the present century against the flaccid materialist positivism of the XIX century. Anti-positivist, yet positive; this is neither a sceptical nor an agnostic, neither a pessimistic nor a supinely optimistic system, as are most of the negative doctrines which place the centre of life outside man; for indeed man can, and must, form his own world by the exercize of his own free will.

Fascism wants men to be active and to engage in activity with all their energy; it requires that they should be manfully aware of the difficulties besetting them and ready to face them. Life is conceived as a struggle in which a man is bound to win for himself a really worthy place, first of all by fitting himself physically, morally and intellectually, and to have the necessary qualities for winning it. As it is for the individual, so is it for the nation, and for all mankind. Hence the high value of culture in all its forms, religious, scientific and artistic, and the outstanding importance of education. Hence also the essential value of work, by which man subdues nature and creates the human world in its economic, political, ethical and intellectual aspects.

This positive conception of life is obviously an ethical one. It covers the entire field of reality as well as the human activities which master it. No action is exempt from moral judgment; no activity can be deprived of the value which a moral purpose confers on all things. Therefore life, as conceived by the Fascist, is serious, austere, religious; all its manifestations take place in a world sustained by moral forces and subject to spiritual responsibilities. The Fascist disdains an easy-going life.

The Fascist conception of life is a religious one in which man is viewed in his permanent relation to a higher law, endowed with an objective will transcending the individual and raising him to conscious membership of a spiritual society. Those who perceive nothing beyond opportunist considerations in the religious policy of the Fascist Regime,[1] fail to realize that Fascism is not only a system of government, but also and chiefly a system of thought.

In the Fascist theory of history, man is such only by virtue of the spiritual process to which he contributes as a member of the family, the social group, the nation and in his relation to history to which all nations have contributed. Hence the great value of tradition in records, in language, in customs and in the rules of social life. Apart from history, man is a nonentity. Fascism is therefore opposed to all individualistic abstractions based on XVIII century materialism; and it is opposed to all Jacobin utopias and innovations. It does not believe in the possibility of happiness on earth as conceived by XVIII century economic writers, and therefore rejects the teleological notion that at some future time the human family will secure a final settlement of all its difficulties. This notion runs counter to experience which teaches that life is in continual motion and undergoing a process of evolution. In politics Fascism aims at realism; in practice it desires to deal only with those problems which are the spontaneous product of historic conditions and which find or suggest their own solution. Only by experiencing reality and getting a firm hold on the forces at work within it, may man influence other men and nature.

Being anti-individualistic, the Fascist system of life stresses

1. This refers to Mussolini's Concordat with the Papacy, signed 1929. In earlier times Mussolini had been a violent critic of the Church.

the importance of the State and recognizes the individual only in so far as his interests coincide with those of the State, which stands for the consciousness and the universality of man as a historic entity. It is opposed to classic Liberalism which arose as a reaction to absolutism and exhausted its historical function when the State became the expression of the consciousness and will of the people. Liberalism denied the State in the name of the individual; Fascism reasserts the rights of the State as expressing the real essence of the individual. And if liberty is to be the attribute of living men and not that of abstract dummies invented by individualistic Liberalism, then Fascism stands for liberty and for the only liberty worth having, the liberty of the State and of the individual within the State. The Fascist conception of the State is all-embracing; outside of it no human or spiritual values may exist, much less have any value. Thus understood, Fascism is totalitarian and the Fascist State, as a synthesis and a unit which includes all values, interprets, develops and lends additional power to the whole life of a people.

No individuals or groups, political parties, associations, economic unions, social classes are to exist apart from the State. Fascism therefore opposes Socialism which rejects unity within the State, obtained by the fusion of all classes into a single ethical and economic reality, since it sees in history nothing more than the class struggle. Fascism likewise opposes trade-unionism as a class weapon. But Fascism recognizes the real needs which gave rise to Socialism and trade-unionism, when they are brought within the orbit of the State, giving them due weight in the corporative system through which widely different interests are coordinated and harmonised for the unity of the State.

Grouped according to their several interests, individuals form classes; they form trade unions when they are organized according to their various economic callings; but first and foremost they form the State which is no mere matter of numbers, the sum-total of individuals forming a majority. Fascism therefore opposes the form of democracy which entrusts the nation to a majority, debasing it to the level of the largest number; but, if the Nation be considered, as it should be, from the point of view of quality instead of quantity, as an idea, it is the purest form of democracy, the mightiest, because it is the most ethical, the most coherent, the truest, the expression of a people through the conscience and will of the few, if not indeed, of a single man. . . .

In so far as it is embodied in a State, this higher personality becomes a Nation. It is not the Nation which produces the State; that is an old-fashioned naturalistic idea which afforded a basis for XIX century publicity in favour of national governments. It is rather the State which forms the Nation, by lending strength and power and real life to a people conscious of its own moral unity.

The right to national independence does not arise from any merely literary and idealistic form of self-consciousness; still less from a more or less passive and unconscious *de facto* situation, but from an active, conscious, political will, expressing itself in action and prepared to assert its rights. It arises, in short, from the existence at least *in fieri*[2] of a State. Indeed, as the expression of a universal ethical will, the State itself creates the right to national independence.

A nation, as expressed in the State, is a living, ethical entity only in so far as it is progressive. Inactivity means death. Therefore the State does not only stand for Authority which governs and confers legal form and spiritual value on individual wills, but it is also Power which makes its will felt and respected beyond its own boundaries, thus affording practical evidence of the universal character of the decisions necessary to ensure its development. This implies organization and expansion, potential if not actual. Thus the State is equal to the will of a single man whose development cannot be checked by obstacles and it proves its own universality by achieving self-expression.

The Fascist State, as a higher and more powerful expression of personality, is a force, but a spiritual one. It sums up all the manifestations in the intellectual and moral life of man. Its functions cannot therefore be limited to that of enforcing law and order, as the Liberal doctrine would have it. It is no mere

2. The Italian words mean "in pride"; a state existing "in pride" and not otherwise is hard to express in English. The reference is to the age when Italy was not united into a single state, but existed "in pride," i.e., in Italian consciousness.

mechanical device for defining the sphere within which the individual may duly exercise his supposed rights. The Fascist State is an inwardly accepted standard and a rule of conduct, a discipline of the whole person; it permeates the will no less than the intellect. It stands for a principle which becomes the central motive of man as a member of civilized society, sinking deep down into his personality; it dwells in the heart of the man of action and of the thinker, of the artist and of the man of science: soul of the soul.

Fascism, in short, is not only a lawgiver and a founder of institutions, but an educator and a promoter of spiritual life. It does not merely aim at remoulding the forms of life, but also their content, man, his character and his faith. To achieve this purpose it enforces discipline and makes use of authority, entering into the mind and ruling with undisputed sway. Therefore it has chosen as its emblem the Lictors' rods,[3] the symbol of uinty, strength and justice.

. . . .

The years preceding the March on Rome[4] cover a period during which the need for action prevented delay and careful theoretical elaborations. Fighting was going on in towns and villages. There were discussions, but there was something more sacred and more important: Death. Fascists knew how to die. A doctrine—fully elaborated, divided into chapters and paragraphs with many notes, may have been lacking, but it was replaced by something far more decisive,—by a creed. All the same if anyone cares to revive the memory of those days he would find with the help of books, articles, resolutions passed at congresses, major and minor speeches, provided he knows how to seek and select, that the doctrinal foundations were laid while the battle was still raging. Indeed, it was during those years that Fascism, though up in arms, refined itself, and proceeded to build up its organization. The problems of the individual and of the State; the problems of authority and liberty; political, social and more especially national problems were discussed; the conflict with Liberal, Democratic, Socialist and Masonic doc-

3. Badge of office for the consuls of ancient Rome.
4. I.e., before Mussolini took power.

trines and those of the *Partito Popolare*,[5] was carried on at the same time as the punitive expeditions. Nevertheless, the lack of a formal system was used by disingenuous opponents as an argument for proclaiming Fascism incapable of elaborating a doctrine at the very same time when that doctrine was being formulated, no matter how tumultuously, first, as in the case of all new ideas, in the guise of violent dogmatic negations; then in the more positive guise of constructive theories, subsequently incorporated in 1926, 1927 and 1928 in the laws and institutions of the Regime.

Fascism is now clearly defined not only as a Regime, but as a doctrine. This means that Fascism, exercizing its critical faculties on itself and on others, has studied from its own special standpoint and judged by its own standards all the problems affecting the material and intellectual interest now causing grave anxiety to the nations of the world, and it is ready to deal with them with its own methods.

As far as concerns the future development of mankind, quite apart from all present-day political considerations, Fascism does not on the whole believe in the possibility or utility of perpetual peace. Pacifism is therefore rejected as a cloak for cowardly supine renunciation as against self-sacrifice. War alone keys up all the energies of man to their greatest pitch and sets the mark of nobility on those nations which have the bravery to face it. All other tests are substitutes which never place a man face to face with himself before the alternative of life and death. Therefore all doctrines which postulate peace at any price as their premiss are incompatible with Fascism. Equally foreign to the spirit of Fascism, even though they may be accepted for their utility in meeting special political situations, are all internationalist or League[6] organizations which, as history amply proves, crumble to the ground whenever the heart of nations is stirred deeply by sentimental, idealist or practical considerations. Fascism carries this anti-pacifist attitude into the life of the individ-

5. Popular Party; a Christian Socialist party, led by Don Luigi Sturzo, a Sicilian priest.

6. League of Nations, established in 1920 as part of the settlement after World War I and intended as an organization to keep international peace.

ual. "I don't care," *me ne frego*, scrawled on his bandages by a wounded man became the proud motto of the storm-troopers, and it is not only an act of philosophical stoicism, it sums up a doctrine which is not merely political; it is the evidence of a fighting spirit which accepts all risks. It stands for a new mode of life of the Italians. The Fascist accepts and loves life; he rejects and despises suicide as cowardly. Life as he understands it means the fulfilment of duty, moral improvement, conquest; life must be lofty and full, it must be lived for oneself but above all for others, both nearby and far off, present and future.

The demographic policy of the Regime is a consequence of these premises. The Fascist loves his neighbour, but that word does not stand for a vague and incomprehensible idea. Love of one's neighbour does not exclude necessary educational severity; still less does it exclude differentiation and rank. Fascism will have nothing to do with universal embraces; as a member of the community of nations it looks other peoples straight in the eyes; it is vigilant, on its guard; it follows others in all their activities and takes note of any change in their interests; and it does not allow itself to be deceived by changing and deceptive appearances.

Such a conception of life makes of Fascism the resolute negation of the doctrine underlying so-called scientific and Marxist Socialism, the doctrine of historic materialism which would explain the history of mankind in terms of the class struggle and of changes in the processes and means of production, to the exclusion of all else.

That the vicissitudes of economic life, the discovery of raw materials, new technical processes, scientific inventions, have their importance nobody denies; but that they are sufficient to explain human history to the exclusion of other factors is absurd. Fascism believes now and always in sanctity and heroism, that is to say in acts wherein no economic motive, immediate or remote, is at work. Having denied historic materialism, which sees in men mere puppets on the fringes of history, appearing and disappearing on the crest of the waves while the real directive forces move and work in the depths, Fascism also denies the immutable and irreparable character of class struggle, which is the natural outcome of that economic conception of history; above all it denies that class struggle is the principal agent in social transformations. Having thus struck a blow at Socialism in the two main points of its doctrine, all that remains of it is the sentimental aspiration, old as humanity itself, towards social relations in which the sufferings and sorrows of the humble will be alleviated. But here again Fascism rejects the economic interpretation of happiness as something to be secured through Socialism, automatically so to say, at a given stage in social evolution, when a maximum of material comfort will be assured to all. Fascism denies the materialist conception of happiness as a possibility, and abandons it to the economists of the mid-eighteenth century. This means that Fascism denies the equation: wellbeing = happiness, by which men are merely considered as animals, happy when they can feed and fatten, thus being reduced to a purely vegetative existence.

Besides Socialism, Fascism points its guns at the whole block of Democratic ideologies and rejects both their premises and their practical application and methods. Fascism denies that numbers, as such, may be the determining factors in human society; it denies the right of numbers to govern by means of periodical consultations; it asserts the incurable and fruitful and beneficent inequality of men, who cannot be levelled by any such mechanical and external device as universal suffrage. Democratic Regimes may be described as those under which the people are deluded from time to time into the belief that they are exercising sovereignty, while all the time real sovereignty belongs to and is exercized by other forces, sometimes irresponsible and secret.

. . . .

In rejecting Democracy Fascism rejects the absurd conventional lie of political equalitarianism, the habit of collective irresponsibility, the myth of felicity and indefinite progress. But if Democracy be understood as a regime in which the masses are not driven back to the outskirts of the State, then the writer of these pages has already defined Fascism as an organized, centralized, authoritarian Democracy.

Fascism is definitely and absolutely opposed to the doctrines of Liberalism, both in the political and in the economic sphere.

. . . .

The Fascist negation of Socialism, Democracy, Liberalism should not, however, be interpreted as implying a desire to drive the world backwards to positions occupied prior to 1789, a year commonly referred to as that which inaugurated the Democratic and Liberal century. History does not travel backwards. The Fascist doctrine has not taken De Maistre[7] as its prophet. Monarchist absolutism is of the past, and so is Church rule. Dead and done for are feudal privileges and the division of society into closed, secluded castes. Neither has the Fascist conception of authority anything in common with that of the police-ridden State.

A party wielding totalitarian rule over a nation is a new departure in history. There are no points of reference nor of comparison. From beneath the ruins of Liberal, Socialist and Democratic doctrines, Fascism recovers the elements which are still vital. It preserves what may be described as the "acquired facts" of history; it rejects all else. That is to say, it rejects the idea of a doctrine suited to all times and to all peoples. Granted that the XIX century was the century of Socialism, Liberalism, Democracy, this does not mean that the XX century must also be the century of Socialism, Liberalism and Democracy. Political doctrines pass; nations remain. We are free to believe that this is the century of authority, a century tending to the Right, a Fascist century. If the XIX century was the century of the individual—Liberalism implies individualism—we are free to believe that this is the collective century, and therefore the century of the State. It is quite logical for a new doctrine to make use of the elements of other doctrines which are still vital. No doctrine ever came to life as a totally new, fresh and unheard-of idea. It is always connected, even if the connection be only historical, with those which came before it and those which will follow. Thus the scientific Socialism of Fourier, Owen, Saint-Simon and others; thus XIX century Liberalism traces its origin back to the XVIII century illuministic movement, and the doc-

7. Joseph de Maistre (1753-1821), French political writer and advocate of reactionary policies during and immediately after the French Revolution.

trines of Democracy to those of the Encyclopaedists. All doctrines aim at directing men's activities towards a given aim; but these activities in their turn react on the doctrine, modifying and adjusting it to new needs, or outstripping it. A doctrine must therefore be a vital act and not a verbal display. Hence the manifold characteristics of Fascism, its will to live, its attitude towards violence, and its value.

The key-stone of the Fascist doctrine is its conception of the State, of its essence, its functions and its aims. For Fascism the State is absolute, individuals and groups relative. Individuals and groups are admissible in so far as they act in accordance with the State. Instead of directing the nation and guiding the material and moral progress of the community, the Liberal State restricts its activities to recording results. The Fascist State is wide awake and has a will of its own. For this reason it can be described as "ethical." At the first quinquennial assembly of the Regime in 1929, I said:

"The Fascist State is not a night-watchman, only solicitous of the personal safety of the citizens; nor is it organized exclusively for the purpose of guaranteeing a certain degree of material prosperity and relatively peaceful conditions of life; a board of directors could do that. Neither is it exclusive and holding itself aloof from the manifold activities of the citizens and the nation. The State as conceived and built up by Fascism, is a spiritual and ethical entity for securing the political, juridical and economic organization of the nation, an organization which is an expression of the spirit in its origin and growth. The State guarantees the safety of the country at home and abroad, and it also safeguards and hands down the spirit of the people, elaborated through the ages in its language, its customs and its faith. The State is not only the present, it is also the past and above all the future. Transcending the individual's brief spell of life, the State stands for the inherent conscience of the nation. The forms in which it finds expression change, but the need for it remains. The State educates its members to citizenship, makes them aware of their mission, urges them to unity; its justice harmonizes their divergent interests; it hands down to future generations the conquests of the mind in the fields of science, art, law, human solidarity; it leads them up from primitive tribal life to imperial rule, the highest expression of human power. The State hands down to future generations the memory of those who laid down their lives to ensure its safety or to obey its laws; it sets up as examples and records for future ages the names of captains who enlarged its territory and of the men of genius who have made it famous. Whenever respect for the State declines and the disintegrating and centrifugal tendencies of individuals and groups prevail, nations are headed for decay."

Since 1929, economic and political developments have everywhere emphasized these truths. The importance of the State is rapidly growing. The so-called crisis[8] can only be settled by State action and within the orbit of the State. . . .

If Liberalism spells individualism, Fascism spells collectivism. —The Fascist State, however, is an unique and original creation. It is not reactionary but revolutionary, for it anticipates the solution of certain universal problems which have been raised elsewhere in the political field by the disgregation of parties, the usurpation of powers by parliaments, the irresponsibility of assemblies; in the economic field by the increasingly numerous and important functions discharged by trade unions and trade associations with their disputes and agreements, affecting both capital and labour; in the ethical field by the need felt for order, discipline, obedience to the moral principles of patriotism.

Fascism desires the State to be strong and organic, based on solid foundations of popular support. The Fascist State lays claim to rule in the economic field no less than in others; it makes its action felt throughout the length and breadth of the country by means of its corporate, social and educational institutions, and all the political, economic and spiritual forces of the nation, organized in their respective associations, spread all over the State.

A State based on millions of individuals who recognize its authority, feel its action, and are ready to serve its ends is not the tyrannical State of a mediaeval lordling. It has nothing in common with the despotic State existing prior to or subsequent

8. A reference to the depression of the early 1930's which was near its depth when this article originally appeared.

to 1789. Far from crushing the individual, the Fascist State multiplies his energies, just as a soldier in a regiment is not weakened but rather strengthened by the number of his fellow soldiers.

The Fascist State organizes the nation but it leaves the individual adequate elbow-room. It has curtailed useless or harmful liberties, while preserving those which are essential. In such matters not the individual but the State alone can be the judge.

The Fascist State is not indifferent to religious phenomena in general nor does it maintain an attitude of indifference to Roman Catholicism, the special, positive religion of the Italians. The State possesses a moral code rather than a theology. The Fascist State sees in religion one of the deepest of spiritual expressions and for this reason it not only respects, but it defends and protects religion. The Fascist State does not attempt, as did Robespierre at the height of the revolutionary delirium of the Convention, to set up a "god" of its own; nor does it vainly seek, like Bolshevism, to efface God from the soul of man. Fascism respects the God of ascetics, saints and heroes, and it also respects God as conceived by the ingenuous and primitive heart of the people, the God to whom their prayers are raised.

The Fascist State expresses the will to exercise power and to command. Here the Roman tradition is embodied in a conception of strength. Imperial power, as understood by the Fascist doctrine, is not only territorial or military or commercial; it is also spiritual and ethical. An Imperial nation, that is to say a nation which is directly or indirectly a leader of others, may exist without the need of conquering a single square mile of territory. Fascism sees in the Imperialistic spirit—namely, in the tendency of nations to expand—a manifestation of their vitality. In the opposite tendency, which would limit their interests to the Fatherland, it sees a symptom of decadence. People who rise or revive are Imperialists; renunciation is characteristic of dying peoples. The Fascist doctrine is that best suited to the tendencies and feelings of a people which, like the Italian, after lying fallow during centuries of foreign servitude, is now reasserting itself in the world.

But Imperialism implies discipline, the coordination of efforts, a profound sense of duty and a spirit of self-sacrifice. This explains many aspects of the practical activities of the Regime, and the direction taken by many of the forces of the State as also the severity which has to be exercised towards those who oppose this spontaneous and inevitable movement of XX century Italy by harping on the outgrown XIX century theories, theories which have been rejected whenever daring experiments in political and social transformation are being attempted.

Never before have the nations thirsted for authority, direction, order as they do now. If every age has its own doctrine, then numberless signs point out Fascism as the doctrine of our age. That it is a vital one is proved by the fact that it has aroused a faith; that this faith has conquered souls is proved by the fact that Fascism can point out its fallen heroes and its martyrs.

Fascism has now acquired throughout the world the universality which belongs to all doctrines which, by achieving self-expression, represent a moment in the history of human thought.

Race as Refuge for the Lost Soul

Adolf Hitler (1889–1945) dictated *Mein Kampf* (My Battle) during the months of his imprisonment following an unsuccessful *coup d'état* attempted in November 1923. When he was released from prison (having served only nine months of a five-year sentence) he returned to political agitation. He first reorganized the National Socialist German Workers' Party to make it completely subject to his will; he then made it strong enough to take full advantage of the severe economic depression that hit Germany in 1930. Both Nazi and Communist votes swelled at the expense of more moderate parties, and street-fighting erupted between the two rivals for power.

Army politicians, seeking mass support for their nationalist and conservative policies, persuaded President Paul von Hindenburg to appoint Hitler Chancellor of Germany in January 1933. Hitler demanded and received special powers and used them to destroy the democratic constitution that had emerged from defeat in World War I. Hitler substituted a personal dictatorship and used his power to restore German military strength. His relentless efforts to upset the hated Versailles settlement of 1920 met with initial success but provoked World War II in 1939. As Germany's defeat became obvious, Hitler committed suicide in May 1945.

The first portions of *Mein Kampf* reproduced below deal with Hitler's early life when, after his mother's death, he left Linz where he had grown up and went to Vienna, hoping to become an artist. Instead he had to make a living doing odd jobs; and his life centered more and more on the feelings of rejection that gnawed at him and his emotionally intense effort to find out why his dreams would not come true. By blaming Jews and Marxists (Social Democrats), he explained his failure to his own satisfaction and prepared himself to become the spokesman for millions of Germans when, after 1918, the German nation as a whole experienced feelings of rejection and failure on a massive scale.

The passage dealing with propaganda shows Hitler's cynical side; the last excerpt describes in suitably romanticized style how Hitler first came into contact with the party he was soon to dominate and use to dominate Germany. These passages are more autobiographical than most parts of *Mein Kampf*, which consists largely of digressions: mainly *obiter dicta* on politics and shrill denunciation of everyone whom Hitler disliked.

ADOLF HITLER: MEIN KAMPF

What I knew of Social Democracy during my youth was precious little and mostly wrong.

I was secretly glad to know that it fought for general suffrage and the secret ballot. My reason already told me that this would lead to the weakening of the Habsburg régime which I hated so much. In the conviction that the State on the Danube could never be preserved unless the German nationality was sacrificed, and that even paying the price of the gradual Slavicizing of the German element would in no way have guaranteed the survival

From Adolf Hitler, *Mein Kampf, Complete and Unabridged*, trans. by Ralph Manheim (New York: Reynal & Hitchcock, 1940), pp. 50-56, 65-68, 72-74, 79-81, 232-34, 237-38, 240, 291-300.

of the State, as it was doubtful if the Slavic nationality could have accomplished this, I therefore welcomed every development which in my opinion would lead to the breakdown of the State which had pronounced the death sentence on ten million German people. The more the linguistic *tohuwabohu* [Hebrew—Genesis 1:2—meaning chaos, confusion, hubbub] ate into and tore at the parliament, the sooner would come the hour of doom of this Babylonian realm, and with it, the day of freedom for my German–Austrian people. Only in this way could the *Anschluss* with the old motherland[1] be achieved.

I rather liked the activity of Social Democracy. The fact that it finally endeavored to raise the standard of living of the working class—in those days my innocent mind was foolish enough to believe this—seemed to speak rather in its favor than against it. But what disgusted me most was its hostile attitude towards the fight for the preservation of the German nationality, its pitiful courtship of the Slav "comrades," who readily accepted this wooing as long as it meant practical allowances, but were otherwise arrogantly aloof, thus paying the intruding beggars the wages they deserved.

At the age of seventeen I had rarely heard the word "Marxism," whereas "Social Democracy" and "Socialism" were identical ideas to me. Here, too, the hand of Fate had to open my eyes to this unprecedented betrayal of the people.

Till then I had known the Social Democratic Party only from a spectator's point of view, on the occasion of various mass demonstrations, without having the slightest insight into the mentality of its followers or the meaning of its doctrine; but now I suddenly came into contact with the products of its education and view of life; I now achieved in a few months what otherwise might have taken decades: the realization that it was a pestilential whore covered with the mask of social virtue and brotherly love, and that mankind must rid the world of her as soon as possible, or otherwise the world might easily be rid of mankind.

While I was employed as a building worker, my first encounter with Social Democracy took place.

It was not a very enjoyable experience from the beginning.

1. I.e., union with Germany.

My clothes were still in good shape, my language was refined, and my manners reserved. I still was so preoccupied with my own affairs that I did not bother much with my surroundings. I looked for work to prevent me from starving, thus hoping to find the possibility for further training, however slow it might be. Perhaps I would not have troubled about my new surroundings at all if something had not happened on the third or fourth day which forced me to take a stand. I was asked to join the organization.

My knowledge of unions was nil at that time. I would not have been able to prove the suitability or the uselessness of their existence. When I was told that I had to join, I refused. I gave as my reason that I did not understand the whole affair and that, on the whole, I would not let myself be forced into anything. The first was perhaps the reason why I was not thrown out immediately. Perhaps they hoped that in a few days I would be converted or would give in. In any event, they were thoroughly mistaken. After two weeks I was not allowed to wait any longer, even if I had wanted to. During these two weeks I had become better acquainted with my surroundings, so that no power on earth could have induced me to join an organization whose representatives had meanwhile shown themselves in so unfavorable a light.

The first few days I was annoyed.

At noon some of the men went into the nearest public houses, while others remained on the spot where they in most cases ate a very frugal meal. These were the married ones whose wives brought them their noonday soup in battered dishes. . . . Now politics were discussed.

I drank my bottle of milk and ate my piece of bread somewhere on the side, cautiously studying my new surroundings or pondering over my miserable fate. Yet I heard more than enough; also, more than once it seemed to me as if they approached me intentionally in order to draw me out. In any case, what I heard served to annoy me extremely. Everything was rejected: the nation as an invention of the "capitalistic" classes—how often was I to hear just this word!—; the country as the instrument of the bourgeoisie for the exploitation of the workers;

the authority of the law as a means of suppressing the proletariat; the school as an institution for bringing up slaves as well as slave drivers; religion as a means for doping the people destined for exploitation; morality as a sign of sheepish patience, and so forth. Nothing remained that was not dragged down into the dirt and the filth of the lowest depths.

In the beginning I tried to keep silent. But finally I could hold back no longer. I began to take part and to contradict. But soon I realized that this was entirely hopeless as long as I did not possess at least a certain knowledge of the subjects under argument. Thus I began to look into the sources from which the others drew their so-called wisdom. I studied book after book, pamphlet after pamphlet.

On the job the arguments often became heated. Being daily better informed about their knowledge than my adversaries themselves, I argued till finally one day they applied the one means that wins the easiest victory over reason: terror and force. Some of the leaders of the other side gave me the choice of either leaving the job at once or of being thrown from the scaffold. As I was alone and resistance seemed hopeless, I preferred to follow the former, enriched by a new experience.

I went away, disgusted, but at the same time I was so stirred that it would have been impossible for me to turn my back on the whole affair. No; after my first indignation had passed, my stubbornness gained the upper hand. I firmly resolved to return to another construction job. This decision was encouraged by Poverty, who, after I had eaten up my small savings in the course of a few weeks, clasped me in her unfeeling arms. Now I had to, whether I wanted to or not. The game began again from the beginning, only to end in a similar way as it had the first time.

My mind was tormented by the question: Are these still human beings, worthy of being part of a great nation?

A torturing question it was; if answered in the affirmative, then the fight for a nation is no longer worth the trouble and the sacrifices which the better ones have to make for such outcasts; if the answer is in the negative, then our nation is poor in *human beings.*

During these days of pondering and reflection I watched with uneasiness the mass of those who could no longer be counted as belonging to the nation grow into a threatening legion.

How different were my feelings when one day I stared at the endless columns of a mass demonstration of Viennese workers, marching by in rows of four! For nearly two hours I stood there and watched with bated breath this terrible human dragon creeping slowly along. Depressed and anxious I left the square and walked home. On my way I saw in a tobacco shop a copy of the *Arbeiterzeitung*, the mouthpiece of the old Austrian Social Democracy. It was also available in a cheap coffee shop where I sometimes used to go to read the newspapers; but so far I had not been able to bring myself to look at this wretched paper for more than two minutes, for the effect of its language on me was like that of spiritual vitriol. Under the depressing influence of the demonstration, an inner voice now urged me to buy the paper for once and to read it thoroughly. I did this in the evening, though I sometimes had to fight down the rage rising in me because of this concentrated solution of lies.

The daily reading of the Social Democratic newspapers enabled me better to study the inner meaning of these ideas than all of the theoretic literature put together.

What a difference between the phrases about liberty, beauty, and dignity, the delusive swaggering which attempted to express the deepest wisdom, the disgusting and humane morality—everything was written with an iron-faced prophetic certainty—contained in the theoretic literature and this doctrine of salvation of a new mankind in a daily press which did not shrink from any baseness whatsoever, and which operated with the most brutal forces of calumny and a virtuosity for lying that was outrageous! The one is intended for the innocent simpletons of the middle, and, of course, the upper, classes of the "intelligentsia"; the other for the masses.

For me the concentration on the literature and press of this organization and its doctrine was my return to my people.

What I first had looked upon as an impassable chasm now spurred me on to a greater love for my country than ever before.

Aware of the terrible workings of this poison, only a fool

would condemn the victim. The more independent I became in the following years, the greater the distance, the wider were my eyes opened to the inner causes of the Social Democratic successes. Now I understood the brutal demand to subscribe only to red newspapers, to attend only red meetings, to read only red books, and so on. My eyes saw with plastic clarity the enforced result of this doctrine of intolerance.

The psyche of the great masses is not receptive to half measures or weakness.

Like a woman, whose psychic feeling is influenced less by abstract reasoning than by an undefinable, sentimental longing for complementary strength, who will submit to the strong man rather than dominate the weakling, thus the masses love the ruler rather than the suppliant, and inwardly they are far more satisfied by a doctrine which tolerates no rival than by the grant of liberal freedom; they often feel at a loss what to do with it, and even easily feel themselves deserted. They neither realize the impudence with which they are spiritually terrorized, nor the outrageous curtailment of their human liberties, for in no way does the delusion of this doctrine dawn on them. Thus they see only the inconsiderate force, the brutality and the aim of its manifestations to which they finally always submit.

If Social Democracy is confronted by a doctrine of greater truthfulness, carried out with the same brutality, then the latter will be victorious, though the struggle may be hard.

. . . .

The more insight I gained into the externals of Social Democracy, the greater became my longing to penetrate to the nucleus of its doctrine.

The official literature of the party, of course, was of little use. As far as economic problems are concerned, it is wrong in assertion and proof; as regards the political aims, it lies. In addition, I was disgusted with its modern pettifogging methods and its writing. With an enormous amount of words of unclear content or unintelligible meaning it piles up sentences which are supposed to be as ingenious as they are meaningless. Only the decadent bohemianism of our big cities may feel at home in this labyrinth of reason, to pick up an "inner experience" from the dung heap of this literary dadaism, supported by the proverbial modesty of part of our people, which senses deepest wisdom in the most incomprehensible things.

However, by balancing the theoretical untruth and the nonsense of this doctrine with the reality of its appearance, I gradually gained a clear picture of its inner intention.

In such hours I had sad forebodings and was filled with a depressing fear. I was faced by a doctrine consisting of egoism and hatred; it could be victorious, following mathematical laws, but at the same time it could bring about the end of mankind.

Meanwhile I had learned to understand the connection between this doctrine of destruction and the nature of a race, which hitherto had been unknown to me.

Understanding Jewry alone is the key to the comprehension of the inner, the real, intention of Social Democracy.

He who knows this race will raise the veil of false conceptions, and out of the mist and fog of empty social phrases there rises the grinning, ugly face of Marxism.

Today I would find it difficult, if not impossible, to say when the word "Jew" gave me cause for special thoughts for the first time. At home, as long as my father lived, I cannot remember that I ever heard the word. . . .

There were only a very few Jews in Linz. In the course of the centuries their external appearance had become European and human; yes, I even looked upon them as Germans. The nonsense of this notion was not clear to me, since I saw the only distinguishing mark in their strange religion. The fact that they had been persecuted on that account (as I believed) turned my aversion against unfavorable remarks about them almost into abhorrence.

I had no idea at all that organized hostility against the Jews existed.

And so I arrived in Vienna.

Captivated by the mass of architectural impressions, depressed by the burden of my fate, I was at first unaware of the classification of the population in the huge city. Although Vienna in those years already had two hundred thousand Jews among its two million inhabitants, I did not see them. During the first weeks, my eyes and my senses were unable to take in the rush of so many new values and ideas. Only after settling down, when the confused pictures began to grow clearer, did I look at my new world more attentively, and then I also came upon the Jewish problem.

I cannot say that I particularly liked the way in which I was to become acquainted with them. I still saw nothing but the religion in the Jew, and for reasons of human tolerance I continued to decline fighting on religious grounds. In my opinion, therefore, the language of the anti-Semitic Viennese press was unworthy of the cultural traditions of a great race. I was depressed by the memory of certain events in the Middle Ages which I did not wish to see repeated. Since the newspapers in question had not a high reputation generally—for what reason I myself did not exactly know—I saw in them more the products of envious annoyance rather than the results of a fundamental but incorrect opinion.

. . . .

When . . . my opinions in regard to anti-Semitism also slowly began to change in the course of time, it was probably my most serious change.

This change caused me most of my severe mental struggles, and only after months of agonizing between reason and feeling, victory began to favor reason. Two years later feeling had followed reason, and from now on became its most faithful guard and monitor.

In the period of this bitter struggle between spiritual education and cold reasoning, the pictures that the streets of Vienna showed me rendered me invaluable services. The time came when I no longer walked blindly through the mighty city as I had done at first, but, with open eyes, looked at the people as well as the buildings.

One day when I was walking through the inner city, I suddenly came upon a being clad in a long caftan, with black curls.

Is this also a Jew? was my first thought.

At Linz they certainly did not look like that. Secretly and cautiously I watched the man, but the longer I stared at this strange face and scrutinized one feature after the other, the more my mind reshaped the first question into another form:

Is this also a German?

As was my custom in such cases, I tried to remove my doubts by reading. For the first time in my life I bought some anti-Semitic pamphlets for a few pennies. They all started with the supposition that the reader already knew the Jewish question in principle or understood it to a certain degree. Finally, the tone was such that I again had doubts because the assertions were supported by such extremely unscientific arguments.

I then suffered relapses for weeks, and once even for months.

The matter seemed so monstrous, the accusations so unbounded that the fear of committing an injustice tortured me and made me anxious and uncertain again.

However, even I could no longer actually doubt that they were not Germans with a special religion, but an entirely different race; since I had begun to think about this question; since my attention was drawn to the Jews, I began to see Vienna in a different light from before. Wherever I went I saw Jews, and the more I saw of them, the sharper I began to distinguish them from other people. The inner city especially and the districts north of the Danube Canal swarmed with a people which through its appearance alone had no resemblance to the German people. . . .

I gradually realized that the Social Democratic press was headed primarily by Jews; but I did not attach special importance to this fact, as it was the same with the other newspapers. But one thing struck me: there was not one paper that employed Jews which had a really national tendency, as I understood it, based on my education and attitude.

Now, although I made an effort and tried to read these Marxian products of the press, my aversion was intensified; I tried to get better acquainted with the producers of this mass of knavery.

They all were Jews from the publishers downwards.

I took all the Social Democratic pamphlets I could get hold of and traced the names of their authors: they all were Jews. I memorized the names of all the leaders; the greater part of them were also members of the "chosen people"; no matter if they were representatives of the Reichsrat or secretaries of the unions, presidents of organizations or street agitators. One always found the same uncanny picture. The name Austerlitz, David, Adler, Ellenbogen, and so forth, will remain in my memory forever.

One thing had become clear to me: the party with whose little representatives I had to fight the hardest struggle during many months were almost entirely in the hands of a foreign race; it brought me internal happiness to realize definitely that the Jew was no German.

Only now I learned thoroughly to know the seducers of our people.

Only a year of my stay in Vienna had sufficed to convince me that no worker was so stubborn as not to give in to better knowledge and better arguments. Gradually I became acquainted with their own doctrine and I used it as a weapon in the battle for my own internal conviction.

Now success was nearly always on my side.

It was possible to save the great masses, but only after the greatest sacrifices of time and patience.

But it was never possible to free a Jew from his convictions. . . .

One did not know what to admire more: their glibness of tongue or their skill in lying.

I gradually began to hate them.

. . . .

All propaganda has to be popular and has to adapt its spiritual level to the perception of the least intelligent of those towards whom it intends to direct itself. Therefore its spiritual level has to be screwed the lower, the greater the mass of people which one wants to attract. But if the problem involved, like the propaganda for carrying on a war, is to include an entire people in its field of action, the caution in avoiding too high spiritual assumptions cannot be too great.

The more modest, then, its scientific ballast is, and the more it exclusively considers the feelings of the masses, the more striking will be its success. This, however, is the best proof whether a particular piece of propaganda is right or wrong, and not the successful satisfaction of a few scholars or "aesthetic" languishing monkeys.

This is just the art of propaganda that it, understanding the great masses' world of ideas and feelings, finds, by a correct psychological form, the way to the attention, and further to the heart, of the great masses. That our superclever heads never understand this proves only their mental inertia or their conceit.

But if one understands the necessity of the attitude of the attracting skill of propaganda towards the great masses, the following rule then results:

It is wrong to wish to give propaganda the versatility of perhaps scientific teaching.

The great masses' receptive ability is only very limited, their understanding is small, but their forgetfulness is great. As a consequence of these facts, all effective propaganda has to limit itself only to a very few points and to use them like slogans until even the very last man is able to imagine what is intended by such a word. As soon as one sacrifices this basic principle and tries to become versatile, the effect will fritter away, as the masses are neither able to digest the material offered nor to retain it. Thus the result is weakened and finally eliminated. . . .

The people, in an overwhelming majority, are so feminine in their nature and attitude that their activities and thoughts are motivated less by sober consideration than by feeling and sentiment.

This sentiment, however, is not complicated but very simple and complete. There are not many differentiations, but rather a positive or a negative; love or hate, right or wrong, truth or lie; but never half this and half that, or partially, etc.

The English propaganda understood and considered all this in the most ingenious manner. There were really no half measures which perhaps might have given cause for doubt.

The proof of this brilliant knowledge of the primitiveness of feeling of the great masses was to be found in the atrocity propaganda that had been adapted to this, thus ruthlessly and ingeniously securing moral steadfastness at the front, even during the greatest defeats, and further in the just as striking pinning down of the German enemy as the only party guilty of the War's outbreak; a lie, the unsurpassed, impudent, and biased stubbornness of which and how it was brought forth took into account the sentimental and extreme attitude of this great people and therefore gained credence.

But how effective this kind of propaganda is is shown most strikingly by the fact that after four years it was not only able to make the enemy hold his own, but it even began to eat into our own people. . . .

All advertising, whether it lies in the field of business or of politics, will carry success by continuity and regular uniformity of application.

Here, too, the enemy's war propaganda set a typical example. It was limited to a few points of view, calculated exclusively for the masses, and it was carried out with untiring persistency. Basic ideas and forms of execution which had once been recognized as being right were employed throughout the entire War, and never did one make even the slightest change. At the beginning it was apparently crazy in the impudence of its assertions, later it became disagreeable, and finally it was believed. After four and a half years a revolution broke out in Germany the slogan of which came from the enemy's war propaganda.

In England, however, one understood one thing more: that for this spiritual weapon the possible success lies only in the mass of its application, but that success amply covers all expenses.

There, propaganda was considered a weapon of the first order, whereas with us it was the last bread of the politician without office, and a pot-boiler for the modest hero.

All in all, its effect was just nil.

. . . .

One day I received orders from my headquarters[2] to find out what was behind an apparently political society which, under the name of "German Workers' Party," intended to hold a meeting on one of the following days, in which also Gottfried

2. Hitler was officially demobilized but still carried on his company's rolls and living in barracks in 1919 when these events took place. Unlike Mussolini, Hitler served throughout World War I as a front-line soldier, rose to the rank of corporal, and won two decorations for bravery. With such a war record high ranking army officers were glad to use him for confidential activities.

Feder[3] was supposed to speak; I was to go there and to look at the society and to report upon it. . . .

When in the evening I entered the "Leiber" room which later on was to become of historical importance for us, of the former Sterneckerbräu in Munich, I met there about twenty to twenty-five people, chiefly from among the lower walks of life.

Feder's lecture was already familiar to me from the courses, and therefore I could devote myself to looking at the assembly proper.

Its impression on me was neither good nor bad; a new foundation like so many others. . . .

After listening for about two hours I did not judge the "German Workers' Party" from any different point of view. I was glad when Feder finally finished. I had seen enough and was just about to go when the open discussion, which was announced at that moment, made me decide to stay after all. But here also everything seemed to take an unimportant course, till suddenly a "professor" was given the floor who first expressed doubts of the correctness of Feder's reasons, and then, after the latter had replied very ably, planted himself on the ground of "facts," not without recommending, however, to the young party to take up the "severance" of Bavaria from "Prussia" as an especially important point of the party program. The man had the cheek to pretend that, in that case, German Austria especially would immediately link itself to Bavaria, and that then the peace would be a far better one, and other similar nonsense. Thereupon I could not help but announce my intention to speak, in order to give this learned man my opinion on this point, with the result that the gentleman who had just spoken left the scene like a drenched poodle, even before I had finished. When I spoke they had listened with astonished faces, and only when I was about to say good-night to the assembly, a man came running after me, introduced himself (I even did not understand his name correctly), and handed me a small booklet, obviously a political

3. Prominent as an economic theorist in the early days of the Nazi movement, and principal author of the party program, adopted in 1920 and declared "immutable" in 1926, Feder later sank to insignificance in the days of Nazi power.

pamphlet, with the urgent request that I read this by all means.

This was very agreeable to me, for now I could hope that perhaps in this way I could become acquainted with this boring society in an easier manner, without being forced again to attend such interesting meetings. For the rest, this man who was apparently a worker, had made a good impression on me. With this now I went away.

In those days I still lived in the barracks of the Second Infantry Regiment, in a tiny room which still showed very clearly the traces of the Revolution. During the day I was out, mostly with the Rifle Regiment 4, or at meetings or lectures with some other army unit, etc. Only at night I slept in my quarters. As I used to wake up in the morning before five o'clock, I had gotten into the habit of throwing pieces of bread or hard crusts to the little mice which spent their time in the small room, and then to watch these droll little animals romp and scuffle for these few delicacies. I had already known so much misery during my lifetime that I was able to imagine only too well the hunger, and therefore also the pleasure, of the little things.

On the morning after this meeting, towards five o'clock, I was lying awake in my cot and looking at this bustle and activity. Since I could not go to sleep again, I suddenly thought of the previous evening, and now I remembered the booklet which the worker had given to me. And so I began to read. It was a little pamphlet in which the author, this particular worker, described how, out of the medley of Marxist and unionist phrases, he again arrived at thinking in national terms; this explained the title, "My Political Awakening." Once I had started, I read the entire little document with interest; for in it an event was reflected which I had gone through personally in a similar way twelve years ago. Involuntarily I saw thus my own development come to life again before my eyes. In the course of the day I thought about it several times and was finally just about to put it away when, less than a week later, to my astonishment, I received a postcard with the news that I had been accepted as a member of the "German Workers' Party"; I was requested to express my opinion about this, and for that purpose I was expected to come to a committee meeting of the party on the following Wednesday.

I was actually more than astonished at this manner of "winning" members, and I did not know whether to be annoyed or to laugh at it. I had no intention of joining a ready-made party, but wished to found a party of my own. This unreasonable demand was really out of the question for me.

I was just about to send the gentlemen my written reply, when curiosity gained the upper hand and I decided to appear on the day fixed in order to define my reasons orally.

Wednesday arrived. The restaurant in which the said meeting was to take place was the Alte Rosenbad in the Herrenstrasse; a very poor restaurant, to which only once in a blue moon somebody seemed to find his way by mistake. This was not surprising in the year 1919, when the menus of even the larger restaurants were able to attract customers but very modestly and poorly. But until then I had not known this inn at all.

I passed through the sparsely lit guestroom where not a soul was present, looked for the door to the adjoining room, and then I was face to face with the "meeting." In the twilight of a half-demolished gas lamp four young people were sitting at a table, among them also the author of the little booklet, who immediately greeted me in the most friendly terms and welcomed me as a new member of the "German Workers' Party."

Now I was somewhat taken aback. As I was informed that the actual "Chairman for the organization in the Reich" was still to come, I intended holding back my explanation. The latter finally appeared. . . .

Meanwhile my curiosity was again aroused and I was full of expectation for the things to come. . . .

Now the minutes of the last session were read, and the confidence of the assembly was expressed to the secretary. Next followed the treasury report (there were all in all 7 Marks and 50 Pfennings in the possession of the party), for which the assurance of the general confidence was expressed to the treasurer. Now this again was put down in the minutes. Then followed the First Chairman's reading of the answers to a letter from Kiel to one from Düsseldorf and to one from Berlin; everybody agreed to them. Now the documents received were read: a letter from Berlin, one from Düsseldorf, and one from Kiel, the arrival of which seemed to be accepted with great satisfaction. One explained this growing correspondence as the best and most visible symptom of the spreading importance of the "German Workers' Party." Then a lengthy discussion about the answers to be made took place.

Terrible, terrible; this was club-making of the worst kind and manner. And this club I now was to join?

Then the new memberships were discussed, that means, my being caught.

Now I began to ask questions. Apart from a few leading principles, nothing existed; no party program, no leaflets, nothing in print at all, no membership cards, not even a miserable rubber stamp; only visibly good faith and good will.

My smile had disappeared again, for what was all this but the typical symptom of utter helplessness and complete despair covering all previous parties, their programs, their intentions and their activities? What made these four young people come together to an outwardly so ridiculous activity was actually only the expression of their inner voice which, emotionally rather than consciously, made all the previous doings of parties appear as no longer suitable for a rise of the German nation as well as for the healing of its internal damages. I quickly read through the leading principles which were available in a typed copy, and in them I saw a seeking rather than knowledge. Many things were dim or uncertain, many things were missing, but nothing was there which in its turn could not be looked upon as a symptom of struggling toward realization.

I, too, knew what these people felt; it was the longing for a new movement which was to be more than a party in the previous sense of the word.

When I went home to the barracks on that evening, I had already formed my opinion of this society.

Now I was faced by perhaps the most serious question of my life: was I to join or was I to refuse? . . .

Now Fate itself seemed to give me a hint. I should never have joined one of the existing parties, and later on I will state the reasons for this; for this reason, however, this ridiculously small foundation with its handful of members seemed to me to have the advantage that it had not yet hardened into an "organization," but seemed to offer to the individual the chance for real personal activity. For this was the advantage which was bound to result: here one would still be able to work, and the smaller the movement was, the easier it would be to bring it into the right shape. Here the contents, the goal, and the way could still be fixed, something that with the existing great parties was impossible from the beginning.

The longer I tried to think about it, the more the conviction grew in my mind that just here, out of such a small movement, some day the rise of the nation could be prepared, but never from the political parliamentarian parties which clung much too much to the old ideas or even shared the advantages of the new régime. For what was to be announced now was a new view of life and not a new election slogan.

After two days of agonized pondering and reflection I finally arrived at the decision to take the step.

It was the most decisive decision of my life.

There could not, and must not, be a retreat.

Thus I registered as a member of the German Workers' Party[4] and received a provisional membership ticket with the number seven.

4. The party name was officially changed in April 1920 to National Socialist German Workers' Party. Hitler quickly became the party leader, but he did not establish absolute control until after becoming Chancellor, and then only through a "Blood Purge" in which his potential rivals within the Party were killed.

Freedom as Cure for the World's Ills

When President Franklin D. Roosevelt took office in January 1933, he had to face a major economic depression. Hasty and unsystematic improvization, modeled in part on patterns of war mobilization in 1917–19, met the crisis of massive unemployment more or less successfully; and in the years that followed, longer range reforms of many kinds were written into law. Then, toward the end of Roosevelt's second term of office, World War II broke out in Europe (September 1939) and a new focus of attention quickly came to dominate American public life.

Important elements in Congress and amongst the public at large felt that the United States had been mistaken in intervening in World War I, and tried to see that the error would not be repeated by preventing the economic involvements with Great Britain and France that had helped to entangle the United States in Europe's quarrels in 1917. The President, however, took a different line. He wished to use American economic power and productive capacity to strengthen the foes of Hitler and his Axis partners. Roosevelt argued that victory for Nazi Germany would create a serious and direct threat to the United States, so that arming others to fight against Hitler was a kind of insurance policy, protecting the national interest in the cheapest possible fashion.

Roosevelt also remembered the role President Wilson had played during World War I in voicing ideals that had seemed worth fighting for. In particular, the repudiation of American participation in the League of Nations seemed to many Americans including Roosevelt, to have been a great mistake and one of the causes for the outbreak of World War II. In January 1941, when the debate over United States foreign policy was still being very vigorously pursued by both "isolationists" and "interventionists"—as the two sides were called by their opponents—President Roosevelt therefore took the occasion of his annual "State of the Union" report to Congress to strike a Wilsonian note once more by defining the goals toward which the United States and the whole world ought, in his view, to strive.

The "Four Freedoms" first enunciated in the speech reprinted below later served as a sort of slogan to define the kind of world the American government wished to see emerge from the war.

FRANKLIN D. ROOSEVELT: STATE OF THE UNION ADDRESS, 1941

Mr. President, Mr. Speaker, Members of the Seventy-seventh Congress, I address you, the Members of the Seventy-seventh

From the *Congressional Record*, 77th Congress, First Session, Volume 87, Part 1, pp. 44-47.

Congress, at a moment unprecedented in the history of the Union. I use the word "unprecedented," because at no previous time has American security been as seriously threatened from without as it is today.

The Army and Navy, however, have made substantial progress during the past year. Actual experience is improving and speeding up our methods of production with every passing day. And today's best is not good enough for tomorrow.

I am not satisfied with the progress thus far made. The men in charge of the program represent the best in training, ability, and patriotism. They are not satisfied with the progress thus far made. None of us will be satisfied until the job is done.

No matter whether the original goal was set too high or too low, our objective is quicker and better results.

To give two illustrations:

We are behind schedule in turning out finished airplanes; we are working day and night to solve the innumerable problems and to catch up.

We are ahead of schedule in building warships; but we are working to get even further ahead of schedule.

To change a whole nation from a basis of peacetime production of implements of peace to a basis of wartime production of implements of war is no small task. And the greatest difficulty comes at the beginning of the program, when new tools and plant facilities and new assembly lines and shipways must first be constructed before the actual matériel begins to flow steadily and speedily from them.

The Congress, of course, must rightly keep itself informed at all times of the progress of the program. However, there is certain information, as the Congress itself will readily recognize, which, in the interests of our own security and those of the nations we are supporting must of needs be kept in confidence.

New circumstances are constantly begetting new needs for our safety. I shall ask this Congress for greatly increased new appropriations and authorizations to carry on what we have begun.

I also ask this Congress for authority and for funds sufficient to manufacture additional munitions and war supplies of many kinds, to be turned over to those nations which are now in actual war with aggressor nations.

Our most useful and immediate role is to act as an arsenal for them as well as for ourselves. They do not need manpower. They do need billions of dollars' worth of the weapons of defense.

The time is near when they will not be able to pay for them in ready cash. We cannot, and will not, tell them they must surrender merely because of present inability to pay for the weapons which we know they must have.

I do not recommend that we make them a loan of dollars with which to pay for these weapons—a loan to be repaid in dollars.

I recommend that we make it possible for those nations to continue to obtain war materials in the United States, fitting their orders into our own program. Nearly all of their matériel would, if the time ever came, be useful for our own defense.

Taking counsel of expert military and naval authorities, considering what is best for our own security, we are free to decide how much should be kept here and how much should be sent abroad to our friends who, by their determined and heroic resistance, are giving us time in which to make ready our own defense.

For what we send abroad we shall be repaid, within a reasonable time following the close of hostilities, in similar materials or, at our option, in other goods of many kinds which they can produce and which we need.

Let us say to the democracies, "We Americans are vitally concerned in your defense of freedom. We are putting forth our energies, our resources, and our organizing powers to give you the strength to regain and maintain a free world. We shall send you, in ever-increasing numbers, ships, planes, tanks, guns. This is our purpose and our pledge."

In fulfillment of this purpose we will not be intimidated by the threats of dictators that they will regard as a breach of international law and as an act of war our aid to the democracies which dare to resist their aggression. Such aid is not an act of war, even if a dictator should unilaterally proclaim it so to be.

When the dictators are ready to make war upon us, they will not wait for an act of war on our part. They did not wait for

Norway or Belgium or the Netherlands to commit an act of war.

Their only interest is in a new one-way international law, which lacks mutuality in its observance and, therefore, becomes an instrument of oppression.

The happiness of future generations of Americans may well depend upon how effective and how immediate we can make our aid felt. No one can tell the exact character of the emergency situations that we may be called upon to meet. The Nation's hands must not be tied when the Nation's life is in danger.

We must all prepare to make the sacrifices that the emergency —as serious as war itself—demands. Whatever stands in the way of speed and efficiency in defense preparations must give way to the national need.

A free nation has the right to expect full cooperation from all groups. A free nation has the right to look to the leaders of business, of labor, and of agriculture to take the lead in stimulating effort, not among other groups but within their own groups.

The best way of dealing with the few slackers or trouble makers in our midst is, first, to shame them by patriotic example; and if that fails, to use the sovereignty of government to save government.

As men do not live by bread alone, they do not fight by armaments alone. Those who man our defenses, and those behind them who build our defenses, must have the stamina and courage which come from an unshakable belief in the manner of life which they are defending. The mighty action which we are calling for cannot be based on a disregard of all things worth fighting for.

The Nation takes great satisfaction and much strength from the things which have been done to make its people conscious of their individual stake in the preservation of democratic life in America. Those things have toughened the fiber of our people, have renewed their faith and strengthened their devotion to the institutions we make ready to protect.

Certainly this is no time to stop thinking about the social and economic problems which are the root cause of the social revolution which is today a supreme factor in the world.

There is nothing mysterious about the foundations of a

healthy and strong democracy. The basic things expected by our people of their political and economic systems are simple. They are:

Equality of opportunity for youth and for others.

Jobs for those who can work.

Security for those who need it.

The ending of special privilege for the few.

The preservation of civil liberties for all.

The enjoyment of the fruits of scientific progress in a wider and constantly rising standard of living.

These are the simple and basic things that must never be lost sight of in the turmoil and unbelievable complexity of our modern world. The inner and abiding strength of our economic and political systems is dependent upon the degree to which they fulfill these expectations.

Many subjects connected with our social economy call for immediate improvement.

As examples:

We should bring more citizens under the coverage of old-age pensions and unemployment insurance.

We should widen the opportunities for adequate medical care.

We should plan a better system by which persons deserving or needing gainful employment may obtain it.

I have called for personal sacrifice. I am assured of the willingness of almost all Americans to respond to that call.

A part of the sacrifice means the payment of more money in taxes. In my Budget message I recommend that a greater portion of this great defense program be paid for from taxation than we are paying today. No person should try, or be allowed, to get rich out of this program; and the principle of tax payments in accordance with ability to pay should be constantly before our eyes to guide our legislation.

If the Congress maintains these principles, the voters, putting patriotism ahead of pocketbooks, will give you their applause.

In the future days, which we seek to make secure, we look forward to a world founded upon four essential human freedoms.

The first is freedom of speech and expression everywhere in the world.

The second is freedom of every person to worship God in his own way everywhere in the world.

The third is freedom from want, which, translated into world terms, means economic understandings which will secure to every nation a healthy peacetime life for its inhabitants everywhere in the world.

The fourth is freedom from fear—which, translated into world terms, means a world-wide reduction of armaments to such a point and in such a thorough fashion that no nation will be in a position to commit an act of physical aggression against any neighbor—anywhere in the world.

That is no vision of a distant millennium. It is a definite basis for a kind of world attainable in our own time and generation. That kind of world is the very antithesis of the so-called new order of tyranny which the dictators seek to create with the crash of a bomb.

To that new order we oppose the greater conception—the moral order. A good society is able to face schemes of world domination and foreign revolutions alike without fear.

Since the beginning of our American history we have been engaged in change—in a perpetual peaceful revolution—a revolution which goes on steadily, quietly adjusting itself to changing conditions—without the concentration camp or the quicklime in the ditch. The world order which we seek is the cooperation of free countries, working together in a friendly, civilized society.

This Nation has placed its destiny in the hands and heads and hearts of its millions of free men and women; and its faith in freedom under the guidance of God. Freedom means the supremacy of human rights everywhere. Our support goes to those who struggle to gain those rights or keep them. Our strength is in our unity of purpose.

To that high concept there can be no end save victory.

VII

Human Condition

A Nineteenth-Century View

Winwood Reade: The Martyrdom of Man

A Twentieth-Century View

A Nineteenth-Century View

Voltaire criticized orthodox Christianity in the name of reason and common sense. In the nineteenth century, the evolutionary biology of Darwin, the historical materialism of Marx and Engels, and the anthropological investigations of primitive cultures all provided new challenges to fundamental Christian dogma. The selection reprinted here, a portion of the final chapter of Winwood Reade's *The Martyrdom of Man,* is the climax of a biological and anthropological argument for the liberation of mankind from superstition.

Reade (1838–75) came from a middle-class English landowning family. His uncle Charles wrote the historical novel *The Cloister and the Hearth*; Winwood's father worked with the British East India Company. Winwood enrolled at Oxford but left without a degree. By 1862 he had published three long, unsuccessful novels, including the strongly anticlerical *Veil of Isis.* At age twenty-four he gave up writing, borrowed some money on his inheritance, and went to Africa, ostensibly to investigate the habits of the gorilla.

He returned to Africa twice more, in 1869 and 1873, and used his experiences as the basis of a second, more profitable literary career. He served as special correspondent to the London *Times,* and wrote several volumes about his explorations. He published *The Martyrdom of Man* in 1872; in the book, he used his knowledge of primitive societies to support his evolutionary arguments.

WINWOOD READE: THE MARTYRDOM OF MAN

A Nineteenth-Century View

We do not wish to extirpate religion from the life of man; we wish him to have a religion which will harmonise with his intel-

From Winwood Reade, *The Martyrdom of Man* (New York, C. P. Somerby, 1876), pp. 535-43.

lect, and which inquiry will strengthen, not destroy. We wish, in fact, to *give* him a religion, for now there are many who have none. We teach that there is a God, but not a God of the anthropoid variety—not a God who is gratified by compliments in prose and verse, and whose attributes can be catalogued by theologians. God is so great that he cannot be defined by us. God is so great that he does not deign to have personal relations with us human atoms that are called men. Those who desire to worship their Creator must worship him through mankind. Such, it is plain, is the scheme of Nature. We are placed under secondary laws, and these we must obey. To develop to the utmost our genius and our love—that is the only true religion. To do that which deserves to be written, to write that which deserves to be read, to tend the sick, to comfort the sorrowful, to animate the weary, to keep the temple of the body pure, to cherish the divinity within us, to be faithful to the intellect, to educate those powers which have been entrusted to our charge and to employ them in the service of humanity—that is all that we can do. Then our elements shall be dispersed, and all is at an end. All is at an end for the unit, all is at an end for the atom, all is at an end for the speck of flesh and blood with the little spark of instinct which it calls its mind; but all is not at an end for the actual man, the true being, the glorious One. We teach that the soul is immortal; we teach that there is a future life; we teach that there is a heaven in the ages far away—not for us single corpuscules, not for us dots of animated jelly, but for the One of whom we are the elements, and who, though we perish, never dies, but grows from period to period, and who by the united efforts of single molecules called men, or of those cell-groups called nations, is raised towards the divine power which he will finally attain. Our religion, therefore, is virtue; our hope is placed in the happiness of our posterity; our faith is the perfectibility of man.

A day will come when the European God of the nineteenth century will be classed with the gods of Olympus and the Nile; when surplices and sacramental plate will be exhibited in museums; when nurses will relate to children the legends of the Christian mythology as they now tell them fairly tales. A day will come when the current belief in property after death (for is not existence property, and the dearest property of all?) will be accounted a strange and selfish idea, just as we smile at the savage chief who believes that his gentility will be continued in the world beneath the ground, and that he will there be attended by his concubines and slaves. A day will come when mankind will be as the family of the forest, which lived faithfully within itself according to the Golden Rule in order that it might not die. But love, not fear, will unite the human race. The world will become a heavenly commune to which men will bring the inmost treasures of their hearts, in which they will reserve for themselves not even a hope, not even the shadow of a joy, but will give up all for all mankind. With one faith, with one desire, they will labour together in the sacred cause—the extinction of disease, the extinction of sin, the perfection of genius, the perfection of love, the invention of immortality, the exploration of the infinite, and the conquest of creation.

You blessed ones who shall inherit that future age of which we can only dream—you pure and radiant beings who shall succeed us on the earth—when you turn back your eyes on us poor savages grubbing in the ground for our daily bread, eating flesh and blood, dwelling in vile bodies which degrade us every day to a level with the beasts, tortured by pains and by animal propensities, buried in gloomy superstitions, ignorant of Nature which yet holds us in her bonds; when you read of us in books, when you think of what we are and compare us with yourselves, remember that it is to us you owe the foundation of your happiness and grandeur—to us who now in our libraries and laboratories and star-towers and dissecting-rooms and workshops are preparing the materials of human growth. And as for ourselves, if we are sometimes inclined to regret that our lot is cast in these unhappy days, let us remember how much more fortunate we are than those who lived before us a few centuries ago. The working man enjoys more luxuries to-day than did the king of England in Anglo-Saxon times; and at his command are intellectual delights which but a little while ago the most learned in the land could not obtain. All this we owe to the labours of other men. Let us therefore remember them with gratitude; let us follow their glorious example by adding something new to the knowledge of mankind; let us pay to the future the debt which we owe to the past.

All men, indeed, cannot be poets, inventors, or philanthropists; but all men can join in that gigantic and god-like work the progress of creation. Whoever improves his own nature improves the universe of which he is a part. He who strives to subdue his evil passions—vile remnants of the old four-footed life—and who cultivates the social affections; he who endeavours to better his condition and to make his children wiser and happier than himself; whatever may be his motives, he will not have lived in vain. But if he act thus not from mere prudence, not in the vain hope of being rewarded in another world, but from a pure sense of duty as a citizen of Nature, as a patriot of the planet on which he dwells, then our philosophy which once appeared to him so cold and cheerless will become a religion of the heart, and will elevate him to the skies; the virtues which were once for him mere abstract terms will become endowed with life, and will hover round him like guardian angels, conversing with him in his solitude, consoling him in his afflictions, teaching him how to live and how to die. But this condition is not to be easily attained. As the saints and prophets were often forced to practise long vigils and fastings and prayers before their ecstasies would fall upon them and their visions would appear, so virtue in its purest and most exalted form can only be acquired by means of severe and long-continued culture of the mind. Persons with feeble and untrained intellects may live according to their conscience, but the conscience itself will be defective. To cultivate the intellect is therefore a religious duty; and when this truth is fairly recognised by men, the religion which teaches that the intellect should be distrusted, and that it should be subservient to faith, will inevitably fall. . . .

. . . .

It is incorrect to say "theology is not a progressive science." The worship of ancestral ghosts, the worship of pagan deities, the worship of a single god, are successive periods of progress in the science of divinity. And in the history of that science, as in the history of all others, a curious fact may be observed. Those who overthrow an established system are compelled to attack its founders, and to show that their method was unsound, that their reasoning was fallacious, and that their experiments were incomplete. And yet the men who create the revolution are made in the likeness of the men whose doctrines they subvert. The system of Ptolemy was supplanted by the system of Copernicus, yet Copernicus was the Ptolemy of the sixteenth century. In the same manner, we who assail the Christian faith are the true successors of the early Christians, above whom we are raised by the progress of eighteen hundred years. As they preached against gods that were made of stone, so we preach against gods that are made of ideas. As they were called atheists and blasphemers, so are we. And is our task more difficult than theirs? We have not, it is true, the same stimulants to offer. We cannot threaten that the world is about to be destroyed; we cannot bribe our converts with a heaven, we cannot make them tremble with a hell. But though our religion appears too pure, too unselfish for mankind, it is not really so, for we live in a noble and enlightened age. At the time of the Romans and the Greeks the Christian faith was the highest to which the common people could attain. A faith such as that of the Stoics and the Sadducees could only be embraced by cultivated minds, and culture was then confined to a chosen few. But now knowledge, freedom, and prosperity are covering the earth. For three centuries past, human virtue has been steadily increasing, and mankind is prepared to receive a higher faith. But in order to build we must first destroy. Not only the Syrian superstition must be attacked, but also the belief in a personal God, which engenders a slavish and Oriental condition of the mind; and the belief in a posthumous reward, which engenders a selfish and solitary condition of the heart. These beliefs are therefore injurious to human nature. They lower its dignity; they arrest its development; they isolate its affections.

We shall not deny that many beautiful sentiments are often mingled with the faith in a personal Deity, and with the hopes of happiness in a future state; yet we maintain that, however refined they may appear, they are selfish at the core, and that if removed they will be replaced by sentiments of a nobler and a purer kind. They cannot be removed without some disturbance and distress, yet the sorrows thus caused are salutary and sublime. The supreme and mysterious Power by whom the universe has been created, and by whom it has been appointed to run its course under fixed and invariable law; that awful One to whom it is profanity to pray, of whom it is idle and irreverent to argue and debate, of whom we should never presume to think save with humility and awe; that Unknown God has ordained that mankind should be elevated by misfortune, and that happiness should grow out of misery and pain.

I give to universal history a strange but true title—*The Martyrdom of Man*. In each generation the human race has been tortured that their children might profit by their woes. Our own prosperity is founded on the agonies of the past. Is it therefore unjust that we also should suffer for the benefit of those who are to come? Famine, pestilence, and war are no longer essential for the advancement of the human race. But a season of mental anguish is at hand, and through this we must pass in order that our posterity may rise. The soul must be sacrificed; the hope in immortality must die. A sweet and charming illusion must be taken from the human race, as youth and beauty vanish never to return.

A Twentieth-Century View

Pierre Teilhard de Chardin (1881–1955) was a geologist, a Jesuit priest and a man of wide-ranging synthetic mind. His championship of the universality of evolution (including evolution of religious truths) led his ecclesiastical superiors to dismiss him from a teaching post at Paris in 1925. They sent him to China, where he helped to discover "Peking man." At the time of its discovery, the skull dug up in a cave near Peking was one of the oldest known evidences of human evolution. Such a find required re-evaluation of older ideas of how men had evolved. Teilhard de Chardin became one of the world experts on this question through writings that set out to fit the new discoveries into what had been known before. In the 1930's he took part in several expeditions to remote regions of east Asia looking for additional evidences of early men. Toward the end of his life, however, he concluded that he had been searching in the wrong place, for numerous finds after World War II seem to show that the cradle of mankind was in Africa.

Teilhard de Chardin always connected his interest in human origins with an effort to fit the contemporary scene into a cosmic frame of reference. A vast time scale, he believed, was needed to understand what was happening in the world; and a clear grasp of really important trends could even generate foresight into the shape of things to come. His principal work dealing with such speculations, *The Phenomenon of Man*, was published 1938–40, but attracted little attention until after his death. (An English translation appeared in 1959.)

The essay, approximately one-third of which is reproduced below, was written in the last year of Teilhard de Chardin's life, 1954–55. It thus constitutes his final effort to define man's place in the universe as he saw it. The editors have eliminated some of the original footnotes, mainly references to other authors. A few short passages have also been omitted where the author's private technical jargon seemed too difficult to follow without excessively elaborate commentary.

PIERRE TEILHARD DE CHARDIN: THE SINGULARITIES OF THE HUMAN SPECIES

Considered in its pre- or para-sapiens phase, the human zoological group shows in its structures, as I noted a moment ago, distinct traces of the divergent ramification usual in all pre-human phyla. But this is not all. In addition—another indication of its immature state—it does not seem, in a period covering some hundreds of thousands of years, to have succeeded in notably spreading beyond the frontiers of the territory in which it was born. It is curious that, except in southern and western Europe,

From Pierre Teilhard de Chardin, *The Appearance of Man*, translated by J. M. Cohen, pp. 232-252.

the Quaternary area of the old "biface" implements more or less coincides with that of the great Pliocene anthropoids.

From the beginning of the *sapiens* stage (upper Palæolithic), on the other hand, events come thick and fast in the field of geographical extension. First a visible movement of the principal focus of hominisation (C1) from subtropical Africa northwards, in the direction of the Mediterranean. And then, departing from this new base, in less than twenty thousand years the *sapiens* sheet spreads without appreciable breaks (either anatomical or cultural) over the whole of northern Europe—and passing beyond Siberia into America north and south. The sheet is apparently not very coherent at the beginning; but through it a continuity of type and custom is maintained sufficient, despite its wide extension, to make the formation of fresh cleavages between human communities henceforth very difficult. This is clear both to anthropologists and ethnographers.

In fact, with the *sapiens* type (I was going to say "thread") at last found, the Noosphere[1] begins once and for all to be woven: a Noosphere still loose of course, but one in which we already recognize the strong envelope of thought in which we exist today: that of a humanity finally joined together at all its edges—and traversed by a network of links which, latterly becoming aerial and "'ethereal," more and more literally present, in the immensity of their organism, the image of a nervous system.

Simply observed from a biological point of view, the history of this bursting into flower is nothing short of amazing.

But it is just here that, instead of admiring, many people on the contrary begin to be afraid.

"For, after all," they cry, "interesting though it is scientifically, since it shows us the secret ways of matter, may not this

1. Mental world. Nous=Greek for "mind." The author coined this term as a twin to "biosphere," meaning the realm of living things on and near the Earth's surface, and "lithosphere," meaning the envelope of rock surrounding the Earth's moulten core. This is a fundamental concept for Teilhard de Chardin. It allows him to conceive of thought and the changes thought makes in the world as part of an evolutionary cosmic process, in which the emergence of life, the formation of molecules and atoms, etc., were prior less complex, less fully conscious stages. [Eds.]

vast movement of planetary arrangement happen (unfortunately) to be one of these blind natural phenomena that once launched rush madly onwards until they destroy themselves? Perhaps last century saw the transient optimum of the accommodation on earth of a species which then reached the comfortable limits of its expansion and interconnections. But may not this state of things be now rapidly deteriorating by running out of control?

"Only look at what is happening at this very moment all around us.

"As the combined effect of an almost vertical growth of population and a no less rapid increase in the radius of action (that is to say the *volume*) of each individual on the surface of the globe, the Noosphere—as you call it—after comfortably expanding into still unoccupied domains, is obviously beginning to be compressed upon itself. And is not this progressive closing of the vice bringing all kinds of disquieting symptoms with it?

"*a* A rapid exhaustion of the nutritional and industrial resources of the earth.

"*b* Disappearance and levelling, under a layer of neutral and homogeneous culture, of the differences effected in the course of history by the rich variety of human products.

"*c* Mechanisation (at the same time by industry, institutions and propaganda) of individual values and thoughts.

"*d* Fissure and breaking up of countries, split apart by the very excess of the pressure that brings them togther.

"For reasons inescapably linked with the biological forces of reproduction, with the physically increasing power of reflexion, and lastly with the closed curvature of the earth, it is correct that the species is contracting on itself and totalising, both in a single movement. There is no way of escaping the squeeze. But how can one help seeing in all this that at the same time the human quality in us, very far from perfecting itself, is becoming degraded and dehumanized."

This is what they are repeating, in the name of realism or even of science and in a variety of tones, at the present time.

Now it is precisely this view that I have set out to rebut with all my strength in these pages.

It is impossible of course to disagree with the premisses of the judgement passed. At the end of a period of expansion covering all historical time (and the end of prehistory) humanity has suddenly entered a painful state of compression on itself. This is a fact. After the initial step of individual reflexion—after the decisive emergence of the forces of co-reflexion in *Homo sapiens* at his beginnings—now for a fully extended humanity comes the dangerous passage from dilation to contraction: the delicate change of phase (see Fig. 1).

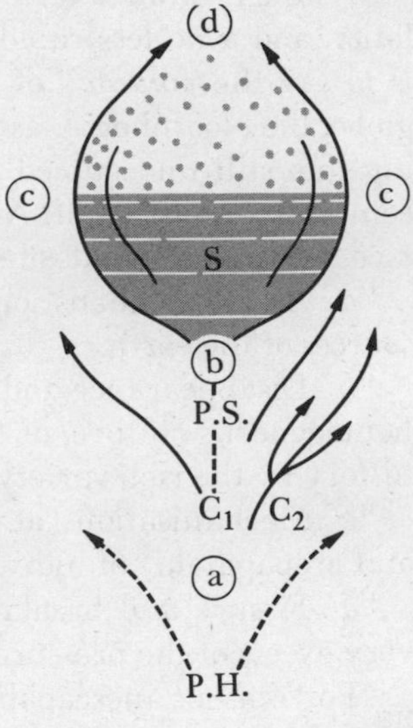

Fig. 1. Diagram explaining the history of the structure of the human phylum
P.H., pre- or para-hominians (Australopitheci, etc.)
P.S., Men of the *pre-* or *para-sapiens* type (Pithecanthropoids, Neaderthaloids, etc.)
S., *H. sapiens*
a., Initial critical point of reflexion[2] (beginnings of hominisation)
b., Decisive emergence, with *H. sapiens*, of Co-reflexion[3]
c.c., (Present-day) passage for humanity, in the course of co-reflexion, from the dilated to the compressed phase of his evolution
d., Position presumed (by extrapolation of a higher critical point of *supra*-reflexion[4] (Point "Omega")
C_1 and C_2, African and Southern Asiatic focuses of hominisation (C_2 miscarrying with the Pithecanthropines)

At the moment of taking a step into the unknown it is natural that we should hesitate. But have we nothing to reassure us? Can we not tell ourselves that if the first two special situations faced by our species in the past both clearly represent a success

2. A technical term here. Means using symbols (words mainly) to guide action, affecting interaction with the world, i.e., "knowing."

3. Knowing that one knows, involving consciousness of self, individually and collectively.

4. An as yet largely undefinable intensification of Noospheric interaction.

for life, the third (I mean the totalisation into which we are entering) has every chance, despite certain appearances to the contrary, of also marking in its way a step forward?

Can twentieth-century humanity be a species approaching its end? Not at all, as I shall attempt to show; on the contrary, and by very virtue of the powers heating and forging it, a species entering on the plenitude of its *particular* genesis; something quite new to biology that is beginning.

Biological interpretation of the socialisation of humanity: Humanity, a phylum converging on itself

Whenever a new human individual comes into the world, he finds other humans around him, to reassure him and accustom him to the people and things on which he opens his eyes.

The continuously growing tragedy of men-taken-as-a-whole is that they are in an opposite situation; by the very conditions of the cosmic situation engendering them, *reflexion* and *co-reflexion* (at least in the first evolutionary stage where we still are) is like waking all alone in the night. For the individual man is essentially family, tribe, nation. Humanity, on the other hand, has not yet found other humanities around it, to lean down and tell it where it is going.

Considering this darkness and isolation from birth, it is only too easy to understand the anxiety that has seized our generation, suddenly confronted with the reality of a tide that forces us upon one another, body and soul, on an increasingly contracting globe, and threatens to stifle us.

How can we help feeling that, linked though it is to the very mechanism of cosmogenesis, this anxiety might take an unwonted and monstrous form if it were to continue much longer? At the point of biological evolution which we have reached (that is to say in order to balance within us the rising forces of reflexion) we have an absolute need to find a compass and a road. Without them we shall panic! Unless we suppose the world to be intrinsically pathless (and the very fact of our existence denies this), how can we help thinking that both are within hand's reach if we search carefully?

Let us see whether it may not be possible for us to escape from the anxiety into which we have been thrown at this moment by the dangerous power of thought—simply by thinking still better. And to do so, let us begin by ascending till we are above the trees that hide the wood. That is to say, by forgetting for a moment the details of economic crises, political tensions and class wars which block our horizon, let us raise ourselves high enough to observe as a whole and dispassionately the general progress of hominisation over the last fifty or sixty years.

Placed at this favourable distance, what do we see immediately, and what would be *specially* noticed by a possible observer coming from the stars?

Two major phenomena without doubt.

1. First, that in the course of half a century technology has made incredible progress: not technics of a dispersed and local kind but a true *geo-technology* extending the closely interdependent network of its enterprises over the whole earth.

2. And secondly, that during the same period, at the same rate and on the same scale of planetary co-operation and accomplishment, science has transformed in all directions (from the infinitely small to the vast and the vastly complicated) our common vision of the world and our common power of action.

Henceforth I shall have continuously to insist on the *strictly* (and not only *metaphorically*) biological nature of these two conjoint events. But prior to all discussion of the organic, additive and universal character of the effects of co-reflexion, we must surely be struck at first glance by the reappearance in this context of the famous *pair* complexity/consciousness, the spiral ascent of which characterises, as we have seen, the appearance and developments of life throughout the geological periods.

Here, a material arrangement generating psychic growth. And there, the awakening of a psyche generating still more arrangement.

Seeing this well-known sign, how can we for a moment doubt that in the spasm of human totalisation, it is evolution itself, and the *main current* of evolution, that is continuing its march forward in the form of what we call *civilisation*.

What leads us astray here, *in casu*,[5] is of course the change of order in the scale of operations. Applied in turn to atoms, then molecules, then cells, the idea of a progressive "centro-complexification" of matter seems to us a genuinely organic affair. We accept it unblinkingly. Extended, on the other hand, to living autonomous individuals (that is to say ultimately to ourselves) it tends to appear to us unreal if not shocking. As if in acquiring our little ego, we had become too grand still to have the faculty for being integrated as elements in any physical unity of a higher order than our own. It is as if we were actually free to deny its *natural* value to the immense and universal biological process of socialisation.

Socialisation.

We can no longer deceive ourselves about the implacable determinism of the phenomenon itself. Multiplied by the play of reproduction, living individuals no longer align themselves only, conforming to the laws of speciation, in a system of ramified phyla. From the very lowest zological forms they (all, though in different degrees) at the same time manifest an evident tendency to join together: sometimes by links of a mainly physiological kind, giving birth to kinds of poly-organisms (colonies of Cœlenterata); and sometimes by mainly psychic links (colonies of insects) leading to true societies. No individual without a population. And no population without association.

We know all this, and moreover in the course of our lives we experience it.

Then why, through a misconceived instinct of self-defence or out of intellectual habit, should we persist in treating this capacity and inclination of all living beings (the more living they are) to draw together and co-ordinate as something accidental or para-biological? Why, in defiance of the facts, still refuse to recognise in the irresistible rise through the biosphere of the effects of socialisation a superior form of what I have already called "the cosmic process of corpusculation"?

Would not the whole spectacle of the world become clearer to our eyes if only, looking what is new and extraordinary in the

5. Latin: "in this case."

face, we could make up our minds to admit that, after the atoms, the molecules and the cells, it is whole animals, it is men themselves for whom the moment has now come: that the universe is now engaging them in its syntheses in order that the *vortex* of evolution may continue to coil on itself?

From this point of view (see Fig. 1) would not what we have so far called the Noosphere be structurally and genetically only a privileged realm of space in which . . . a *whole phylum* . . . is assembling on itself to form a single gigantic corpuscle?

Is this really something to be afraid of? Should we not rather feel reassured?

For, in the course of this unprecedented biological operation of a whole species "imploding" on itself, we stand at this moment precisely at the sensitive, "equatorial" point; here the evolution of *Homo sapiens,* having hitherto been expansive, is now beginning to become compressive. Inevitably this change of condition, at its onset, gave us a kind of vertigo. But enlightened at last by a little more knowledge, we now see that we can face the high pressures of the upper hemisphere, which we have just entered, without fear. Without fear, I say; for, by the very mechanism of cosmogenesis the forces of planetary contraction at present being released will inevitably win our consent to more arrangement, that is to say, in the long run, to more consciousness—provided that we obey them.

Here then are the compass and road we needed and were looking for, both contained in this very simple formula:

"Under all circumstances always advance upwards, where technically, mentally and affectively everything (in us and around us) *most rapidly converges.*"

. . . .

Beneath the ups and downs of human history: the accumulation of a co-reflective

I have just pleaded the urgency of an integration (without confusion) of the Social with the Biological. Such ideas are habitually met with arguments based on the apparently unstable and superficial character of human acquirements in all their forms.

"For, after all," they object, "is not a child coming into the world today in Paris or New York born just as ignorant and helpless as a little Neanderthaler?" And if tomorrow we should run out of grain, iron or coal (a possible eventuality) should we not be forced back to the age of cave-dwelling—neither more nor less? Let us have no illusions! All the time he has been socialising in the *sapiens* state, man has not changed physically or spiritually. Only strip him of his varnish of civilisation and you'll find him neither more nor less than he was in Cro-Magnon times.

This would-be dogma of the present invariability of human nature could be met scientifically with serious reservations. Whatever the assurance of our modern neo-Darwinians when they come to refute anything that looks like Lamarckism, one cannot quite see how in the case of animals (notably insects), a number of instincts, surely hereditary today, can possibly have become established without a chromosomic fixation of certain *acquired habits* (methods of making nests, hunting, etc.) which have gradually become germinal by force of *repeated* education (with or without social pressure) on a sufficiently great number of generations. Anatomically, it is true, man does not seem to have appreciably changed for some thirty thousand years.[6] But psychically, it is certain that we are the same? That is to say, are we quite certain, for example, that we are not born today with the faculty of perceiving and accepting, as instantly evident and natural, certain dimensions, certain relationships, certain evidences[7] that escaped our forebears? And would not this alone afford sufficient indication that, biologically speaking, we are still on the move?

But let us leave this point aside since it is still under discussion. And, free to return to the question later, let us provisionally admit that in his physical and mental structure the individual *sapiens* is in fact a definitely fixed animal form. How, I

6. Perhaps simply because the interval of time is too short; or perhaps because we still lack any means of directly following the possible progress of cerebration on the level of the neurons. [Au.]

7. The evolutionary structure of the universe, for example; or the absolute value of the individual; or the primacy of human solidarity. [Au.]

ask, would this fixity (if proved) prevent him, any more than an atom of hydrogen or carbon, from finding himself engaged, in *combination*, in corpuscular structures of a higher order than himself? As an element, of course, man would no longer be able to change himself. But would it not still be a very real method of evolution for him to form an integral part of a system (the Noosphere) in full evolution? . . .

. . . .

It is already a great deal, no doubt, but it is not yet enough to recognise . . . that, within the Noosphere, by reason of the intraphyletic convergence proper to the human species, zoological evolution has changed its methods and its ways of invention. Still more important is the fact that, correlatively with its change of motion this *New Evolution* has become capable of utilising for its ends an equally *new* form of *heredity*, much more flexible and richer, without being any the less "biological" on that account. It is no longer a matter only of combinations of chromosomes transmitted by fertilisation, but *educative* transmission of a complex, continuously modified and augmented by conduct and thought. Within and in virtue of this complex, individual human beings are so subtly developed through the centuries that it is strictly impermissible to compare any two men who are not contemporaries—that is to say are taken from two quite different times t and t^1 of the Noosphere.

By what mysterious labour of groping and selection is it formed, this *additive and irreversible* kernel of institutions and viewpoints to which we adjust ourselves at birth and which we each contribute to enlarge, more or less consciously and infinitesimally, throughout our lives? What is it that makes one invention or idea among millions of others "take on," grow and, finally, fix itself unchangeably as a human axion or *Consensus*? We should find it difficult to say. But the very fact that beneath the cultural oscillations analysed by Spengler, Toynbee and others, the tide of a common *Weltanschauung*, the gradual perception of a *Direction of History* is continuously rising, without change of course, within the Noosphere—this material fact, I say, is indisputable.

There are technical discoveries (Fire, Nuclear Physics, etc.) and *there are* intellectual revelations (the rights of the individual, the reality of a cosmogenesis, etc.), which once made or received are man's for ever. And the human acquirement thus accumulated through the ages is not to be confused with an inert residue (the "very least common multiple") slowly deposited by the experience of centuries. It is a living force impregnating and completing, in its most essential humanity, each new fraction of human material as it newly appears.

No, it is certainly untrue that, as is still said, the human being in us starts from zero with each new generation. The truth is, on the contrary, that by the accumulated effect of co-reflexion, it takes off each time at a higher turn of the spiral, in a world constantly more orderly and better understood—*orthogenetically*.

So it is principally by trying thoroughly to analyse the evolutionary possibilities and requirements of this *collectively thought* Universe (in which our thinking individualities ultimately find their continuity and consistency) that we can best hope ultimately to glimpse in broad outline the continuation and end of hominisation on earth.

The Terminal Singularity of the Human Species. An Upper Critical Point of Ultrareflexion?

Reflexion entails foresight.

The more, therefore, man collectively reflects on himself, the more inevitable it is that the problem of his destiny will take a place of urgency in his mind. And the more natural it will become for a sort of resentment to arise in his heart because his isolation in the Universe causes him to be ignorant of it. How long is the life of a living planet? To what heights does it rise, and how does it end?

There has, of course, been no lack of attempts at an answer. . . .

But what surprises one on reading these various anticipations of the future, is the absence of all firm principle as a basis for the conjectures put forward. Chance groupings into the future, rather than serious *extrapolations*.

Without pretending to be more clairvoyant than the rest, I want . . . to point out how, by logically extending a certain law of recurrence recognised once and for all as having universal validity, one finds onself impelled not, of course, to draw an imaginative picture of the sequel for humanity but at least to recognise the existence of certain conditions, of certain contours without which our world of tomorrow would be inconceivable; since it would be in contradiction to certain positive and definite characteristics of our world today.

Let us briefly repeat what we have learnt above . . . by the broadest possible survey of the facts actually placed at our disposal by the investigations and reconstructions of science. One can reduce this lesson to the following three points:

a. By the *reflective* nature of his psychism, individual man appears in the field of our experience to be the extreme form so far attained in an isolated element by the cosmic process (or drift) of complexity/consciousness.

b. In the species man (so far as we can judge from the phenomena of planetary arrangement and co-reflexion) *one more step*—a dizzy step—is in course of being taken in the complexification and (psychic) interiorisation of the cosmic material. By dint of *social* links operating in a reflective field, a whole phylum is coagulating and organo-psychically synthesising with itself on the scale of the whole earth.

c. Far from appearing to be slowing up or reaching its ceiling around us, this biological movement of pan-human convergence has simply been entering (for the last century) into a *compressive phase*, in which it is bound to accelerate from now on. It is conceivable that certain abnormal individuals will exercise their liberty of refusal and break free (to their loss) from this aspiration of the "evolutionary vortex." But such evasions can only be viewed as a loss. In fact, on the scale of the species, the process of totalisation is, *by its nature, unstoppable*, linked as it appears to be to two cosmic curves on which our will has no effect: on the one hand, the geometrical curvature of a planet which, relative to our number and radius of action, continues rapidly to contract; and on the other, the psychic curvature of a collective thinking that no force in the world could prevent from concentrating on itself.

Clearly these three propositions, taken together and simply extrapolated, leave only one possible prognostic for the future, which can be formulated like this:

"Structurally and notwithstanding any impression or appearance to the contrary, man is at present engaged in a process within which (by the very use of his liberty—that is to say in order to survive and transcend) he is compelled (*at least* statistically) to an ever increasing biological self-unification. Therefore, right in front of us in time, a *peak* of hominisation must necessarily exist—a peak which, to judge by the enormous *quantity of unarranged humanity* still all around us, must certainly lie *very far above* us in consciousness, if not so far from us in time as we might at first be tempted to suppose."

So, as I have already pointed out, we are far from being lost in the universe; since thick though the mist is on the horizon, the cosmic law of the "convergence of reflexion" is there to show, with the certainty of radar, the presence of a peak in front of us—a peak representing for our phylum a natural emergence from the processes of speciation.

Indeed there is no longer any possible doubt that the play of the planetary forces of complexity/consciousness, *normally extended*, summons us to and destines us for this peak of hominisation (or, as I have become accustomed to calling it the *point Omega*).

But in the brutal reality of events, do not many things go wrong that *should have* succeeded? A flower fails to bloom. An experience is lacking. A loaf burns in the oven.

Have we all that we need for attaining the biological paroxysm to which, if my calculations are right, every Noosphere is naturally summoned? Have we the means of knowing that, in fact, there will be no wayside failure of the forces of hominisation in the particular case of the earth? We have set out, sure enough—and we are already climbing the slope. But shall we actually have *enough time to reach the top*? Shall we have the necessary *material resources*? And, most important of all, shall we have enough *inner* genius and drive?

. . . .

A. TIME

On the subject of the "end of the world," the first idea that comes to our minds—and that one in fact finds at the basis of all popular beliefs or fears—is the possibility of destruction or at least rapid planetary change. A sidereal collision, for example. Or a sudden cooling of the globe. Or alternatively (a new danger recently discovered by science), the disappearance of the absorbent layer of ozone which protects us from certain destructive rays.

This idea of an accident that will destroy humanity continues to attract our imagination by its simplicity and finality. But scientifically speaking, we must acknowledge that it is becoming increasingly improbable. For the better we realise, by the use of isotopes, how slowly the globe has evolved (a matter of billions of years) in comparison with the average "life" of species (some 20 or 30 million years only) the more aware we are that no interference between these two phenomena is to be feared. Even if humanity could be considered as "an ordinary species," the chances that anthropogenesis might be interrupted in its course by an appreciable stopping or modification of the geogenesis would already be negligible. But how can we fail to see that our vulnerability to "cosmic accident" is even further diminished by the fact that humanity is *not* a species like the rest?

Since by escaping, as we have seen, from the framework of systematisation, humanity has reached the astonishing biological situation of constituting by itself a new "envelope" of the earth, one must believe that its probable longevity in comparison with that of the other animal groups has vastly increased.

In fact the evidence of its extreme speed of evolution leads us to exactly the contrary conclusion.

It is certainly not more than a million years since man appeared, isolated and unarmed, in one corner of the earth. And this short time has been enough (see Fig. 1) to contain the whole *dilating phase* of his phyletic development. Now that he is embarking in all his strength on the second major stage of his evolution, why should this phase of accelerated compression last much longer than its predecessor; that is to say, why should it take much more than another million years?

Now though at the continually increasing speed at which human affairs are going, another million years of hominisation may be startling to the Noosphere, from the astronomical point of view this space of time is quite negligible!

No. Having opened like a flower "for a few hours" on the tree of life, the human species will be more secure than any other branch that has appeared on that truck; it will in fact have nothing serious to fear from a disturbance in the heavens.

We can be reassured on this first score. Between now and the moment when we reach the biological peak, whatever it is, towards which evolution is driving us, if anything eventually fails us it will not be the ground that we stand on. In one or two or three million years the earth will certainly still be there beneath our feet—and still as habitable as it is today both in its temperature and its land-masses.

But, before that supreme moment comes, shall we not perhaps, with our lack of foresight, have already destroyed what the earth had by its nature the power and duty to give us, so that we should not fail on the road? . . .

B. THE MATERIAL RESOURCES

Until man appeared on earth, a loose and flexible equilibrium was constantly maintained between the litho- and bio-spheres. Thanks to the populations of microbes deep within the decomposed rocks and the plant life which absorbed the sun's rays, an "autotrophic" basis (of bacteria and vegetation) proportionate to the nourishment required by an always increasing number of higher animals had been gradually constituted, and became increasingly consolidated in the course of time. Periodically, of course, large desert patches formed here and there in the vegetation; or advances of glaciation bared the sterile rock over vast spaces. But these local wounds were very soon healed. The momentary effects of famine diminished. And on the whole, biogenesis continued regularly, from age to age, its complicated play of multiplication, speciation and selection on the earth's surface.

This, I repeat, until the biological crisis of hominisation took place.

But from that fateful moment, what a change!

In considering the historical phenomenon that terrestrial consciousness became at one of its points *reflective*, we have so far confined ourselves to discussing the evolutionary leap, that is to say the triumphal inauguration of a new era in planetary life. The moment has now come to point out the *physiologically* dangerous aspect of this indisputable victory. When life became reflective, not only did a hitherto unknown capacity for invention appear on earth. But also, correlatively, two fundamental biological functions, those of *multiplication* and *consumption*, suddenly leapt into an unprecedented importance for the higher forms of life. Suddenly the whole economy of the planet was called into question.

The fact is undeniable.

Thanks to his psychic superiority, which allowed him to supplant all other life, man (especially since Neolithic times) has so reproduced himself and "worked" so well—with stone, iron and fire—that his activities have finally succeeded in breaking the old state of equilibrium between the soil and himself.

It has certainly taken him some time to become aware of his carelessness! Was it not only yesterday that our economists began to draw up a balance-sheet of the earth? But today—following an incredibly rapid rise in the world population—and following a no less incredibly rapid rise in the *daily ration* required by a human individual for survival (a ration not only of bread and water but of substances and energies of all sorts), the danger of dearth is becoming so obvious that cries of alarm can be heard from all quarters. At the rate things are going (too many people and too much careless wastage by them), the soil and sub-soil of the continents are in danger of being exhausted in very few centuries. Our evolutionary capital is disappearing before our eyes. I was speaking just now of a *peak* of co-reflexion lying one or two million years ahead of us. But is not this fine dream of the future brutally dispelled by the evidence that if there is indeed a maximum of expected hominisation for the Noosphere, this maximum will have to arrive very quickly (immediately even) since hominisation can only be maintained by absorbing a mathematically increasing quantity of energy, and never again (as certain specialists maintain) will man possess the abundance of resources (alimentary and industrial) that our civilisation is so unthinkingly burning up today.

In face of a situation the reality and gravity of which I should be the last to underestimate, I nevertheless refuse to be pessimistic. On the contrary, without ceasing, I hope, to be realistic, I maintain that from an economic point of view nothing prevents us from still thinking that for man "life begins tomorrow." And these are my reasons:

As an inevitable result of the acceleration in consumption, we are rapidly (even too rapidly) exhausting our beds of iron, oilfields and coal measures: this is clear. As a result of our accelerated reproduction, an increasingly great gap is at the same time tending to develop between the total extent of our arable land and the needs of the world population: this is no less evident. But, on the other hand, at this appointed moment, do we not find our physicists just putting their hands on nuclear energy—and our chemists gradually reducing the problems of organic synthesis? Who can say where this movement will stop? Humanity has been irreverently compared to a flower appearing transitorily on the mineralised corpse of millions of years of buried life. But why not think instead that like those aircraft which require an outside force[8] to launch them, our species, in order to become autotrophic and autonomous, needed during its first phase (which is just ending) to find an abundant source of ready prepared energy beside it? After which it will be able to fly with its own wings.

In the hundreds of millions of years during which the psychic temperature of the earth has been rising, without ever falling back, life must have found many obstacles in its path. Today when it has taken its full momentum, could it possibly fail precisely in the magnificent act of completely reflecting on itself?

Admitting this (I mean that it must exist, and that a definite solution will finally be found to the problem of human nourishment), how are we going to manœuvre ourselves through the

8. Or, more topically still, to those Hymenoptera that, to perform their metamorphosis, have to find food ready prepared for them by their mother lying beside them as they hatch out. [Au.]

dangerous pass in which we stand at present? By what methods of soil conservation, by what balanced economy of raw materials, by what new course of prudence in the reproduction of the species, can we gain the necessary time to discover and acclimatise to our civilisation a whole world of new energies? What, in other words, are we to do in order that, in the year 3000, humanity may be, *as it must be*, better nourished and even better equipped than it is today for its efforts to confront the biological expectations of its continued destiny?

No one could yet give an exact answer to these questions. But in the meantime one thing at least is certain. The survival of material plenty (required, I repeat, by the normal predictable course of hominisation) can only be assured by still more science, and still more ambition, and still more wisdom.

So (despite appearances) it is not so much on the quantity of our economic resources, but rather on the increased intensity of our reflective and affective powers that the ultimate success or failure of humanity basically depends.